DOCTOR ON BOARD

Ship's Medicine Chest and Care
on the Water

BY WILLIAM W. FORGEY, M.D., FAWM, CTH®

SHERIDAN
HOUSE

Guilford, Connecticut

DEDICATION

This book is dedicated to my good friend and colleague Lorenzo Peder Giatgen Marcolongo, M.D., who has shared adventures with me from the Arctic to below the equator.

HERIDAN
OUSE

An imprint of The Rowman & Littlefield Publishing Group, Inc.
4501 Forbes Blvd., Ste. 200
Lanham, MD 20706
www.rowman.com

Distributed by NATIONAL BOOK NETWORK

British Library Cataloguing in Publication Information available
Library of Congress Cataloging-in-Publication Data available

ISBN 978-1-4930-5663-7 (paper)
ISBN 978-1-4930-5664-4 (electronic)

CONTENTS

Chapter 1: Introduction to Nautical Medicine **1**

Chapter 2: Patient Assessment **3**

Assessment and Care **3**
How to Use This Book

Initial Assessment **6**
Survey the Scene • Check the Airway and Breathing •
Check Circulation • Check for Severe Bleeding • Check
the Cervical Spine

Focused Assessment **8**
The Physical Exam • General Principles of the Focused
Assessment

Vital Signs **9**
Level of Responsiveness • Pulse • Respirations •
Skin Signs • Blood Pressure • Temperature • Oxygen
Saturation

Medical History and Physical Examination **12**
Head • Neck • Chest • Abdomen • Back • Pelvis/Hip •
Legs • Shoulders and Arms

Chapter 3: Stabilization Of The Patient **15**

Shock **15**

Difficult Respirations **17**
Foreign Body Airway Obstruction • Adult
One-Rescuer CPR • Adult Two-Rescuer CPR •
Defibrillator • Rapid Breathing

Cardiac Evaluation and Care **23**
Heart Attack—Myocardial Infarction • Rapid Heart
Rate—Tachycardia • Slow Heart Rate—Bradycardia

Chapter 4: Symptom Management **29**

Fever/Chills **30**

Lethargy **32**

Pain. **33**

Mild Pain • Severe Pain

Itch **35**

Hives. **36**

Hiccups. **37**

Headache **37**

Chapter 5: Seasickness (*mal de mer*) and Sopite Syndrome. **39**

Chapter 6: Eye. **45**

Eye Patch and Bandaging Techniques **46**

Foreign Body Eye Injury. **47**

Contact Lenses **49**

Eye Abrasion. **52**

Ultraviolet Eye Injury **53**

Conjunctivitis **54**

Iritis. **55**

Allergic Conjunctivitis **56**

Sties and Chalazia. **56**

Spontaneous Subconjunctival Hemorrhage **57**

Blunt Eye Trauma. **57**

Glaucoma **58**

Chapter 7: Nose. **61**

Nasal Congestion **61**

Nasal Foreign Body. **61**

Nosebleed—Epistaxis **62**

Broken Nose **63**

Chapter 8: Ear **65**

Earache. **66**

Outer Ear Infection—Otitis Externa **66**

Middle Ear Infection—Otitis Media **67**

Foreign Body in Ear **69**

Ruptured Eardrum **69**
Temporomandibular Joint Syndrome **70**

Chapter 9: Mouth and Throat **71**
Sore Throat **71**
Infectious Mononucleosis **72**
Mouth Sores **72**
Dental Care. **74**
Gum Pain or Swelling • Mouth Lacerations • Dental
Pain • Lost Filling • Cavity • Loose or Dislodged
Tooth • Pulling a Tooth

Chapter 10: Chest **81**
Bronchitis/Pneumonia **81**
Pneumothorax. **82**
Pulmonary Embolus **83**

Chapter 11: Abdomen **85**
Abdominal Pain **85**
Gall Bladder Problems and Appendicitis
Vomiting. **90**
Diarrhea **90**
Constipation **93**
Hemorrhoids. **93**
Hernia. **94**
Bladder Infection **95**
Urinary Retention. **96**
How to Insert a Foley Catheter

Chapter 12: Reproductive Organs. **99**
Venereal Diseases **99**
Vaginal Discharge and Itching **100**
Menstrual Problems **101**
Spontaneous Abortion **102**
Ectopic Pregnancy **102**
Pregnancy **103**

Painful Testicle **104**

Chapter 13: Poisoning. **107**
Plant or Food Poisoning **107**
Petroleum Products. **107**
Ciguatera Poisoning **108**
Scombroid Poisoning **108**
Pufferfish Poisoning **109**
Paralytic Shellfish Poisoning. **109**

Chapter 14: Managing Diabetes **111**

Chapter 15: Water Safety, Fluid Replacement **113**
Oral Fluid Replacement **113**
Water Purification
Drinking Seawater **119**

Chapter 16: Soft Tissue Care and Trauma Management . . . **121**
Stop the Bleeding **126**
Hemostatic Dressings. **127**
Wound Cleaning. **131**
Antibiotic Guidelines
Wound Closure Techniques **135**
Tape Closure Techniques • Stapling • Suturing
Special Wound Considerations. **139**
Shaving the Wound Area • Bleeding from Suture or
Staple Use
Scalp Wounds. **139**
Eyebrow and Lip Closure **140**
Mouth and Tongue Lacerations **140**
Control of Pain
Dressings. **141**
Abrasions **142**
Puncture Wounds **143**
Splinter Removal **143**

Fishhook Removal **144**
*Push Through, Snip Off Method • The String Jerk
Method • The Dissection Method*

Friction Blisters. **147**

Thermal Burns **148**

Human Bites. **152**

Animal Bites **152**

Finger and Toe Problems **153**
*Ingrown Nail • Paronychia (Nail Base Infection) •
Felon • Blood Under Nail (Subungual Hematoma)
• Wound Infection and Inflammation • Abscess •
Cellulitis • Skin Rash • Fungal Infection • Allergic
Dermatitis • Bacterial Skin Rash • Seabather's
Eruption*

Chapter 17: Orthopedics. **163**

Muscle Pain—No Acute Injury **164**

Muscle Pain—Acute Injury **165**

Joint Pain—No Acute Injury **167**

Joint Pain—Acute Injury **168**

Fractures—Broken Bones **170**
Open Fracture • Diagnosis and Care Protocols

Head Fractures—Unconscious **174**
Neck • Spine

Collarbone—Clavicle **179**

Shoulder **181**
Shoulder Blade—Scapula

Upper Arm Fractures (Near the Shoulder) **184**

Upper Arm Fractures (Below the Shoulder) **185**

Elbow Trauma. **186**

Forearm Fractures **188**

Wrist Fractures and Dislocations **189**

Thumb Sprains and Fractures **192**

Hand Fractures and Injuries **192**
Finger Fractures and Sprains

Hip Dislocation and Fracture **194**

Thigh (Femur) Fractures **196**
Kneecap (Patella) Dislocation **197**
Knee Sprains, Dislocations, and Fractures **198**
Ankle Sprains, Dislocations, and Fractures **199**
Foot Injuries **200**
Chest Injuries **200**

Chapter 18: Bites and Stings 203
Anaphylactic Shock **203**
Use of Epipen • Snake Bites
Spider Bites **210**
Black Widow Spider • Brown Recluse Spider
Ticks **212**
Caterpillar Reactions **213**
Millipede Reactions **213**
Centipede Bites **213**
Mosquitoes **213**
Black Flies **216**
No-See-Ums and Biting Gnats **216**
Scorpion Stings **217**
Ants/Fire Ants **217**
Aquatic Stings, Cuts, and Rash **218**
Sea Urchin
Jellyfish **218**
Coral Stings **219**
*Coral and Barnacle Cuts • Stingray • Catfish •
Scorpion Fish • Sponge Rash*

Chapter 19: Infectious Disease 221
Diagnosis of Infectious Diseases **221**
*So, What Is the Approach to Infectious Disease?
• Anaplasmosis • Babesiosis • Blastomycosis •
Chikungunya Fever • Cholera • Coccidioidomycosis
• Colorado Tick Fever • Coronavirus • Dengue •
Echinococcus • Ehrlichiosis • Encephalitis • Giardiasis
• Hantavirus • Hepatitis A • Hepatitis B • Hepatitis
C • Hepatitis D • Hepatitis E • Hepatitis G •*

Leptospirosis • Lyme Disease • Malaria • Measles (Rubeola) • Meningococcal Meningitis • Mumps • Plague • Rabies • Relapsing Fever • Rocky Mountain Spotted Fever • Rubella (German Measles, 3-Day Measles) • Schistosomiasis • Stari • Tapeworms • Tetanus • Tick Paralysis • Trichinosis • Trypanosomiasis, African (African Sleeping Sickness) • Trypanosomiasis, American (Chagas Disease) • Tuberculosis • Tularemia • Typhoid Fever • Endemic Typhus, Flea-Borne • Epidemic Typhus, Louse-Borne • West Nile Virus • Yellow Fever • Zika Virus

Chapter 20: Environmental Injuries **255**

Hypothermia. **256**
   Chronic Hypothermia • Acute Hypothermia • Cold Water Submersion

Cold-Stress Injuries **260**
   Frostnip • Frostbite • Cold-Induced Bronchospasm • Immersion Foot (Trench Foot, Cockpit Foot) • Chilblains

Heat Stress Injuries. **264**
   Dilutional Hyponatremia • Heat Cramps • Heat Exhaustion • Heat Stroke • Prickly Heat

Lightning **270**
   Ship Damage • Crew Injury

Chapter 21: The Ship's Medicine Chest **277**

Alternative Improvisation **280**
Lifeboat Kit versus Ship's Medicine Chest **280**
Topical Medication and Bandaging Kit **281**
   Coverlet Bandage Strips • Spenco 2nd Skin • Hemostatic Dressings • Nu-Gauze Pads • Silverlon Bandage • Waterproof Tape • Sam Splint • Elastic Bandages • Maximum Strength Triple Antibiotic Ointment with Pramoxine, 1 oz Tube • Lanacane Cream 1 oz. (30 g) Tube • Chlorhexidine Surgical Scrub • Opcon-A Eye Drops • Hydrocortisone Cream 1%, 1 oz Tube • Clotrimazole Cream 2%, ½ oz Tube • Cavit Dental Filling Paste • Protective Gloves •

*Irrigation Syringe • Surgical Kit • Foley Catheter Kit
• Automatic External Defibrillator*

Non-Rx Oral Medication Kit **288**

*Percogesic Tablets (Pain, Fever, Muscle Spasm,
Sleep Aid, Anxiety, Congestion, Cough, and
Nausea) • Ibuprofen Tablets (200 mg) (Pain,
Fever, Bursitis, Tendonitis, Menstrual Cramps) •
Diphenhydramine Tablets (25 mg) (Antihistamine,
Antianxiety, Cough, Muscle Cramps, Nausea,
Motion Sickness Prevention) • Bisacodyl Tablets
(5 mg) (Constipation) • Loperamide Tablets (2 mg)
(Diarrhea) • Famotidine (20 mg) (Heartburn,
Certain Allergic Reactions)*

Rx Oral/Topical Medication Kit. **291**

*Doxycycline Tablets (100 mg) (Antibiotic) •
Azithromycin Tablets (500 mg) (Antibiotic)
• Levofloxacin Tablets (750 mg) (Antibiotic)
• Diflucan Tablets (150 mg) (Antifungal) •
Norco-10/325 Tablets (Pain, Cough) • Hydroxyzine
Tablets (25 mg) (Nausea, Anxiety, Antihistamine,
Pain Medication Augmentation) • Meloxicam
(Mobic) 15 mg Tablets (Pain Medication, Anti-
Inflammatory, Fever) • Desoximetasone (Topicort)
Ointment (0.25%, 0.5 oz Tube) (Skin Allergy) •
Tobradex Ophthalmic Drops (2.5 ml) (Eye and
Ear Antibiotic, Anti-Inflammatory) • Tetracaine
Ophthalmic Solution (Drops), 0.5%, 15 ml Bottle
(Eye and Ear Anesthetic) • Penciclovir (Denavir)
Cream, 1%, 5 gm Tube (Antiviral, Lip and Mouth
Sores) • Butorphanol (Nubain) Nasal Spray (Severe
Pain) • Dexamethasone (Decadron) Tablets (4 mg)
(Allergy, Specific Trauma Situations) • Metronidazole
(Flagyl) Capsules (250 mg) (Trichomonas or Giardia
Infection) • Famciclovir Capsules (250 or 500 mg)
(Cold Sores, Herpes Viral Infections) • Atovaquone
and Proguanil (Malarone) (250 mg/100mg For
Adult; 62.5 mg/25 mg Pediatric)*

Rx Injectable Medication Kit **297**

*Nalbuphine (Nubain) (20 mg/ml, 10 ml Vial)
• Lidocaine 1% (10 ml Vial) • Dexamethasone
(Decadron) (4 mg/ml, 5 ml Vial) • Ceftriaxone*

(Rocephin) (500 mg Vial) • Hydroxyzine (Vistaril) (50 mg/ml, 10 ml Vial) • Epinephrine Auto Inject Pens (Epipen, Epipen Jr. and Symjepi®)

Cardiac Medication Kit **298**
Aspirin (81 mg Chewable Tablets) • Nitroglycerin Sublingual Tablets (0.4 mg) • Clopidogrel (Plavix) Tablets (75 mg) • Atenolol (Tenormin®) Tablets (25 mg)

Clinical Reference Index. 301
About the Author. 315

CHAPTER 1
INTRODUCTION TO NAUTICAL MEDICINE

So, you are the Doctor on Board!

Obviously, open ocean and even coastal sailing requires forethought regarding food, water supplies, navigation, and communication—all areas of significant technical preparation that require obtaining skill sets and supplies. Self-reliant medical care is no exception. Even advanced first aid classes, such as Wilderness First Responder and Tactical Combat Casualty Care (TCCC), all rely eventually on evacuation as part of the treatment protocol. Under the situation of impractical or impossible evacuation, a means of providing a plan for long-term management must be available.

This book provides the basis of prevention, identification, and long-term management of survivable medical conditions and can be performed with minimal training. It helps you identify sources of materials you will need and should stock, it discusses storage issues, and it directs you to sources for more complex procedures that require advanced concepts of field-expedient techniques that could be of use to trained medical persons such as surgeons, anesthesiologist, dentists, or midwives.

While at sea, you should be able to directly handle many of the medical issues you and your crew might experience, from prevention to treatment of most injuries, motion sickness, and environmental exposure. More complex situations may require your issuing a distress call for advice or help. For these to be properly managed you will need to have appropriate communication and signaling skills and to be able to appropriate request "Pan Pan" or "Mayday" assistance. And just as important, to know when to initiate this help. Knowledge of appropriate communication and signaling technologies are required for any ship's master certification and the responsibility of both owner and master. The *Navigation Rules & Regulations Handbook* by the Department of Homeland Security, United States Coast Guard (USCG), published rules for navigation as well as communications. A copy of this booklet can be obtained from Paradise Cay Publications at www.paracay.com.

Upon establishing the need for help, a report must be made that is coherent and precise to the recuing party. Ship's name, location, number of souls aboard, and other pertinent information for identification and the degree of risk to ship or patient need to be explained. Historically "Pan, Pan" was the expression requesting help for an individual while "Mayday, Mayday" indicated an entire crew and ship are at risk and require assistance.

The *International Health Regulations* (IHR) (2005) is the key international health document that is legally binding across 196 countries, including all World Health Organization (WHO) member states. This includes provisions for the use of various health documents that must be presented, if requested, to health authorities on arrival at ports. These include the International Certificate of Vaccination and Prophylaxis and depending upon circumstances the Maritime Declaration of Health. You should download *A Boaters Guide to the Federal Requirements for Recreational Boats and Safety Tips* by the Department of Homeland Security located at https://www.uscgboating.org/images/420.PDF. This document describes various communications devices and signal requirements and availability.

The Master should have a medical record of every crew member. Each crew member going on an international trip should carry the International Immunization Certificate as well as their passport, upon arrival at international ports. An example of personal medical forms and medical incident reports can be found at www.doctor-on-board.com.

CHAPTER 2

PATIENT ASSESSMENT

ASSESSMENT AND CARE

The technique of providing aid to a victim with an injury is similar to giving appropriate treatment to someone who complains of sickness or sudden pain from a noninjury cause. Proper care can result only if several basic steps are performed properly. The basics are straightforward. You should not be intimidated by this process. The problem with medicine in general is that there are so many possible diagnoses and treatments that the whole thing can seem overwhelming. It is not, however, if you follow certain logical steps.

These logical steps form the basis of starting the decision tree that will lead almost automatically to a correct course of action. They simplify the process into a much less scary proposition. The initial phase is assessment, the second phase is stabilization, and the third phase is treatment. While the first aid approach only includes assessment and stabilization, this book is concerned with developing approaches to definitive treatment that could be reasonably performed in remote areas by relatively untrained (and undoubtedly genuinely concerned) friends of the suddenly impaired.

How to Use This Book

There are four ways to rapidly identify where to find the information you need.

FIRST

A quick glance through the Table of Contents can lead you to the proper chapter and subject.

SECOND

The initial assessment (pages 6–8) and the focused assessment (pages 8–9) not only describe how to perform a physical examination and what to look for, but these sections also refer you to the page of the book that tells you what to do if something is wrong.

THIRD

Throughout the book, various sections have diagnostic tables with references to further evaluate or explain treatment options. For problems that fall into these categories, you can refer directly to the tables indicated in the following list.

List of Diagnostic Tables/References

Abdominal pain and problems	(Table 11.1 Symptoms & Signs), pages 85–89
Bites and stings	page 203
Ear problems	(Table 8.1 Symptoms + Signs), page 65
Environmental injuries	page 255
Eye problems	(Table 6.1 Symptoms + Signs), page 45
Infectious diseases	Table 19.1 (on set of Infectious Disease Time of Exposure), page 221
	Table 19.2 (Herd Hummunity) page 223
Orthopedic injuries	page 163
Shock	page 15–16
Soft tissue care and trauma management	page 121
Symptom management (Gen, System Care Guide)	Table 4.1, page 29 and Table 4.2, page 30

FOURTH

The Clinical Reference Index, starting on page 301, provides a comprehensive cross-reference between symptoms, conditions, and treatments. Subjects are listed using both medical jargon and vernacular descriptions.

Assessment is divided into two phases called the initial assessment and focused assessment. What good is an assessment if you don't know what to do with the information? During rescue operations, what you do with the information is record it. This recorded information, which includes periodic reassessment data, can be valuable to physicians at treatment centers, as it indicates either a stable or a deteriorating patient, and helps direct the future course of action. For those of us stuck with caring for the patient in a remote area, these data can be used to enter a decision tree that will help determine our best course of action. Sometimes this will be definitive treatment; other times it will amount to minimizing the damage and striving to keep the victim as functional as possible, or sometimes just alive. If you call for advice from a shore-based medical consult team, you will need to be concise with your description. When you make your next port of call, you will want to be able to comply with IHR regarding reporting any ill, injured, or deceased crew member. An example of a medical incident form and patient evaluation form is available at www.doctor-on-board.com.

Assessment and Care	Chapter 2, page 3
Initial Assessment	Chapter 2, page 6
Survey the Scene	Chapter 2, page 6
Check the Airway and Breathing	Chapter 2, page 6
Check Circulation	Chapter 2, page 7
Check Severe Bleeding	Chapter 2, page 7
Check the Cervical Spine	Chapter 2, page 7
Focused Assessment	Chapter 2, page 8
The Physical Exam	Chapter 2, page 8
Vital Signs	Chapter 2, page 9
Level of Responsiveness	Chapter 2, page 10
Pulse	Chapter 2, page 10
Respirations	Chapter 2, page 10
Skin Signs	Chapter 2, page 10
Blood Pressure (BP)	Chapter 2, page 11
Temperature	Chapter 2, page 11
Oxygen Saturation	Chapter 2, page 11
Medical History and Physical Examination	Chapter 2, page 12
Head	Chapter 2, page 12
Neck	Chapter 2, page 12

Chest	Chapter 2, page 12
Abdomen	Chapter 2, page 13
Back	Chapter 2, page 13
Pelvis/Hip	Chapter 2, page 13
Legs	Chapter 2, page 13
Shoulders and Arms	Chapter 2, page 13
Shock	Chapter 3, page 15–16
Difficult Respirations	Chapter 3, page 17
Foreign Body Airway Obstruction	Chapter 3, page 17–18
Adult One-Rescuer Cardiopulmonary Resuscitation (CPR)	Chapter 3, page 18–21
Adult Two-Rescuer CPR	Chapter 3, page 21–22
Defibrillator	Chapter 3, page 22
Rapid Breathing	Chapter 3, page 22–23
Cardiac Evaluation and Care	Chapter 3, page 23
Heart Attack—Myocardial Infarction (MI)	Chapter 3, page 23–26
Rapid Heart Rate (Tachycardia)	Chapter 3, page 26
Slow Heart Rate (Bradycardia)	Chapter 3, page 27

INITIAL ASSESSMENT

Survey the Scene

Before assessing the patient, assess the scene! Accidents tend to multiply. Make sure the scene is safe for the rescuers and the victim. Ensure that the situation does not become worse. This step can include such diverse aspects as avoiding further avalanches or rockfalls and ensuring an adequate clothing and food supply for rescuers. Initially, however, scene assessment should consist of looking for immediate hazards that might result in more casualties among the group attempting to help the victim.

Check the Airway and Breathing

Check the airway. If the victim can talk, his airway is functioning. In an unconscious patient, place your ear next to his nose/mouth and your hand on his chest and look, listen, and feel for air movement.

No air movement: Check to see whether the tongue is blocking the airway by pushing down on the forehead while lifting the chin.

In case of possible neck injury, the airway can be opened with a lift of the jaw without movement of the neck. Open the victim's mouth and visually inspect, removing any objects you can see.

Still no air movement: Pinch his or her nose and seal your mouth over his or hers and try to breathe air into his or her lungs. If the first attempt to breathe air into the victim fails, you should reposition the victim's head and try again.

Still no air movement: Perform chest thrusts, similar to the compressions of CPR; see page 20. Perform 30 compressions followed by attempts to breathe in air as directed earlier.

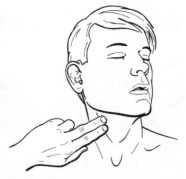

Once you are able to establish air movement, continue until the victim can take over on his or her own.

Check Circulation

Check circulation by placing several of your fingertips lightly into the hollow below the angle of the patient's jaw. See figure 2.1.

Figure 2.1
Position of fingers to check carotid pulse.

No pulse: Start CPR; see page 20.

Check for Severe Bleeding

Check quickly for severe blood loss. Check visually and with your hands. Slide your hand under the victim to ensure that blood is not leaking into the deck and check inside bulky garments for hidden blood loss.

Severe bleeding: Use direct pressure and/or a tourniquet; see page 126.

Check the Cervical Spine

During the primary assessment, keep the head and neck as still as possible if there is any suspicion of a cervical spine injury. This may certainly be the case if the patient is unconscious or suffering from an accident such as a steep fall, a sudden stop, or significant blows to the head. See treatment of spine injuries, pages 177–179.

Buck Tilton and Frank Hubbell, in their excellent book *Medicine for the Backcountry* (Globe Pequot Press, 1999), state, "Do not let fear of spinal cord injury blind you to more immediate threats to life. If the scene is not safe, the patient may need to be carefully moved. If the airway is not open, grasp the sides of your patient's head firmly, and pull with steady, gentle traction, and attempt to align the head and neck with the rest of the body. Gentle traction should be maintained until mechanical stabilization can be improvised." See spinal cord management, pages 177–179.

FOCUSED ASSESSMENT

The Physical Exam

While the purpose of the initial assessment (formerly called the primary or hasty survey) is to rapidly find and correct life-threatening conditions, the focused assessment (formerly identified as the secondary survey) is an attempt to identify all of the medical problems that the patient might have. This requires a thorough examination because sometimes an obvious injury can be distracting. A broken bone may cause both you and the victim to not notice a less painful but potentially more serious injury elsewhere.

The only way to perform a focused assessment is to do it thoroughly, using both your vision and sense of touch, asking simple questions, and being methodical in the approach. Sense of touch is important. Sliding your hand under the victim might find areas of tenderness, or even considerable blood loss, that would otherwise be unnoticed. It is surprising how much blood can be flowing under a wounded victim and not even be noticed until your hand encounters it.

The mission of the focused assessment is not only to discover various medical problems, but also to record and keep track of them during periodic reassessments. The reassessment information is even more important than the first set of information taken during the initial focused assessment. How often the focused assessment needs to be repeated, and how extensive it needs to be, depends primarily on the history of the event. Very serious-appearing events could initially require total body reassessment every 15 minutes. There can be no hard and fast rule concerning how often to repeat reassessments and how extensive they must be. There is no escaping the use of common sense. Eventually reassessment every few hours, even discontinuing this process, will become proper. This is particularly appropriate when the examination is unchanged and stable, the patient is alert, and you have obviously effectively dealt with the injuries. The scheme for recording this information is in the form of a SOAP note (which stands for Subjective, Objective, Assessment, and Plan).

The most significant difference between medical care at sea and urban first aid is that the focused assessment when you are at sea must also lead to treatment protocols. This methodical examination should generally start at the head and work its way to the feet. The exception could be children, where you might want to alleviate their apprehension by starting with their legs before examining their heads. Generally starting at the head is best.

General Principles of the Focused Assessment

1. Start at the top and work your way down.
2. Move the patient as little as possible and try not to aggravate known injuries while looking for others.
3. Constantly communicate with the patient during the examination, even if she seems unconscious.
4. Look for damage, even cutting away clothing, if necessary, to visualize suspected injuries.
5. Ask about pain, discomfort, and abnormal sensations constantly during the exam.
6. Gently feel all relevant body parts for abnormalities.

VITAL SIGNS

While even accurate measurements of the body's functions may not indicate what is wrong with a patient, the second and subsequent measurements indicate how well the patient is doing. You will need to use common sense to determine how often the signs are taken, but certainly close monitoring of the patient should be continued until he or she is obviously stable.

Vital signs consist of several elements: level of responsiveness, pulse, respirations, skin signs, BP, and temperature.

Level of Responsiveness

Is the patient alert, or does he or she respond only to verbal or painful stimulus? Or is he or she unresponsive? He or she should know who he or she is, where he or she is, what happened to him or her, and about what time of the day it is. Responsiveness ranges from alert, to verbal (responsive to spoken contact), to pain (not responsive to verbal contact but responsive to being pinched or rubbed on the shin), to unresponsive.

Pulse

Check and record rate, rhythm, and quality (thready, normal, or bounding) of the pulse. If an injury has been sustained by a limb, check pulses on both injured and uninjured limbs and compare.

Shock, see page 15.

Deformed fracture causing a decreased pulse, see page 170.

Respirations

Note the rate, rhythm, and quality of respirations (labored, with pain, flaring of nostrils, or noise such as snores, squeaks, gurgles, or gasps). An adult normally breathes 12 to 18 times per minute, while children breathe faster.

Respiratory difficulties, see page 17.

Skin Signs

Check skin color, particularly in the nonpigmented areas of the body, and note whether skin is hot/cold and moist/dry.

Hot, fever, see page 31; heat stress, see page 264.

Cold, shock, see page 31; hypothermia, see page 256.

Blood Pressure

BP can be measured with a stethoscope and BP cuff or by estimating. If you can feel a pulse in the radial artery at the wrist, the BP top (systolic) pressure is probably at least 80 mm. If you can only feel the femoral pulse in the groin, the pressure is no lower than 70 mm. When only the carotid pulse in the neck is palpable, the systolic is probably at least 60 mm. Normal systolic BPs range from 100 to 140. Low upper BP with normal pulses (say the 70 to 85 beats per minute range) is safe. But an increased pulse rate with a low pressure is an indication of shock.

Temperature

Oral thermometers will give the most accurate field temperatures, unless the ambient temperature is close to the room temperature of a Ritz-Carlton resort. Then forehead infrared or ear temperature thermometers are convenient, until their batteries wear out. Plastic direct-contact thermometers also require a similar ambient temperature range for accuracy. An estimation of fever can be made if the person's normal resting pulse rate is known. Each degree Fahrenheit will generally result in a 10-beats-per-minute pulse increase. There are exceptions, such as typhoid fever, when there can be a relatively slow heart rate for a high fever (see page 250).

Oxygen Saturation

A pulse oximeter is very reasonable piece of equipment to manage, from both acquisition cost and weight. A pulse oximeter is only $30, available over the counter at most pharmacies.

This device is attached to the index finger and will provide a continuous measure of heart rate and oxygen saturation. At sea level, the normal oxygen saturation reading will be 94% or greater.

Figure 2.2
Pulse oximeter.

MEDICAL HISTORY AND PHYSICAL EXAMINATION

Taking a medical history allows you to factor in your patient's previous or current illnesses as they may relate to the situation at hand. Before or during your actual physical examination, if the patient is not in an acute stage, ask about any allergies, medications that your patient is taking, past history of his or her health, last food or drink, and about the events that led up to the accident. If he or she is in pain, ask what provokes it, what action (if any) decreases its intensity, whether it radiates, how severe it is, what type it is (burning, sharp, dull), and when it started.

Part of the medical history should include a list of the personal medications that the person has brought on board. This is discussed further in chapter 21.

Head

Look for damage, discoloration, and blood or fluid draining from ears, nose, and mouth. Ask about loss of consciousness, pain, or any abnormal sensations. Feel for lumps or other deformities.

Losses of consciousness, see page 10.

Headache, see page 37; ear trauma, see page 69; eye trauma, see page 57; nose trauma, see page 63.

Mouth trauma, see pages 75 and 140.

Neck

Look for obvious damage, or deviation of the windpipe (trachea). Ask about pain and discomfort. Feel along the cervical spine for a pain response.

Cervical spine trauma, see pages 7 and 177.

Chest

Compress the ribs from both sides, as if squeezing a birdcage, keeping your hands wide to prevent the possibility of too much direct pressure on fractures. Look for damage or deformities. Ask about pain. Feel for instability.

Chest trauma, see page 200.

Difficulty breathing, see page 17.

Abdomen
With hands spread wide, press gently on the abdomen. Look for damage. Ask about pain and discomfort. Feel for rigidity, distention, or muscle spasms.

Abdominal pain, see pages 85–86.

Back
Slide your hands under the patient, palpating as much of the spine as possible. Note if there is an area of point tenderness over the bones along the spine (the spinous processes). If there is, suspect spine trauma. Check also for signs of local bleeding if you cannot observe the back directly during this check.

Spine trauma, see pages 177–179.

Pelvis/Hip
Place your hands on the top front of the pelvis on both sides (the iliac crests), pressing gently down and pulling toward the midline of the body. Ask about pain. Feel for instability.

Hip or pelvis pain, see pages 194–196.

Legs
With your hands surrounding each leg, one at a time, run from the groin down to the toes, squeezing as you go. Note especially if there is a lack of circulation, sensation, or motion in the toes.

Bone injury, see pages 194–200.

Shoulders and Arms
One at a time, with hands wide, squeeze each shoulder, and run down the arms to the fingers. Check for circulation, sensation, and motion in the fingers.

Shoulder trauma, see pages 181–183.

Joint trauma, see page 184.

Broken bone, see pages 170–174.

CHAPTER 3
STABILIZATION OF THE PATIENT

SHOCK

Shock is a deficiency in oxygen supply reaching the brain and other tissues as a result of decreased circulation. An important aspect of the correction of shock is to identify and treat the underlying cause. Shock can be caused by burns, electrocution, hypothermia, bites, stings, bleeding, fractures, pain, hyperthermia, illness, rough handling, allergic reaction (anaphylaxis), damage or excitement to the central nervous system, dehydration from sweating, vomiting, or diarrhea, or loss of adequate heart strength. Each of these underlying causes is discussed separately in this book.

Shock can progress through several stages before death results. The first phase is called the compensatory stage, during which the body attempts to counter the damage by increasing its activity level. Arteries constrict and the pulse rate increases, thus maintaining the BP. The next phase is called the progressive stage (or decompensatory stage), when suddenly the BP drops and the patient becomes worse, often swiftly. When he or she has reached the "irreversible stage," vital organs have suffered from loss of oxygen so profoundly that death occurs even with aggressive treatment.

Consider the possibility of shock in any victim of an accident or when significant illness develops. Ensure that an adequate airway is established (see further discussion under Adult One-Rescuer CPR, page 18). Assess the cardiovascular status. Place your hand over the carotid artery (figure 2.1) to obtain the pulse. In compensatory shock, the patient will have a weak, rapid pulse. In adults, the rate will be over 140; in children, 180 beats per minute. If there is doubt about a pulse being present, listen to the bare chest. If cardiac standstill is present, begin one-person or two-person CPR (see pages 18–21). Elevate the legs to 45 degrees to obtain a better return of venous blood to the heart and head. However, if there has been a severe head injury, keep the person flat. If he or she has trouble breathing, elevate the chest and head to a comfortable position. Protect the patient from the environment with insulation underneath and shelter above him. Strive to make him comfortable. Watch your spoken and body language. Reassure without patronizing and let nothing that you say or act out cause him or her increased distress.

Attempt to treat the underlying cause of the shock. The primary or secondary assessment and history may well elicit the cause of shock, and appropriate treatment can be devised from the field-expedient methods listed in this book.

Shock due to severe allergic reactions is called anaphylactic shock and is discussed on pages 15–16.

Vasovagal syncope is a common form of shock. Sometimes called fainting, the clue is a very slow heartbeat in the patient. Generally something has happened to the patient to precipitate this reaction, such as witnessing blood loss in himself or herself or another person, receiving an injection (or even witnessing someone else receiving one), or perhaps attending one of my medical lectures. (See slow heart rate, pages 26–27.)

Decision/Care Table

If no breathing is present—from whatever cause,
  see Adult One-Rescuer CPR, pages 18–21

If no heartbeat is present—from whatever cause,
  see Adult One-Rescuer CPR, pages 18–21

If associated with cold conditions,
  see Hypothermia, page 254

If body temperature is over 100°F with cough,
  see Bronchitis/Pneumonia, pages 81–82

If body temperature is over 100°F without cough,
  see Fever/Chills, pages 30–32

If severe pain, sudden onset after trauma,

see Chest Injuries, pages 200–201

If severe pain, sudden onset, no trauma:

see Pneumothorax, page 82

see Pulmonary Embolus, page 83

see Cardiac Evaluation and Care, page 23

If associated with hysterical reaction:

see Rapid Breathing, pages 22–23

If associated with choking:

see Foreign Body Airway Obstruction, pages 17–18

If associated with dull ache in middle of chest:

see Cardiac Evaluation and Care, pages 23–24

DIFFICULT RESPIRATIONS

It has been stated that you can live 3 minutes without air, 3 days without water, 3 weeks without food, and 3 months without love. While some feel that they may stretch these time limits to 4, others feel the shorter periods would be all they could survive. Without any question, adequate respirations are the most significant demand of the living creature. When respiratory difficulties start, it's urgent to find the reason and alleviate it. When breathing stops, reestablishing air flow is critical.

Foreign Body Airway Obstruction

If a conscious adult seems to be having distressed breathing, ask, "Are you choking?" A choking victim cannot talk but may be making a high-pitched sound during attempts to breathe. He or she will rapidly become a bluish color and unconscious if the blockage is total. If the victim is apparently choking, perform an abdominal thrust to relieve foreign body airway obstruction. If the victim is standing or sitting, stand behind and wrap your arms around the patient, proceeding as follows: make a fist with one hand. Place the thumb side of the fist against the victim's abdomen, in the midline slightly above the navel and well below the breastbone. Grasp your fist with the other hand. Lift your elbows away from the victim's body and press your fist into the victim's abdomen with a quick, upward thrust. Each new thrust should be a separate and distinct movement. It may be necessary to repeat the thrust multiple times to clear the airway. If the person is obese or pregnant, use chest thrusts in the same manner as just described, but with your arms around the lower chest and your fists on the center of the victim's sternum.

If the victim becomes unconscious and is on the ground, he or she should be placed on his or her back, face up. Perform a tongue-jaw lift, open the mouth, and remove any visible objects. With the airway open, try to ventilate. If still obstructed, reposition the head and try to ventilate again. If still obstructed, give 30 chest thrusts, followed by two attempts

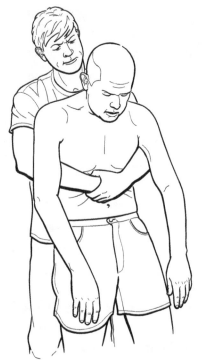

Figure 3.1
The abdominal thrust, formerly called the Heimlich maneuver, used to treat a foreign body causing an airway obstruction

to ventilate as described earlier. Each time you open the mouth to ventilate the victim, check for a visible obstruction and remove it if you see one. Repeat these steps until effective. Obviously this person should be evacuated to professional care immediately (see figure 3.1).

Adult One-Rescuer CPR

Note: This brief presentation of the basics of CPR reflects research, indicating the importance of immediately reestablishing circulation via chest compressions. If you are without training in rescue breathing, you may choose to perform hands-only CPR.

To establish unresponsiveness, first try talking—clearly and loudly—to the victim, asking questions such as "Are you OK? Can you hear me?" If there is no response to your verbal contact, make gentle physical contact by touching the victim's shoulder and repeating your questions. If gentle contact fails, apply a painful stimulus, such as a pinch to the back of the arm. If the patient remains unresponsive, in civilization activate the EMS system (call 911) prior to attempting CPR. When at sea, immediately proceed with the following steps:

> Check for signs of circulation that include coughing, breathing, or movement. If you have been trained, you may also check for a carotid pulse. This is found by placing your hand on the voice box (larynx). Slip the tips of your fingers into the groove beside the voice box and feel for the pulse (see figure 2.1). Check for circulation for a maximum of 10 seconds.

If the victim is unresponsive with no signs of circulation, start chest compressions.

Chest compressions are performed by the rescuer kneeling at the victim's side, near his chest. Place the heel of one hand on the center of the sternum. Place the other hand on top of the one that is in position on the sternum (see figure 3.3). Be sure to keep your fingers off the ribs. The easiest way to prevent this is to interlock your fingers, thus keeping them confined to the sternum. With your shoulders directly over the victim's sternum, compress downward, keeping your arms straight. Depress the sternum at least 2 inches. Relax the pressure completely, keeping your hands in contact with the sternum at all times, but allowing the sternum to return to its normal position between compressions. Both compression and relaxation should be of equal duration.

Perform 30 external chest compressions at a rate of at least 100 per minute. Push down hard and push down fast.

Open the airway using the head-tilt/chin-lift or jaw-thrust technique (see figure 3.3). Place one hand on the victim's forehead and apply firm, backward pressure with the palm to tilt the head back. Place the fingers of the other hand under the bony part of the lower jaw near the chin and lift to bring the chin forward and the teeth almost shut, thus supporting the jaw and helping to tilt the head back, as indicated in figure 3.2. In case of suspected neck injury, use the chin-lift without the head-tilt technique. The nose is pinched shut by using the thumb and index finger of the hand on the forehead.

The chin-lift method will place tension on the tongue and throat structures to ensure that the air passage will open.

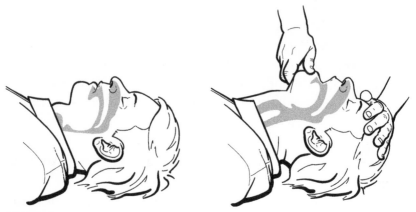

Figure 3.2
The head/tilt method of opening the airway in an unconscious person.

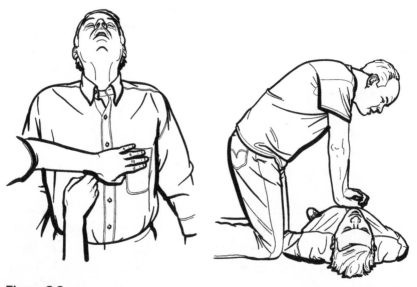

Figure 3.3
(A) Position of hands and (B) position of rescuer.

If breathing is absent, give 2 slow breaths (about 1 second per breath), watching the chest rise. Then allow for exhalation between breaths. The breathing rate should be once about every 6 seconds. Using slow breaths reduces the amount of air that tends to enter the stomach and cause gastric distention.

After 5 cycles of 30:2 compressions and ventilations (about 2 minutes), reevaluate the patient. Check for the return of circulation. If it is absent, resume CPR with 30 compressions followed by 2 breaths, as indicated earlier. If it is present, continue to the next step. Check breathing. If present, monitor breathing and pulse closely.

If absent, perform rescue breathing at 1 breath about every 6 seconds and monitor pulse closely.

If CPR is continued, do not interrupt CPR for more than 5 seconds except in special circumstances. Once CPR is started, it should be maintained until professional assistance can take over the responsibility, or until a physician declares the patient dead. If CPR has been continued for 30 minutes without regaining cardiac function, and the eyes are fixed and nonreactive to light, the patient can be presumed dead. The exceptions would be hypothermia (see page 256) and lightning injuries (page 270). In these circumstances, if professional help does not intervene, CPR should be continued until the rescuers are exhausted.

Some authorities in remote area rescue have felt that the survival rate is so low without defibrillation within 4 minutes by paramedics that CPR should not be started when cardiac standstill is due to a heart attack. It certainly should not be started or maintained under these conditions when its performance might endanger the lives of members of the rescue party. Regardless, CPR is an important skill that every person should master. The only way to learn this technique is to take a CPR course—it cannot be properly self-taught.

Adult Two-Rescuer CPR

The two-rescuer technique differs in that Rescuer One will take a position by the head and Rescuer Two assumes the position as described under one-rescuer CPR.

After establishing unresponsiveness (and activating the EMS system if in civilization), and after finding no signs of circulation, Rescuer Two begins chest compressions with his or her hands on the center of the patient's sternum, at a rate of at least 100 compressions per minute, and compressing the chest at least 2 inches with each compression.

After 30 compressions, Rescuer One opens the airway (head-tilt/chin-lift or jaw-thrust), takes a quick look for obstructions and removes any that are visible, and then gives 2 breaths of about 1 second each. After 5 cycles of 30:2, the two rescuers may switch places if one rescuer is experiencing fatigue.

Two-person CPR is not generally taught to the public in basic courses to avoid confusion. However, in the ocean where prolonged CPR might be necessary, being familiar with this technique can help alleviate the tremendous fatigue that CPR induces in rescuers.

Defibrillator

While not inexpensive, ships carrying older members of their party should consider purchasing and learning to use a defibrillator. Most are automated so that they inform you if the patient has a cardiac rhythm that requires a shock. The machine then "talks" you through the process. Any course that teaches CPR can also teach the use of an automatic defibrillator.

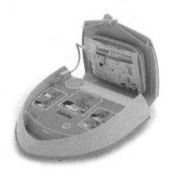

Rapid Breathing

Rapid breathing (hyperventilation syndrome or tachypnea) can represent either a serious medical condition or can be the result of a harmless panic attack. This symptom in a diabetic is very dangerous, as it represents a very high blood sugar level, but it can be prevented by proper diabetic management.

Figure 3.4

AED. Expect this device to cost approximately $3,000. They will require monthly testing, appropriate protections from the elements, and need to be calibrated yearly.

The feeling of panic that results in very shallow breathing causes the victim to lose excessive amounts of carbon dioxide from the bloodstream. The resulting change in the acid-base balance of the blood (respiratory alkalosis) will cause a numb feeling around the mouth and in the extremities, and if the breathing pattern persists, it can even lead to violent spasms of the hands and feet. This form of hysteria can appear in teenagers and healthy young adults. It would be helpful for victims to rebreathe their air from a stuff sack to increase the carbon dioxide level in the bloodstream. They need to be reassured and told to slow down the breathing. It is fine for them to draw long, deep breaths, as it is the rapid breathing that causes the loss of so much carbon dioxide.

If necessary, from the Non-Rx Oral Medication Kit give Percogesic®, 2 tablets, or from the Rx Oral/Topical Medication Kit give Atarax® 25 mg, 2 tablets. From the Rx Injectable Medication Kit, Vistaril®, 50 mg intramuscularly (IM), is also helpful in treating hyperventilation. These drugs are being used in this instance as antianxiety drugs. Atarax and Vistaril are brand names of hydroxyzine.

Diabetics must have access to a glucometer to check their blood sugar levels, even if they do not use insulin. A high sugar reading causing rapid breathing is a medical emergency requiring rapid evacuation. The management of diabetes is beyond the scope of this book but must be well understood by diabetics caring for themselves at sea.

CARDIAC EVALUATION AND CARE

Heart Attack—Myocardial Infarction

The following symptoms are fairly classical for a person having an inadequate oxygen supply to the heart: chest heaviness or pain with exertion; pain or ache radiating into the neck or into the arms; sweating; clammy, pale appearance; shortness of breath. The pain is called angina and results from the heart muscle starving for oxygen. If the blockage is profound, heart muscle will die. This is called an MI, and it means heart attack and damaged muscle. The cause of death is frequently a profound irregular heartbeat caused by electrical irritation in the damaged muscle. Another cause of death is loss of adequate power to pump blood from weakened heart muscle. A delayed cause of death can be from the sudden rupture of the weakened heart wall.

The most important thing for an individual with these symptoms is rest. Rest causes the oxygen requirement of the heart to be at a minimum. Position the victim for optimum comfort, generally with his head elevated about 45 degrees (see figure 3.5). In some cases, even with an electrocardiogram, it is impossible for a trained physician to determine whether an individual is having a cardiac problem. When in doubt, rest the patient and try to evacuate without having him or her do any of the work. Treat him or her as a total invalid.

Physical rest is preferred, but if air evacuation or litter transport is impossible, the quickest route to the hospital is the best route, even if the victim must walk at a slow pace. Reperfusion therapy (opening the coronary arteries with medications or mechanical means), even up to 36 hours post-infarction, reduces long-term mortality and complications.

Oral therapy can reduce infarction size and improve mortality (see *Wilderness Medical Society Practice Guidelines for Wilderness Emergency Care*, 5th edition, edited by William Forgey, MD, Falcon Guides, 2005).

1. Give the patient 4 chewable baby aspirin tablets (81 mg each) immediately, then 1 daily afterward. Check to see if the victim is carrying any prescription heart medications and note usage instructions on the bottle.

2. Give sublingual glycerin if anyone in the party is carrying it. If you are carrying the Rx Cardiac Medication Kit, you will have nitroglycerin spray. Do not give if the BP is below 100 mmHg systolic. If no BP cuff is available, administer if the pulse is palpable in sitting position and there are no signs of hypotension. Do not give if the pulse is below 60 beats per minute. Do not repeat if syncope (fainting) develops after the initial dose. One tablet, followed by an additional tablet at 10-minute intervals, is appropriate. When using the spray, the dose is 1 or 2 sprays under the tongue, repeating as per the above schedule.

Figure 3.5
A heart attack victim can usually breathe better sitting up.

3. Give Plavix® (clopidogrel), 300 mg, loading dose immediately, then 75 mg daily. Obese patients may require 600 mg loading dose for complete platelet inhibition.

4. Administer metoprolol or atenolol (25 mg) every 6 hours, beginning 30 minutes after onset of chest pain, and repeat every 6 hours even if pain improves. Wait 30 minutes after onset of chest pain to identify patients with severe shock, bradycardia (slow heart rate), or acute pulmonary edema. In other words, do not give if the patient's heart rate is below 60 beats per minute or BP is below 100 mmHg systolic, or if the patient complains of severe shortness of breath or is wheezing.

5. You may give the victim medication adequate to relieve pain (see page 24). From the Rx Oral Kit give Atarax (hydroxyzine), 25 mg orally, or from the Rx Injectable Kit give Vistaril (hydroxyzine), 25 mg IM, if needed, to treat nausea or to help sedate the victim. You may repeat the pain medication and the nausea/sedation medication every 4 hours as needed.

Observe respirations and pulse rate. You will note the comment in the section under Adult One-Rescuer CPR that providing CPR to a heart attack victim who cannot be defibrillated within 4 minutes is a lost cause. The only significant reason for starting CPR, if the person becomes pulseless, is to placate the onlookers. Due to the virtual zero salvage rate, you are treating yourself and the others watching who, after perhaps half an hour, will consider that everything has been done that was possible. This may be a very important part of the emotional support required by individual group members as they reflect upon the event.

Rapid Heart Rate—Tachycardia

A rapid heart rate after trauma or other stress may signify impending shock. The underlying cause should be treated. This may require fluid replacement or pain medication. Body temperature elevations cause an increase in heart rate of 10 beats per minute for each degree above normal. A sudden onset of rapid heart rate with sharp chest pain can indicate a pulmonary embolism or pneumothorax. Treat with pain medication and have the patient sit propped up for ease in breathing.

A very rapid rate of 140 to 220 beats per minute may be encountered suddenly and without warning in very healthy individuals. This PAT (paroxysmal atrial tachycardia) frequently has, as its first symptom, a feeling of profound weakness. The victim generally stops what he or she is doing and feels better sitting down. These attacks are self-limited, but they can be aborted by one of several maneuvers that stimulate the vagus nerve, which in turn slows down the pulse rate. These maneuvers include holding one's breath and bearing down very hard, closing one's eyes and pressing firmly on one of the eyeballs, inducing vomiting with a finger down the throat, or feeling for the carotid pulse in the neck and gently pressing on the enlarged portion of this vessel, one side at a time. Another effective maneuver is to take a deep breath and plunge one's face into ice water. Frequently, however, the victim must just wait for the attack to pass. This arrhythmia will sometimes come on after a spate of activity. No medication is generally required.

Slow Heart Rate—Bradycardia

A slow heart rate is important in two instances: when someone passes out; and when it accompanies a high fever. Generally, fainting or shock is associated with a rapid pulse rate (see compensatory shock, page 15), an attempt by the body to maintain BP. A safety mechanism, which the body employs to prevent BP from elevating too high, is a sensor system in each carotid artery in the neck, called the carotid bodies. If these sensors are stimulated by an elevated BP, a reflex mechanism that relaxes and opens blood vessels throughout the body and lowers the heart rate is generated via impulses from the carotid bodies through the vagus nerve. The vagus nerve can be fooled into inappropriately initiating this reflex mechanism at times. A person watching an accident scene, or even thinking about such an episode, can stimulate the vagus nerve through its connection with the frontal lobe. The resulting slow pulse and relaxed arteries can result in the person passing out (fainting).

As mentioned earlier, the pulse usually increases as the body temperature rises. It also falls as the core temperature lowers into a hypothermia state (see page 256). Several diseases are notable in that the pulse rate is lower than would be expected for the elevated body temperature caused by the disease. Typhoid fever (page 250) is the classic example of this phenomenon.

CHAPTER 4
SYMPTOM MANAGEMENT

Symptoms are indicators of problems. Fever, pain, and itch can sometimes aid you in determining exactly what is wrong with the patient. The various decision tables in this book use one or more symptoms to help identify a diagnosis and plan a treatment.

It is also useful to know how to minimize some of these symptoms. Why itch when you can treat it? The cause of an itch may vary from poison plant dermatitis to an insect bite to liver disease. Regardless of the cause, what can you do to alleviate it?

The best method for reducing symptoms is to successfully treat the underlying problem. Sometimes definitive treatment cannot be accomplished. At other times, the symptom remains after the injury is past and the symptom becomes the greatest part of the problem.

Table 4.1 provides a guide to general symptom care.

Table 4.1 General Symptom Care Guide

Rapid Breathing difficulties	22–23
Cough	293
Diarrhea	90–93
Fever/chills	30
Headache	37
Heart rate, too fast-Tachycardia	26
Heart rate, too slow-Bradycardia	27
Hiccups	37
Hires	36
Itch	35
Lethargy	32
Nausea/vomiting	90
Pain, Mild, & Severe	33–35
Skin Rash	158–159

Table 4.2 General Anatomical Location Guide

Eye	45
Nose	61
Ear	65
Mouth (and dental)	72–77
Chest	81
Abdomen	85
Reproductive organs	99

For a discussion of symptoms localized to a specific body part, refer to table 4.2 for the anatomical or body location and symptom cross-referenced in the Clinical Reference Index, starting on page 301.

Evaluation and management of symptoms relating to injuries and environmental exposure can also be found through the Clinical Reference Index.

FEVER/CHILLS

The average oral temperature of a resting individual is 98.6°F (37°C); in active individuals, it is 101°F (38°C). Rectal temperatures are 0.5°F to 1.5°F higher. A tympanic temperature (taken by an infrared sensor placed in the ear) will range from equaling to being 0.5°F to 1°F higher than oral. An axillary (armpit) reading ranges 0.5°F to 1°F lower than oral. Forehead or temporal readings are, in my opinion, all over the map, depending on ambient temperature, sweating, technique and expense/accuracy of the device, but are generally considered equal to oral. Certainly, they are useful when checking a large number of persons rapidly and give a good guess. A person's temperature increase of 1 degree above their normal will result in the heart rate increasing 10 beats per minute over their normal resting heart rate. This is a useful field method of judging temperature, if everyone knows what his or her resting pulse is. Some diseases cause a peculiar drop in heart rate, even in the face of an obviously high temperature. The most notable of these are typhoid fever (see page 250) and yellow fever (page 252).

Although injury and exposure can cause elevated body temperature, fever is usually the result of infection. The cause of the fever should be sought and treated. If pain or infection is located in the ear, throat, and the like, refer to the appropriate anatomical area listed in the Clinical Reference Index at the end of the book.

If other symptoms beside fever are present (diarrhea, cough, etc.), see the cross-references listing for these symptoms in the Clinical Reference Index to provide treatment to alleviate the suffering of these conditions. This may diagnose the underlying disease, which will have a specific treatment indicated in the text.

The sailor's approach to therapy may be quite different from that used in clinical medicine. While on a voyage beyond medical care, when in doubt about whether a fever is due to viral, bacterial, or other infectious causes, treat for a bacterial infection with an antibiotic from your Rx medication kits. Initially give the patient (Levaquin®) 750 mg, 1 tablet daily, and continue until the fever has been broken for an additional 3 days. This will conserve medication while providing adequate antibiotic coverage for a suspected bacterial infection.

If it is possible that the patient has a strep throat, give azithromycin (Zithromax®) rather than levofloxacin, as described on page 292. If you are not carrying the Rx kit, then treat the symptoms using the medications described in your non-Rx kits. In either case, rest is important until the patient is again free of fever and has a sense of well-being.

Chills are a kind of shivering, accompanied by a feeling of coldness (not related to hypothermia; see page 30). Chills, also called rigors, usually occur when the body temperature is 102°F (38.9°C) or the person has had a sudden rise in body temperature. Chills frequently indicate the onset of a bacterial infection, which should be treated with an antibiotic as described earlier. In tropical countries, serious infections, such as malaria, must be considered (see page 238). People tolerate fevers quite well, and it is possible that elevated temperatures enhance the immune response to infections. However, persons with a history of febrile seizures or a history of heart problems should certainly be treated to lower an elevated temperature.

Generally, it is best to use acetaminophen (paracetamol), but usually ibuprofen and aspirin are safe. Aspirin should be avoided in children with chicken pox or other viral illness due to an increase in Reye's syndrome (a disease of progressive liver failure and brain deterioration) with its use. The Non-Rx Oral Medication Kit contains three products useful in treating fever: ibuprofen, aspirin, and Percogesic. As these are over-the-counter products, the dosage will be listed on the product containers. The Rx Oral kit contains meloxicam and its use is described in that section (see pages 291–297).

LETHARGY

Lethargy, or prolonged tiredness or malaise, is a non-localizing symptom, such as fever or muscle ache (myalgia). Pain, however, is a localizing symptom that points to the organ system that may be the cause of such things as lethargy, fever, or a generally ill feeling. Frequently after a few days of lethargy—or at times even hours—localizing symptoms develop and the cause of the lethargy can be determined to be an infection of the throat, ear, and the like.

Sometimes a chronic condition is the source of the lethargy, such as anemia, leukemia, low thyroid function, occult or low-grade infection, mental depression, or even physical exhaustion. The latter we would expect to be obvious from the history of the preceding level of activity and strength should return within a few days.

Anemia can be present due to chronic blood loss from ulcers, menstrual problems, inadequate formation of iron, leukemia, or other cancers in the bone marrow, and so forth. Chronic anemia can be identified by looking at the color of the skin inside the lower eyelids. Pull the lower lid down and look at it. Compare to another person. Normally this thin skin is very orange-colored, even if the cheeks are pale. If the color is a blanched white, anemia is very likely. Another good indication of anemia is an increase in the pulse rate of more than 30 beats per minute in the standing position, compared to a recumbent position.

If other symptoms are present, such as nausea, one must think of hepatitis (see pages 231–232), or if preceded by a severe sore throat, infectious mononucleosis (see pages 71–72).

See also, Sopite syndrome, a form of lethargy caused as a symptom of seasickness (see chapter 5).

Lethargy is one of the most common presenting complaints that I see in my office. An accurate diagnosis requires careful evaluation, sometimes aided by laboratory tests. If the problem is not depression, then regardless of the cause, the person needs rest, proper nutrition, and adequate shelter.

PAIN

Adequate pain management can involve a mixture of proper medication and attitude—the attitudes of both the victim and the medic are crucial. A calm, professional approach to problems will lessen anxiety, panic, and pain. Pain is an important symptom that tells you something is wrong. It generally "localizes" or points to the exact cause of the trouble, so that pain in various parts of the body will be your clue that a problem exists and that specific treatment may be required to eliminate it. Refer to the Clinical Reference Index (page 301) under specific areas of the body (such as ear or abdomen) to read about diagnosis and specific treatments of the causes of pain.

An application of cold water or ice can frequently relieve pain. This is very important in burns, orthopedic injuries, and skin irritations. Cold can sometimes relieve muscle spasm. Gentle massage and local hot compresses are also effective treatments for muscle spasm.

The alleviation of pain with medication calls for a stepwise increase in medication strength until relief is obtained. Throughout this book, you will be referred to this section for adequate pain management. Use discretion in providing adequate medication to do the job, without overdosing the patient. Remember that a pill takes about 20 minutes to begin working and is at maximum therapeutic strength in about 1 hour. If possible, wait an hour to see how effective the medication has been. But use common sense. If the injury is severe, give a respectable initial dose.

Mild Pain

For mild pain, from the Non-Rx Oral Medication Kit, provide the victim with ibuprofen, 200 mg, 1 or 2 tablets every 4 hours. Meloxicam in the prescription kit is particularly good for orthopedic injuries or whenever muscle sprains and contusions are encountered. It is also ideal for menstrual cramps and tension headache, and it is relatively safe to use in head injuries. It can also be used for the muscle aches and fever from viral and bacterial infections.

Meloxicam, ibuprofen, and aspirin have anti-inflammatory actions that make them ideal for treatment of tendinitis, bursitis, or arthritic pain.

Severe Pain

For severe pain you may have to rely on providing the maximal dose of ibuprofen (800 mg every 6 hours) or meloxicam 15 mg once daily. This can be augmented by giving the victim 1 or 2 Atarax 25 mg tablets every 4 to 6 hours. This medication helps eliminate any associated nausea, and from my experience also potentiates the pain medication so that it works more effectively.

The Rx Oral/Topical Medication Kit also contains nasally inhaled Stadol® (butorphanol tartrate). This very powerful pain medication is about 10 times stronger per milligram than morphine. Spray up one nostril, followed by another spray in the other nostril 5 to 20 minutes later, if necessary. This may be repeated every 3 to 4 hours. This medication is as powerful as any injectable product available. See a full discussion of this medication on page 291. Its rate of onset is rapid. Within 5 minutes relief should start, reaching its maximum effect within 20 minutes. Lock this medication in a secure container in the medical chest.

If you are carrying the Rx Injectable Medication Kit, severe pain can be treated with an injection of 10 mg of Nubain® (nalbuphine). This amounts to 0.5 ml of the strength listed in the kit. This can be potentiated with Vistaril (hydroxyzine), 25 or 50 mg, also by injection. Vistaril and Nubain can be mixed in the same syringe. They both sting upon injection.

Local pain can be eliminated or eased with cold compresses or ice, as mentioned earlier. Applying dibucaine 1% ointment will help skin surface pain, such as from sunburn, abrasions, and the like. Applying a cover of Spenco 2nd Skin® dressing provides cooling relief due to the evaporative action of the water from this safe-to-use gel pad. Deep cuts and painful puncture wounds can be injected with lidocaine 1% from the Rx Injectable Medication Kit. This technique is described on page 297.

ITCH

As itch is a sensation that is transmitted by pain fibers, all pain medications can be used in alleviating itch sensations. Itch also indicates that something is awry and may require specific treatment. The most common causes are local allergic reactions, such as poisonous plants, fungal infections, and insect bites or infestations (or look under specific causes in the index). General principles of treatment include further avoidance of the offending substance (not so easy in the case of mosquitoes). Avoid applying heat to an itchy area, as this makes it flare up worse. Avoid scratching or rubbing; this also increases the reaction. If weeping blisters have formed, apply wet soaks with a clean cloth or gauze. While plain water soaks will help, making a solution of regular table salt will help dry the lesions and alleviate some of the itch. Make an approximately 10% solution weight to volume of water. Cream-based preparations work well on moist lesions, while ointments are more effective on dry, scaly ones. The Topical Bandaging Kit contains 1% hydrocortisone cream, which, while safe to use, is generally not very effective against severe allergic dermatitis. For best results, one should apply it 4 times daily and then cover the area with an occlusive dressing, such as cellophane or a piece of plastic bag. The Rx Oral/Topical Medication Kit contains Topicort® (desoximetasone) 0.25% ointment, which is strong enough to adequately treat allergic dermatitis with light coats applied twice daily. Athlete's foot and skin rashes in the groin or in skinfolds are generally fungal and should not be treated with these creams. They may seem to provide temporary relief, but they can worsen fungal infections. For possible fungal infections, apply clotrimazole cream 1% twice daily from the Topical Bandaging Kit.

Oral medications are frequently required to treat severe skin reactions and itch. The Non-Rx Oral Medication Kit contains Benadryl® (diphenhydramine), 25 mg. Take 1 or 2 capsules every 6 hours. It is one of the most effective antihistamines made, but there are less sedating ones now sold without prescription, such as Claritin, Zyrtec, and Allegra. The Rx Oral Topical Medication Kit contains Atarax (hydroxyzine), 25 mg. It is very effective in treating the symptom of itch and as an antihistamine. Take 1 or 2 tablets every 6 hours. These medications are safe to use on all sorts of itch problems. If one is suffering from an asthma attack, however, they should not be used, as they tend to dry out the lung secretions and potentially make the illness worse. Patients with a history of asthma should use the newer antihistamines mentioned earlier.

HIVES

Hives are the result of a severe allergic reaction. Commonly called welts, these raised red blotches develop rapidly and frequently have a red border around a clearer skin area in the center, sometimes referred to as an annular lesion. As these can and do appear over large surfaces of the skin, treatment with a cream is of little help. Use the diphenhydramine or hydroxyzine, as indicated earlier. Extensive urticaria or allergic dermatitis lesions frequently need to be treated with an oral steroid. The Rx Oral/Topical Medication Kit has Decadron® (dexamethasone) 4 mg tablets; 1 tablet should be taken twice daily after meals.

It should be noted that the Vistaril recommended for the Rx Injectable Kit is also hydroxyzine, as is the oral Atarax. This same kit also has an injectable form of the dexamethasone. For treatment of rash, the oral medications should suffice.

In case of a concurrent asthmatic condition or the development of shock, treat as for anaphylactic shock (see pages 203–205). In case of suspected tick bite, an annular or circular lesion may be a sign of Lyme disease (page 236). If fever is present, one must consider that a rash and itch have resulted from an infection. A diagnosis may be impossible at sea, so treatment with an antibiotic is appropriate on expeditions expected to last longer than several more days. Use doxycycline 100 mg twice daily from the Rx Oral/Topical Medication Kit as a field-expedient solution to the problem. Treat fever as described on page 55.

HICCUPS

Hiccups can be started by a variety of causes and are generally self-limited. Persistent hiccups can be a medically important symptom requiring professional evaluation and help in control. Several approaches to their control in at sea may be tried. Have the victim hold his breath for as long as possible or rebreathe air from a stuff sack. These maneuvers raise the carbon dioxide level and help stop the hiccup reflex mechanism. Drinking 5 to 6 ounces of ice water fast sometimes works; one may also close one's eyes and press firmly on the eyeballs to stimulate the vagal blockage of the hiccup. The other vagus nerve stimulation maneuvers described under Rapid Heart Rate, page 26, can be tried.

If these maneuvers do not work, from the Non-Rx Oral Medication Kit, you may give diphenhydramine, 25 mg, or from the Rx Oral/Topical Medication Kit you may give Atarax, 25 mg, 2 tablets. In the Rx Injectable Medication Kit, Vistaril is an injectable form of Atarax. This medication may be given in a dose of 50 mg IM. These doses may be repeated every 4 hours. Let the patient rest and try to avoid bothering him until bedtime. If still symptomatic at that point, have him rebreathe the air from inside a sleeping bag or under a blanket, to raise the carbon dioxide level in his bloodstream and, if nothing else, to muffle the sounds.

HEADACHE

A variety of problems can cause a headache (refer to table 4.3). Too much sun exposure, dehydration, withdrawal from caffeine, stress, dental or eye problems—the list is almost endless. Be sure to consider the possible underlying problems mentioned in the table as they are the most common.

Table 4.3 Causes of Headache Guide

Dental Care	74–80
Dehydration-Risk Factors for Hear Stress Factors	264–267
TMJ-Temporomandibular Joint Syndrome	70
Heat Exhaustion & Heat Stroke	268–270

CHAPTER 5
SEASICKNESS (*mal de mer*) AND SOPITE SYNDROME

Motion in any vehicle can induce nausea, hence the many etiologies of this disorder, such as seasickness, air sickness, and the dreaded "tilt-a-whirl" induced vomiting at the amusement park. After being exposed to motion for many days—a long nautical trip or train ride—some people become nauseated when the motion suddenly stops, and they are on terra firma.

There are many aspects of "seasickness" that are not identified with this condition. Lethargy, irritability, and depression are common problems that may persist for weeks and have been directly related to a condition called Sopite syndrome.

The motion of the sea is a three-dimensional action, unlike land-based vehicles, which are usually two-dimensional, unless lots of sharp curves in hills are being encountered. The illness, while usually apparent when extreme nausea and vomiting ensues, may be often undiagnosed. The syndrome of fatigue (which can mask as irritability, personality change depression) has been called the "Sopite syndrome" and is considered a form of motion sickness. The same stimulus that causes nausea, the rocking motion, can induce drowsiness, such as the time-worn technique of putting the baby to sleep by rocking. Nausea and vomiting are easily recognized in the new voyageur, but the etiology of drowsiness and mood change may not be correctly identified. So, while a rocking motion may be a good thing when used to put a baby to sleep, it is not so good when a helmsman is on watch.

Susceptibility has been studied in astronauts, seafarers, and now, gaming enthusiasts, due to their use of virtual visual headsets. It has been apparent to physiologists for many years that many internal signals under normal conditions are subject to sensory inhibition, which precludes from consciousness many signals related to the background activity of the body. On a moving ship, when getting one's sea legs, this involves being able to coordinate whole body movements to achieve movement goals (standing, walking, climbing, etc.), in the moving environment while also maintaining appropriate predictable stabilization of the viscera. Visceral nerve controls affect the respiration, heart rate, and vestibular (inner ear and cerebellum of the brain) sensitivity to motion.

It is possible to avoid or attenuate seasickness only by introducing exposure gradually and initially limiting the exposure in the "novel" environment. In fact, incremental exposure, progressively increasing the intensity of stimulation over multiple exposures, is a very effective way to prevent motion sickness. But it is difficult to achieve this, unless you command the boat and can order periodic brief sorties into initially gentle, then more aggressive wave conditions.

Otherwise, everyone is plopped into a boat, off you go, and then what you notice is the difference in various people's ability to withstand this stimulation and how they respond. Initially researchers thought there were two types of responders: those who respond primarily with head symptoms, such as headache and drowsiness, and gut responders who primarily experience nausea and vomiting. Recent research has shown that a person's response depends on the relative provocativeness of the stimulation, his or her relative susceptibility, and prior experience.

Not all motion sickness is created equal. Not all vomiting situations are equally discomforting for all individuals. Some feel total relief after vomiting for a period of time. People with a higher threshold for vomiting may feel much more nauseated until they do, then only gain partial relief. Some are unable to vomit even though they are desperate to do so. They may be more incapacitated than those who do vomit.

Decrease of symptoms various enormously between people during the same exposure. Three things affect sickness development: sensitivity to stimulation, the rate of adaptation to simulation (adaptation constant), and the time constant of decay of elicited symptoms. Experiments have shown that anyone with a normal vestibular function when exposed to provocative physical body motion, disruption of vestibular-ocular reflexes, or optokinetic stimulation can to some extent be made motion sick. Any situation that requires altered control of the head and body is potentially provocative. It is profoundly provocative to make pitch or roll head movements when the plane of the head motion is stimulated while rotating. Under normal, nonrotating conditions, when head movement is made, the semicircular canals are stimulated by the acceleration of the head, but the endolymph fluid in these ear balance canals lags and, as the head decelerates, the fluid signal is restored back to its resting position. This generally occurs within 1 second. The neural output of the semicircular canals is proportional to the head velocity, and the fluid movement essentially performs a mechanical integration. The head velocity signal is used to control compensatory eye movements that are normally appropriate to the situation. In addition, that signal is integrated to give an indication of the angular displacement of the head relative to space.

The importance of the, shall we say, hidden visceral nerve signals in response to muscular action, even anticipated action, is critical to understanding much of what happens in seasickness. Visceral responses to muscular actions are essential. If you wish to lift a weight, even throw a ball, signals must be sent to the urinary sphincter and rectal sphincter to tighten up or, with each movement, you would leak urine and stool.

Another nervous "system" we are not aware of that is constantly functioning is proprioception. These nerves, which are basically active where tendons connect to bones, provide our brain with position awareness. In other words, when you shut your eyes and move your arm upward and hold it in position, these nerves provide constant feedback to your brain, indicating the requested action is actually taking place. It should be apparent that during movements caused by a ship's uneven actions, various muscles are being used to control limb and trunk placement, combined with the visceral nerve signals—all of which are important for the brain to decipher what it wants to happened with feedback input "confirming" that it really happened.

And it is this visceral connection that results in some people having the nausea and vomiting as a result of body position not matching the sensory inputs. The sensory inputs are from the balance sensors of the middle ear, the proprioception position sense, the frontal lobe thinking it knows what is going on, and the pathways in the brain that fine-tune controlling appropriate interpretation of the sudden mismatches of sensory data that a tossing sea throws into the poor sailor's "on-board" computer.

Sopite syndrome is characterized by boredom, apathy, failure of initiative, increased irritability, and even changes in personality, as well as profound drowsiness and persistent fatigue that can develop from either highly provocative stimulation or prolonged exposure to low-intensity motion. This is a frequently unknown aspect of seasickness, while nausea and vomiting are easily recognized as a symptom early in the voyage. A potential behavior marker for Sopite syndrome is yawning.

Studies have shown that virtually anyone with a normal middle-ear vestibular function (the balance input system from the semicircular canals of the middle ear) can have seasickness induced. To minimize motion effects, or getting one's "sea legs," it is important to be able to coordinate whole body movements to achieve desired goals in the moving environment while also maintaining appropriate predictable stabilization of the viscera neural input. The natural method for preventing motion sickness is to look at a point on the horizon, thus minimizing the motion exaggeration. On deck, stare at a distant cloud, or look as far forward on the horizon as possible. It helps to be the helmsman as the need to look at the distant horizon and coordination required to adjust course provides sensory input that minimizes the motion effects. Even passively having your hand on the tiller can be helpful. Reading tends to increase the symptoms. Avoid alcohol and greasy foods on bouncy trips. With repeated exposure to the same sort of motion over many days, you may become adapted and experience less discomfort.

The most effective medication to prevent seasickness is scopolamine. The patch (brand name Transderm Scop® United States or Transderm-V® Canada) is placed behind an ear and may be worn for 3 days. It should be placed about 4 hours prior to embarking. It can cause dry mouth, drowsiness (which is potentially another effect of seasickness anyway), and in elderly people, it can cause extreme agitation. Be careful handling this as touching your eye can result in sudden dilation of the pupil. If this happens, the affected eye may remain dilated for 3 days to 2 weeks! Cruise ship medical personnel report elderly people sometimes become very agitated, even manic, when on this medication.

Various antihistamines help control the impulses from the vestibular nerve and provide anti-nausea prevention and treatment. Meclizine (Antivert®, Bonine®, and other brands) and dimenhydrinate (Dramamine® United States, Gravol® Canada) are examples. All of these medications are available without a prescription.

Many of the most potent drugs used to treat nausea and vomiting induced by food poisoning, chemotherapy, or radiation therapy or poisoning do not work as well on seasickness. These are ondansetron (Zofran®), which works on a chemoreceptor trigger zone, and various phenothiazine derivatives, such as prochlorperazine (Compazine® United States, Stemetil® Canada) and promethazine (Phenergan®). Promethazine is less likely to cause side effects than prochlorperazine. These medications require a prescription to purchase.

While the bad news that a normally very effective antiemetic (anti-nausea and -vomiting) agent like ondansetron does not work well on these symptoms when caused from seasickness, there is another somewhat remarkable agent available—and that is the placebo effect. Studies have shown using a placebo in treating motion sickness to be surprisingly effective, as high as 40%. So, if crewmates want to wear a pressure point bracelet or use a folklore remedy, let them have at it. And don't disparage its use as that will harm the benefit that might otherwise result from the placebo effect.

CHAPTER 6

EYE

Pain and irritation of the eye can be devastating. Causes are listed in table 6.1.

Table 6.1 Symptoms and Signs of Eye Pathology

	VISION LOSS	PAIN	RED	DRAINAGE	TISSUE SWELLING
Trauma (57)	l	n	n	l	l
Foreign body (47)	n	n	n		
Infection					
Bacteria (54)		l		l	l
Viral (54)		l	n	n	
Sty (56)		l			
Allergy (56)	n	l			
Corneal ulcers (52)	l				n
Snow blindness (53)	l		n	n	l
Strain		l			
Glaucoma (58)		l		n	
Spontaneous subconjunctival (57) hemorrhage		n			

Legend	n	A frequent or intense symptom
	l	Common, less intense symptom
	Blank	Less likely to produce this symptom

Note: The page numbers are in parentheses.

EYE PATCH AND BANDAGING TECHNIQUES

In case of evidence of infection, do not use an eye patch or splint but have the patient wear dark glasses or a wide-brimmed hat, or take other measures to decrease light exposure. Wash the eye with clean water by dabbing with wet, clean cloth every 2 hours to remove pus and excess secretions. Apply antibiotics as indicated under Conjunctivitis, page 54.

Eye patch techniques must allow for gentle closure of the eyelid and retard blinking activity. Sometimes both eyes must be patched for this to succeed, but this obviously is a hardship for the patient. Simple strips of tape holding the eyelids shut may suffice. In case of trauma, an annular ring of cloth may be constructed to pad the eye without pressure over the eyeball. A simple eye patch with oversize gauze or cloth may work fine, as the bone of the orbital rim around the eye acts to protect the eyeball, which is recessed.

Serious injury requires patching both eyes, as movement in the injured eye will decrease if movement in the unaffected eye is also controlled. It generally helps to have the victim kept at rest with her head elevated 30 degrees. A severe blow to one eye may cause temporary blindness in both eyes, which can resolve in hours to days. Obviously, a person with loss of vision should be treated by a physician if possible. Eye dressings must be removed, or at least changed, in 24 hours.

If a foreign object has been removed from the eye or the victim has suffered a corneal abrasion, the best splint is the tension patch. Start by placing 2 gauze pads over the shut eye, requesting the patient to keep his eyes closed until the bandaging is completed. The patient may help hold the gauze in place. Three pieces of 1-inch-wide tape are ideal, long enough to extend from the center of the forehead to just below the cheekbone. Fasten the first piece of tape to the center of the forehead, extending the tape diagonally downward across the eye patch. The second and third strips are applied parallel to the first strip, one above and the other below. This dressing will result in firm splinting of the bandaged eye.

FOREIGN BODY EYE INJURY

The most common eye problems that are frequently encountered at sea will be foreign body, abrasion, ultraviolet (UV) light (frequently reflective) blindness, and infection (conjunctivitis). Therapy for these problems is virtually the same, except that it is very important to remove any foreign body that may be present.

The initial step in examining the painful eye is to remove the foreign object. One of the lessons drilled into medical students is to never, ever write a prescription for eye anesthesia agents (such as the tetracaine ophthalmic solution that I recommend for the Rx Oral/ Topical Medication Kit). The reason is the patient may use it, obtain relief, and then not have the eye carefully examined for a foreign body. Eventually this foreign body may cause an ulcer to form in the cornea, doing profound damage.

When using the tetracaine, remember that it is very important to find and remove any foreign body. Pull down on the lower lid and use one drop. If the patient is unable to open her eye due to pain, place 1 or 2 drops in the inner corner of the eye while she is lying face up. Have her blink once or twice to allow the liquid to cover the eyeball. This medication burns when initially placed in the eye. This will increase the level of pain for a brief period until the medication takes effect. After the patient has calmed down, have her open the eye and look straight ahead. Very carefully shine a pen light at the cornea from one side to see if a minute speck becomes visible. By moving the light back and forth, one might see movement of a shadow on the iris of the eye and thus confirm the presence of a foreign body. Mucus can give a gooey appearance to the cornea that may mimic a foreign body. Have the victim blink to move any mucus around. A point that consistently stays put with blinking is probably a foreign body.

In making the foreign body examination, also be sure to check under the eyelids. Evert the upper lid over a Q-tip stick, thus examining not only the eyeball but also the undersurface of the eyelid. This surface may be gently brushed with the cotton applicator to eliminate minute particles. Always use a fresh Q-tip when touching the eye or eyelid each additional time. Some foreign bodies can be removed easily. Have the patient place his face under water and blink. Water turbulence from underwater blinking or turbulence from directing running water from a fast-moving stream or by pouring from a cup may wash the problem away.

When a foreign body has been found embedded in the cornea, take a sterile, or at least a clean, Q-tip and approach the foreign body from the side. Gently prod it with the Q-tip handle until it is loosened. The surface of the eye will indent under the pressure of this scraping action. Indeed, the surface of the cornea will be scratched in the maneuver, but it will quickly heal. Once the foreign body has been dislodged, if it does not stick to the wooden or plastic handle but slides loose along the corneal surface, use the cotton portion to touch it for removal.

A stoic individual, particularly one accustomed to contact lenses, might be able to undergo an uncomplicated foreign body removal without the use of tetracaine 0.5% ophthalmic drops, but using anesthesia makes the patient more comfortable and cuts down on interference from the blink reflex.

Foreign bodies stuck in the cornea can be very stubborn and resist removal. At times it is necessary to pick them loose with the sharp point of a #11-scalpel blade or the tip of a needle (I frequently use an 18-gauge needle). Anesthesia with tetracaine will be a necessity for this procedure. Scraping with these instruments will cause a more significant scratch to the corneal surface, but under these circumstances, it may have to be accepted. I would leave stubborn foreign bodies for removal by a physician in all but the most desperate circumstances. If you have a difficult time removing an obvious foreign body from the surface of the cornea, a wait of 2 to 3 days may allow the cornea to ulcerate slightly so that removal with the Q-tip stick may be much easier. Deeply lodged foreign bodies will have to be left for surgical removal.

A painless foreign body may not be a foreign body. It could be a rust ring left behind after a bit of ferrous, or iron-containing, material has fallen out of the eye after having been lodged for a short time. If what you see is painless, ignore it in the remote setting if physician help is not available.

The history that involves striking an object should alert you to the fact that the injury may have penetrated much more deeply than you would expect from blowing debris hitting the eye. While blowing debris can lodge in the eye surface, a foreign body slamming into the eye due to someone striking an object (say, with a hammer) might have penetrated very deeply into the eyeball. Penetrating injuries are a disaster!

A puncture wound of the eyelid mandates careful examination of the cornea surface for evidence of a penetrating foreign body. These injuries must be seen by a physician for surgical care. Evacuation is necessary. If this is impossible, the eye must be patched, examined for infection twice daily, and treated with antibiotic both by mouth and with ointment.

After removal of a foreign body, or even after scraping the eye while attempting to remove one, apply some antibiotic. The prescription kit should contain Tobradex® ophthalmic drops. There are no nonprescription eye antibiotics. Brand-name Neosporin and Polysporin ointments in 15-g tubes are nonprescription antibiotics that can be used in the eye. However, the manufacturer cannot recommend the use of these over-the-counter products for this purpose.

While the tetracaine will provide local pain relief, continued use may hinder the natural healing process and may disguise a significant injury or the presence of an additional foreign body. Pain relief is best attempted by protecting the eye from sunlight using sunglasses, providing a damp cloth for evaporative cooling, and oral pain medication. There is no evidence that patching an eye with a corneal abrasion is useful. Percogesic or ibuprofen, 200 mg, from the non-Rx kit, both given in a dose of 2 tablets every 4 to 6 hours, may be provided for pain. The prescription analgesic Norco®-10/325, 1 tablet every 4 to 6 hours, would provide significant pain relief.

CONTACT LENSES

The increased popularity of contact lenses means that several problems associated with their use have also increased. The lenses are of two basic types: the hard or rigid lens, which generally is smaller and does not extend beyond the iris, and the soft lens, which does extend beyond the iris onto the white of the eye. Soft lenses have been designed for extended wear. Hard lens use requires frequent removal, as the delicate cornea of the eye obtains oxygen from the environment and nutrients from eye secretions. These lenses interfere with this process and therefore are detrimental to the cornea.

Examine the eyes of all unconscious persons for the existence of hard lenses and remove them if found. It is probably best to remove soft lenses also, as some are not designed for extended use and may also damage the eye. The use of soft lenses when it is expected that you may get to go on an extended voyage and extended time, even attempting to use hard lenses, may mean that you should rethink using contact lenses altogether. Also obtain the proper eyeglass prescription and keep a pair in your bug-out bag!

Leaving most hard contact lenses in the eyes longer than 12 hours can result in corneal ulceration. While not serious, this can be a very painful experience. At times, even iritis may result. This condition almost always resolves on its own within a day. The history is the major clue that the diagnosis is correct. If the condition fails to clear within 24 hours, other problems should be looked into, such as corneal laceration, foreign body, or eye infection.

After removal of the contact lenses, place cool cloths or ice packs on the eyes. The patient should be evaluated by a physician to confirm the diagnosis. Provide protection from sunlight, using sunglasses during the day. Give aspirin or other pain medication, if available. The patient may have pain from the migration of the lens into one of the recesses of the conjunctiva, or possibly only have noted a loss of refractive correction. At times the complaint is a sudden "I have lost my contact lens!" Never forget to look in the eye as the possible hiding spot for the lens. Examine the eye as described in the section on foreign bodies in the eye (see page 47). When dealing with a hard lens, use topical anesthesia as described if necessary and available. If the lens is loose, slide it over the pupil and allow the patient to remove it as he or she usually does. If the lens is adherent, rinse with eye irrigation solution or clean water and try again. If a corneal abrasion exists, patch as indicated above after the lens is removed.

The soft lens may generally be squeezed between the fingers and literally "popped" off. A special rubber pincer is sold that can aid in this maneuver. Hard lenses may also be removed with a special rubber suction cup device.

If the patient is unconscious, the hard lenses will have to be removed. Lacking the suction cup device, there are two different maneuvers that may be employed. One is the vertical technique. In this method, move the lens to the center of the eye over the pupil. Then press down on the lower lid, over the lower edge of the contact lens. Next squeeze the eyelids together, thus popping the lens out between them as indicated in figure 6.1a. In the horizontal technique, slide the lens to the outside corner of the eye. By tugging on the facial skin near the eye in a downward and outward direction, the lens can pop over the skin edge and be easily removed (see figure 6.1b).

The unconscious patient should have antibiotic salve placed in his or her eye and the lids taped or patched shut to prevent drying. These patches should be removed when needed for neurological checks, and certainly upon regaining consciousness.

If removal of the lenses must be prolonged, safe storage will have to be provided. Regarding hard lenses, the ideal would be marked containers that pad the lenses so that they do not rattle around or otherwise become scratched. Small vials, labeled R and L, filled with

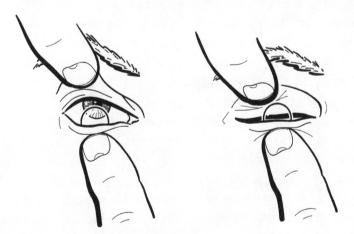

Figure 6.1a
Contact lens removal—vertical technique.

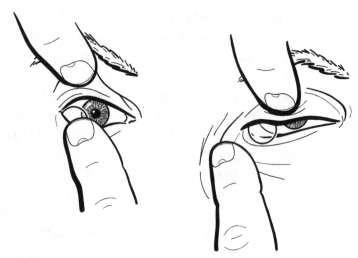

Figure 6.1b
Contact lens removal—horizontal technique.

a fluff of clean material, taped together, and placed in a safe location, would be ideal. Soft contact lenses must be protected from dehydration. It is always proper to store them in normal saline. This solution can be prepared by adding 11/2 ounces of table salt to 1 pint of water. Of course, if the patient has a special solution for her lenses in her possession, use it.

EYE ABRASION

Abrasions may be caused by a glancing blow from a wood chip, a swinging branch, or even from blowing dirt, embers, ice, or snow. The involved eye should be anesthetized with prescription tetracaine and protected with Tobradex ophthalmic drops. Make sure that a foreign body has not been overlooked.

In cold wind, be sure to protect your eyes from the effects of both blowing particles of ice and the wind itself. Grey Owl, in his interesting book, *Tales of an Empty Cabin*, tells how he was walking on one of his long trips through the backwoods along a windswept frozen lake when suddenly he lost sight of the tree line. He felt that he must be in a whiteout, so he turned perpendicular to the wind and hiked toward the shore. Suddenly he bumped into a tree and realized that he was blind! He saved himself only by digging a snow cave and staying put for 3 days. He wondered how many good woodsmen were lost on their trap lines by such a similar incident, apparently, a temporary opacification of the cornea from the cold wind or ice crystal abrasions.

ULTRAVIOLET EYE INJURY

When one thinks of blindness occurring suddenly in the outdoors, the first thing that comes to mind is snow blindness or UV eye damage. "Snow blindness" is a severely painful condition primarily caused by UV B rays of the sun, which are considerably reflected by snow (85%), water (10% to 100%), oceanic and freshwater sea foam (25%), and sand (17%). Boat hulls and sails also reflect varying amounts. Plexiglas windows filter out 65% of UV rays. Thin cloud layers allow the transmission of these rays, while filtering out infrared (heat) rays of the sun. Thus, it is possible on a rather cool, overcast day with bright snow conditions to become sunburned or develop eye injury

Various types of UV eye injury are possible: all are painful. The outer covering of the eye (the cornea) or the lining inside the eyeball (the conjunctiva) can be inflamed by high-dose UV B light. The corneal injury is called a photokeratitis and the corneal injury photoconjunctivitis.

Properly approved American National Standards Institute sunglasses will block 99.8% of the UV B rays. Suitable glasses should be tagged as meeting these standards. Nonprescription glasses must fit properly and ideally provide side protection. A suitable retention strap must be worn, as I finally learned while rafting on the Green River in Colorado. And for those of us who must learn these things more than once, a second pair of glasses—particularly if prescription lenses are worn—is essential. Lacking sunglasses, any field-expedient method of eliminating glare, such as slit glasses made from wood or any material at hand, including the ubiquitous bandanna, will help. An important characteristic of snow blindness is the delayed onset of symptoms. The pain and loss of vision may not be evident until after damaging exposure has been sustained.

Either direct or reflected UV exposure can result in headache or sometimes activate herpes simplex sores on the lips (see page 72). The headache can be treated with pain medication (see page 289) or look for other underlying causes (see page 37).

UV-induced blindness is a self-limiting affliction. However, not only is the loss of vision a problem, but so is the terrible pain, usually described as feeling like red hot pokers were massaging the eye sockets. Lacking any first aid supplies, the treatment would be gentle eye patches, avoiding pressure on the eyes, and the application of cold packs as needed for pain relief. Generally, both eyes are equally affected, with a virtual total loss of vision.

The prescription tetracaine ophthalmic drops will help ease the pain, but long-term use will delay eye surface healing. Oral pain medication will be of help and should be used. The severe pain can last from hours to several days. In case a drainage of pus or crusting of the eyelids occurs, start antibiotic ophthalmic ointment applications as indicated in the section on conjunctivitis. If there is no infection present, eye patching is appropriate. Unfortunately, in a potentially hazardous situation, such as being at sea, patching both eyes makes the person an invalid and increased concern for the person's safety is warranted.

CONJUNCTIVITIS

Conjunctivitis, an infection or inflammation of the eye surface, will be heralded by a scratchy feeling, almost indistinguishable from a foreign body in the eye. The sclera (white of the eye) will be reddened.

Usually the eye will be matted shut in the morning with pus or granular matter.

Infections are generally caused by bacteria, but viral infections also occur. Viral infections tend to have a blotchy red appearance over the white of the eye, while bacterial infections have a generalized red appearance. The drainage in bacterial infections tends to be pus, while viral infections usually cause a watery discharge.

Allergic conjunctivitis will result in a faint pink coloration and a clear drainage. There are frequently other symptoms of allergy such as runny nose, no fever, and no lymph node enlargement. With either viral or bacterial conjunctivitis, look for fever and possibly lymph node enlargement in the neck. Runny nose and sinus infection are frequently present also. Be sure that a foreign body is not the cause of the reddish eye and infection. If so, it must be removed.

Rinse with clean water frequently during the day. Eye infections such as common bacterial conjunctivitis, the most common infection, are self-limiting and will generally clear themselves within 2 weeks. They can become much worse, however, so medical attention should be sought. Do not patch but protect the eyes from sunlight. When one eye is infected, treat both eyes, as the infection spreads easily to the uninfected eye.

There is no suitable nonprescription medication, but note the discussion concerning the use of non-Rx Neosporin or Polysporin in the section on foreign body eye injury. From the Rx supplies, one could use the Tobradex ophthalmic drops 3 times a day for 5 to 7 days. If the infection fails to show improvement within 48 hours, probably the antibiotic will not be effective. Reasons for antibiotic failure include: a missed foreign body; allergy to the antibiotic or to something else, such as pollen; or resistance of an infectious germ to the antibiotic being used. Switch medications in the case of no improvement after 48 hours. When no other antibiotic ointment is available, use an oral antibiotic such as doxycycline 100 mg, 1 capsule twice daily, or the alternative antibiotics suggested for the Rx Oral/Topical Medication Kit. If the eye is improving, continue use as indicated above, continuing for a full 24 hours after symptoms have ceased.

IRITIS

Iritis is an inflammatory disease of the eye having the general appearance of conjunctivitis, but while in the latter the reddish color fades to white near the iris of the eye (the colored part), with iritis the rim of sclera (white of the eye) around the iris is more inflamed or reddened than the white portion further out. The pupil will not constrict when light is shone at it.

Provide sun protection. Give aspirin or other pain medication, if available. This patient requires urgent evacuation to a specialist. The non-Rx treatment will consist of giving the patient ibuprofen, 800 mg every 6 hours, or meloxicam, 15 mg daily. Instill Tobradex ophthalmic drops 4 times a day.

As iritis progresses, the red blush near the iris will become more pronounced and a spasm of the muscle used in the operation of the iris will cause the pupil to become irregular. With further progression, it is possible for the pupil (anterior chamber) to become cloudy, for cataracts and glaucoma to develop, and for serious scarring of eye tissues to develop. Sometimes a profound conjunctivitis or corneal abrasion will cause an iritis that will clear as the problem clears. Some cases of mild iritis can be cleared with agents that dilate the pupil without steroid use. All cases of iritis require treatment by an ophthalmologist.

ALLERGIC CONJUNCTIVITIS

The common outdoor causes of allergic conjunctivitis are sensitivity to inhaled pollens and irritation from fumes. This problem is usually associated with a runny nose (rhinitis) and at times swelling of the eyelids. Rarely there will be a generalized skin itching and the appearance of welts (urticaria). In severe cases, there can be considerable swelling of the conjunctival covering of the white of the eye (sclera), forming what appears as fluid-filled sacs over the sclera of the eye (but not covering the cornea). This puffy tissue generally has a light pink tinge to it. While this can look terrible, it is not serious and will resolve on its own within 48 hours, after further exposure to the causative agent ceases.

From the non-Rx supplies give Percogesic, 1 tablet 4 times a day, and use the Opcon-A® eye drops, 1 in each eye every 3 or 4 hours as needed. Percogesic is used for its decongestant actions, and it will also treat the itchy discomfort of this condition.

STIES AND CHALAZIA

The infections of the eyelid called sties and chalazia can cause scratching of the cornea surface. Often the victim thinks that something is in the eye when, in fact, one of these small pimples is forming. The sty is an infection along a hair follicle on the eyelid margin. The chalazion is an infection of an oil gland on the inner lid margin. The patient will have redness, pain, and swelling along the edge of the upper or lower eyelid. At times the eye will be red with evidence of infection or conjunctivitis. An eyelid may be swollen, without the pimple formation, when this problem first develops. There should not be extensive swelling around the eye. That could represent a periorbital cellulitis, which is a serious infection requiring treatment with injectable antibiotics and urgent evacuation.

Make sure that a foreign body is not causing the symptoms. Check the eye and eyelids as indicated in that section. While so checking, ascertain if a pimple formation confirms the diagnosis. If it is on the upper lid and it is scratching the eye while blinking, patch the eye and send the patient to a physician for treatment. If no medical care is available, have the patient place warm compresses on the eye for 20 minutes every 2 hours to cause the sty to come to a head. When it does, it may spontaneously break and drain. If it does not drain in 2 days, open it with a flick of a sharp blade or needle. Continue the warm compresses and provide medication as below.

If Rx supplies are available, instill Tobradex ophthalmic drops 3 times a day. (Also note that triple antibiotic OTC ointment can be used in the eye if a Rx ointment is not available). If the lid is quite swollen, give the patient doxycycline, 100 mg twice daily, or Levaquin, 750 mg once daily. Once localized and draining, the oral antibiotic will not be necessary.

SPONTANEOUS SUBCONJUNCTIVAL HEMORRHAGE

This condition, an amazingly common problem, presents as bright bleeding over a portion of the white of the eye. (Actually, a hemorrhage has occurred between the white of the eye and the mucous membrane covering it.) It spreads out over a period of 12 to 48 hours, then reabsorbs slowly over the next 7 to 21 days, next turning the conjunctiva yellowish as the blood is reabsorbed. There should not be any pain with this condition, although some people may report a vague "full" feeling in the eye. It normally occurs without cause but can appear after blunt trauma, or violent coughing, sneezing, or vomiting. No treatment is necessary. Evacuation is not required unless associated with trauma.

BLUNT EYE TRAUMA

The immediate treatment is to immobilize the injured eye as soon as possible by patching both eyes and moving the patient only by litter.

Double vision could mean that there has been a fracture of the skull near the eye or that a problem has developed within the central nervous system. Double vision is sometimes caused by swelling of tissue behind the eyelid. A hyphema, a collection of blood in the front or anterior chamber of the eye, may appear. The blood settles in front of the pupil, behind the cornea, and can develop a distinct blood fluid level, becoming easily noticed simply by looking carefully at the pupil and iris.

Patch as indicated in the section on eye patch and bandaging techniques. Patients with a hyphema and serious blunt trauma should be evacuated to a physician for care. Have the patient sit with head up, from 45 to 90 degrees, to allow blood to pool at the lower edge of the anterior chamber. Check the eye twice daily for drainage, which might indicate infection. If infection develops, treat with an oral antibiotic such as the doxycycline, 100 mg twice daily. The Tobradex ophthalmic drops may be instilled 3 times daily. Treat with oral pain medication. Give Atarax, 25 mg 4 times daily as needed, to potentiate the pain medication and help alleviate nausea or 50 mg 4 times daily, if required to calm the patient.

Provide the strongest pain medication required to prevent the injured patient from grimacing and squeezing the injured eye so as not to compromise the eye contents even more. Small corneal or scleral lacerations may require no treatment at all, but these should be seen and evaluated by a physician if possible. Note that severe injury to one eye may even cause blindness to develop in the other eye due to "sympathetic ophthalmia," which is probably an allergic response to eye pigment of the injured eye entering the victim's bloodstream.

GLAUCOMA

Glaucoma is the rise of pressure within the eyeball (intraocular pressure increase). The most common form (open-angle glaucoma) generally is not encountered before the age of 40. The patient notes halos around lights, mild headaches, loss of vision to the sides (peripheral field cuts), and loss of ability to see well at night. The external eye usually appears normal. Glaucoma frequently affects both eyes. This condition is generally of gradual onset, so the patient can consult a physician upon returning to shore.

Initial treatment is with a prescription drug, 1 drop of 0.5% pilo-carpine. It would not be necessary to carry this medication, except to treat this condition. This problem should be detected by the pre-trip physical examination. Everyone over the age of 40 should have their intraocular pressure checked periodically as part of their pre-voyage periodic health assessment.

Acute glaucoma (narrow-angle glaucoma) is much less common than open-angle glaucoma but is much more spectacular in onset. Acute glaucoma is characterized by a rapid rise in pressure of the fluid within the eyeball, causing blurred vision, severe pain in the eye, and even abdominal distress from vagal nerve stimulation. An acute attack can sometimes be broken with pilocarpine, but often needs emergency surgery. A thorough eye examination should be done before the trip to discover those eyes with narrow angles that could result in acute glaucoma. In eyes likely to develop acute glaucoma, a laser iridectomy can be done as an outpatient to prevent an acute narrow-angle glaucoma attack.

Events that might precipitate an acute glaucoma attack can include the use of certain medications, such as decongestants. If any-one develops severe eye pain while taking a decongestant or other nonessential medication, have them stop taking it immediately. Severe eye pain from any cause is a reason for urgent evacuation of the patient.

CHAPTER 7

NOSE

NASAL CONGESTION

Nasal congestion is caused by an allergic reaction to pollen, dust, or other allergens, and viral or bacterial upper respiratory infections. Bacterial infections can be cured with antibiotics, but otherwise all are treated similarly for symptomatic relief. Use Percogesic, 1 tablet every 6 hours as needed, for nasal congestion or discomfort. Drink lots of liquid to prevent the mucus from becoming too thick. Thick mucus will not drain well and can pack the sinus cavities with increasingly painful pressure.

If the patient has no fever, do not give an antibiotic. A low-grade temperature is probably viral and still does not warrant an antibiotic. If a temperature greater than 101°F (38°C) is present, treat with an antibiotic such as doxycycline, 100 mg twice daily, or Zithromax, as indicated on page 291.

NASAL FOREIGN BODY

Foul drainage from one nostril may well indicate a foreign body. In adults the history of something being placed up the nose would, of course, help in the diagnosis. In a child, drainage from one nostril must be a foreign body until ruled out.

Have the patient try to blow his nose to remove the foreign body. With an infant it may be possible for a parent to gently puff into the baby's mouth to force the object out of the nose.

While having a nasal speculum would be ideal, any instrument that can be used to spread the nostrils open will work; for example, the pliers on your Swiss Army knife or Leatherman tool. Spread the tips apart after placing them just inside the nostril. One can stretch the nostril quite extensively without causing pain. Shine a light into the nostril passage and attempt to spot the foreign body. Try to grasp the object with forceps or another instrument. If the foreign material is loose debris—such as a capsule that broke in the patient's mouth and was sneezed into the nostrils—it is best to irrigate this material out rather than attempting to cleanse with a Q-tip, etc. Place a bulb or irrigation syringe in the clear nostril. With the patient repeating an "eng" sound, flush water, and hopefully the debris, out the opposite nostril.

After removing a foreign body, be sure to check the nostril again for an additional one. Try not to push a foreign body down the back of the patient's throat where he may choke on it. If this is unavoidable, have the patient bend over, with the face down, to decrease the chance of choking. After pushing the object further into the nose and into the upper part of the pharynx, hopefully the victim can cough the object out. If you are using this technique, first read the sections on nosebleed and foreign body airway obstruction.

NOSEBLEED—EPISTAXIS

If nose bleeding (epistaxis) is caused by a contusion to the nose, the bleeding can be impressive but is usually self-limited. Bleeding that starts without trauma is generally more difficult to stop. Most bleeding is from small arteries located near the front of the nose partition or nasal septum. The best treatment is direct pressure. Have the victim squeeze the nose between his or her fingers for 10 minutes by the clock (a very long time when there is no clock to watch). If this fails, squeeze another 10 minutes. Do not blow the nose, for this will dislodge clots and start the bleeding all over again. If the bleeding is severe, have the victim sit up to prevent choking on blood and to aid in the reduction of the BP in the nose. Cold compresses can provide a slight amount of help.

Continued bleeding can result in shock. This will, in turn, decrease the bleeding. The sitting position is mandatory to prevent choking on blood from a severe bleed and, as indicated earlier, will aid in the reduction of BP in the nose. Taken to the extreme degree, this position aids in allowing shock to occur.

Another technique that can be tried is to wet a gauze strip thoroughly with the epinephrine from the syringe in the Rx Injectable Medication Kit. The epinephrine can act as a vasoconstrictor to decrease the blood flow and allow clotting.

Those having only nonprescription medical supplies will have to use the Opcon-A eye drops, which will not be as powerful in blood vessel constriction. First, clear the nose of blood clots so the gauze can be in direct contact with the nasal membranes. Have the victim blow his nose or use the irrigation syringe. Place the epinephrine-soaked gauze in the nose and apply pinching pressure. Pinch for 10-minute increments. The gauze may be removed after the bleeding has stopped.

BROKEN NOSE

A direct blow causing a nasal fracture (broken nose) is associated with pain, swelling, and nasal bleeding. The pain is usually point tender, which means a very light touch elicits pain, indicating a fracture has occurred at that location. While the bleeding from trauma to the nose can initially be intense, it seldom lasts more than a few minutes. Apply a cold compress, or a damp cloth that can cool by evaporative cooling. Allow the patient to pinch his nose to aid in reducing bleeding.

If the nose is laterally displaced (shoved to one side), push it back into place. More of these fractures have been treated by coaches on the playing field than have been reduced by doctors. If it is a depressed fracture, a specialist will have to properly elevate the fragments. As soon as the person returns to shore, have him seen by a physician, but this is not a reason for expensive urgent evacuation. Provide pain medication, but this should only be necessary for a few doses. It is rare to need to pack a bleeding nose due to trauma and this should be avoided, if possible, due to the increased pain it would cause.

CHAPTER 8
EAR

Problems with the ear involve pain, loss of hearing, or drainage. Traumas involving the ear could include lacerations, blunt trauma, and hemorrhage (bleeding) in the outer ear tissue, and damage from pressure changes to the eardrum (barotrauma) from diving or high altitude, explosions, or direct blows to the ear. See table 8.1 for signs and symptoms.

Table 8.1 Symptoms and Signs of Ear Pathology

	HEARING LOSS	PAIN	HEAD CONGESTION	EAR	FEVER
Drainage trauma	n	n		l	
Foreign body		l		l	
Infection					
Inner ear	n	n	n	l	n
Outer ear	l	l			l
Allergy	l	l	n		
Dental source		n			
TMJ source		n			
Lymph node source		l			

Legend	n	A frequent or intense symptom
	l	Common, less intense symptom
	Blank	Less likely to produce this symptom

Note: Only if the eardrum ruptures will drainage occur in an inner ear infection. After the rupture, the pain decreases remarkably.

EARACHE

Pain in the ear can be associated with several sources, as indicated in table 8.1. The history of trauma will be an obvious source of pain, as mentioned. Most ear pain is due to an otitis media infection behind the eardrum (tympanic membrane), or to otitis externa infection in the outer ear canal (auditory canal). It can also be caused by infection elsewhere (generally a dental infection, infected tonsil, or lymph node in the neck near the ear). Allergy can result in pressure behind the eardrum and is also a common source of ear pain.

A simple physical examination and the additional medical history will readily (and generally accurately) distinguish the difference between an otitis media or otitis externa infection and sources of pain beyond the ear. Pushing on the knob at the front of the ear (the tragus) or pulling on the earlobe will elicit pain with otitis externa. This will not hurt if the patient has otitis media. The history of head congestion favors otitis media.

A swollen tender nodule in the neck near the ear would be an infected lymph node. If the skin above the swelling is red, the patient probably has an infected skin abscess. The pain from an abscess is so localized that confusion with an ear infection is seldom a problem. One or more tender lymph nodes can hurt to the extent that the exact source of the pain may be in doubt. Swollen, tender lymph nodes in the neck are usually associated with pharyngitis (sore throat), with severe otitis externa, or with infections of the skin in the scalp. The latter should be readily noted by examination—palpate the scalp for infected cysts or abscesses.

Dental caries, or cavities, can hurt to the extent that the pain seems to come from the ear. They can ordinarily be identified during a careful examination of the mouth. If an obvious cavity is not visualized with a light, try tapping on each tooth to see if pain is suddenly elicited (see dental pain, page 74).

OUTER EAR INFECTION—OTITIS EXTERNA

Outer ear infection of the auditory canal (otitis externa), the part of the ear that opens to the outside, is commonly called swimmer's ear. The external auditory canal generally becomes inflamed from conditions of high humidity, accumulation of ear wax, or contact with contaminated water. Scratching the ear after picking the nose or scratching elsewhere may also be a source of this common infection.

Prevent cold air from blowing against the ear. Warm packs against the ear or instilling comfortably warm sweet oil or even cooking oil can help. Provide pain medication. Obtain professional help if the patient develops a fever, if the pain becomes severe, or if the lymph nodes or adjacent neck tissues start swelling. Significant tissue swelling will require antibiotic treatment. At times, a topical ointment will suffice, but with fever or swollen lymph or skin structures, an oral antibiotic will be required.

Triple antibiotic ointment with pramoxine from the Topical Bandaging Kit will work fine for outer ear infections. This is not approved by the FDA for this use, as ear infections are serious, and it is not intended that nonphysicians treat this condition without medical help. From the Rx kit, one could use the Tobradex ophthalmic drops. These medications should be applied with the ear facing up and, in the case of the ointment, allowed to melt by body temperature. This may take 5 minutes per ear. Place cotton in the ear to hold the medication in place. Instill medication 4 times daily and treat for 14 days. If the canal is swollen shut, a steroid ointment may also be used in between applications of the other ointments. From the Topical Bandaging Kit, use the hydrocortisone 1% cream in addition to the triple antibiotic ointment. Tobradex contains enough steroids to be adequate for these purposes.

Swollen tissue and/or fever also require an oral antibiotic. From the Rx Oral/Topical Medication Kit, use doxycycline, 100 mg twice daily, or Levaquin, 750 mg daily. Provide the best pain medication that you can. From your Non-Rx Oral Medication Kit, use 1 or 2 Percogesic every 4 hours.

MIDDLE EAR INFECTION—OTITIS MEDIA

Middle ear infection (otitis media) presents in a person who has sinus congestion and possibly drainage from allergy or infection. The ear pain can be excruciating. Fever will frequently be intermittent, normal at one moment and over 103°F (39°C) at other times. Fever indicates bacterial infection of the fluid trapped behind the eardrum. If the eardrum ruptures, the pain will cease immediately, and the fever will drop. This drainage allows the body to cure the infection but will result in at least temporary damage to the eardrum and decreased hearing until it heals.

There is no increased pain when pulling on the earlobe or pushing on the tragus (the knob in front of the ear) in this condition unless an outer ear infection is also present. If you were to look at the eardrum with an otoscope, it would be red and bulging out from pressure or sucked back by a vacuum in the middle ear.

You do not need an otoscope to diagnose this condition. Many people will complain of hearing loss and think they have wax or a foreign body in the ear canal when they actually have a fluid accumulation behind the eardrum. Consequently, ear drops and washing the ear will not help improve this condition. Beside pain, the key to the diagnosis is head congestion and fever.

There is little that can be accomplished without medication. Protect the ear from cold, position the head so that the ear is directed upward, and provide warm packs to the ear. While drops do not help cure this problem, some pain relief may be obtained with warmed sweet oil (or even cooking oil) drops in the ear.

Treatment will consist of providing decongestant, pain medication, and oral antibiotic. A good decongestant and pain reliever from the Non-Rx Oral Medication Kit is Percogesic, 2 tablets 4 times daily. Rx pain medication is given as needed, as indicated in the previous section. Only the Rx Oral/Topical Kit has the proper antibiotics to treat this condition. Use doxycycline, 1 tablet twice daily, or Levaquin, 750 mg daily, generally for 5 to 7 days.

If the pressure causes the eardrum to rupture, the pain and fever will cease, but there will be a bloody drainage from the ear. Hearing is always decreased with the infection and will remain decreased due to the ruptured eardrum for some time. This generally heals itself quite well but treat with decongestant to decrease the drainage and allow the eardrum to heal. Avoid placing drops or ointments in the ear canal if there is a chance that the eardrum has ruptured, as many medications are damaging to the inner ear mechanisms.

FOREIGN BODY IN EAR

These are generally of three types: accumulation of wax plugs (cerumen), foreign objects, and living insects. Wax plugs can usually be softened with gently warm oil. This may have to be placed in the ear canal repeatedly over many days. Irrigating with room temperature water may be attempted with a bulb syringe, such as the one recommended for wound irrigation in the Topical Bandaging Kit. If a wax-plugged ear becomes painful, treat as indicated in the section on otitis externa.

The danger in trying to remove inanimate objects is the tendency to shove them further into the ear canal or to damage the delicate ear canal lining, thus adding bleeding to your troubles. Of course, rupturing the eardrum by shoving against it would be a real unnecessary disaster. Attempt to grasp a foreign body with a pair of tweezers if you can see it. Do not poke blindly with anything. Irrigation may be attempted as indicated earlier.

A popular method of aiding in the management of insects in the ear canal is the instillation of lidocaine to kill the bug instantly, prior to attempting removal. There are reports of lidocaine making a person very dizzy, especially if it leaks through a hole in the eardrum into the inner ear. This dizziness is very distressing and may result in profound vomiting and discomfort. It is self-limiting, however, and should not last more than a day if it does transpire. An alternative method is to drown the bug with cooking or other oil, then attempt removal. Oil seems to kill bugs quicker than water. The fewer struggles, the less chance for stinging, biting, or other trauma to the delicate ear canal and eardrum. Tilt the ear downward, thus hoping to slide the dead bug toward the entrance, where it can be grasped. Shining a light at the ear to coax a bug out is probably futile.

RUPTURED EARDRUM

Rupture of the eardrum (tympanic membrane perforation) can result from direct puncture, from explosions, and from the barotrauma of diving deep or rapid ascent to high altitude. Being smacked on the ear can also rupture the eardrum, an event that can easily happen during horseplay.

If suffering from sinus congestion, avoid diving or rapid ascents of altitude in vehicles or airplanes. Congestion can lead to blockage of the eustachian tube. Failure to equilibrate pressure through this tube between the middle ear and the throat, and thus the outside world, can result in damage to the eardrum. In case of congestion, take a decongestant and pain medication combination such as Percogesic, 2 tablets every 4 hours, until clear. Cancel any diving plans if congested. Also, if a gradual pressure squeeze is causing pain while diving, the dive should be terminated.

When flying, it will be noted that blocked eustachian tubes will cause more pain upon descent than ascent. When going up, the pressure in the inner ear will increase and blow out through the eustachian tube. When coming down, increased outer atmospheric pressure is much less apt to clear the plugged tube, and a squeeze of air against the eardrum will result. Try to equalize this pressure by pinching the nose shut and gently increasing the pressure in your mouth and throat against closed lips. This will generally clear the eustachian tube and relieve the air squeeze on the eardrum. Do not overdo this; that can also be painful. If barotrauma results in eardrum rupture, the pain should instantly cease. There may be bloody drainage from the ear canal. Do not place drops in the ear canal, but drainage can be gently wiped away, or frequently changed cotton plugs used to catch the bloody fluid.

TEMPOROMANDIBULAR JOINT SYNDROME

The temporomandibular joint (TMJ) syndrome is actually a problem of the jaw, but the pain radiates into the ear so often that we will consider it primarily as a source of ear pain. The TMJ is the hinge joint of the jaw, located just forward of the ear. You can easily feel it move if you place a fingertip into your ear canal. When this joint becomes inflamed, it will frequently cause ear pain. It will then be painful to apply fingertip pressure directly on the joint. No swelling should be noted. Tenderness is increased with chewing, and pain and popping or locking may be noted when opening the jaw widely. The pain radiates into the temple area and when severe, the entire head hurts.

Treatment is with local heat. The use of ibuprofen or Percogesic can be very helpful. Do not eat foods that are hard to chew or that require opening the mouth widely.

CHAPTER 9
MOUTH AND THROAT

SORE THROAT

The most common cause of a sore throat, or pharyngitis, is a viral infection. While uncomfortable, this malady requires no antibiotic treatment—in fact, antibiotics will do no good whatsoever. Strictly speaking, the only sore throat that needs to be treated is the one caused by a specific bacteria (beta hemolytic streptococcus, Lancefield group A), as it has been found that antibiotic treatment for 10 days will avoid the dreaded complication of rheumatic fever, which may occur in 1% to 3% of people who contract this particular infection. Many purists in the medical profession feel that no antibiotics should be used until the results of a throat culture or antibody screen proving this infection have been returned from the lab. On a short trip the victim can be taken to a doctor for a strep culture to determine if the sore throat was indeed strep. On a voyage lasting longer than 2 weeks, it would be best to commit the patient to a full course of antibiotic therapy, realizing that the symptoms will soon pass and the patient seem well, but that it is essential to continue the medication for the full treatment regimen. The number of days of treatment differs depending upon which antibiotic is being used.

There are textbook differences in the general appearance of a viral and strep sore throat. The lymph nodes in the neck are swollen in both cases; they are more tender with bacterial infections, but people with a low pain threshold will complain bitterly about soreness regardless of the source of infection. The throat will be quite red in bacterial infection and a white splotchy coating over the red tonsils or the back portion of the throat generally means a strep infection—at least these classic indications are present 20% of the time. Sore throats caused by some viral infections (namely infectious mononucleosis and adenovirus) may mimic all the above. From the Rx Oral/Topical Medication Kit, use Zithromax 500 mg, as described. The 3-tablet dose provides a therapeutic blood level for 10 days.

INFECTIOUS MONONUCLEOSIS

Infectious mononucleosis, a disease of young adults (teens through 30 years of age), generally presents as a terrible sore throat, swollen lymph nodes (normally at the back of the neck, and not as tender as with strep infection), and a profound feeling of fatigue. It is self-limited, with total recovery to be expected after 2 weeks for most victims—some, unfortunately, are bedridden for weeks and lethargic for 6 months. Spleen enlargement is common. The most serious aspect of this disease is the possibility of splenic rupture, but this is rare. Avoid palpating the spleen (shoving on the left upper quadrant of the abdomen) and let the victim rest (no hiking, etc.) until the illness and feeling of lethargy has passed. The first 5 days are the worst, with fever and excruciating sore throat being the major complaint. Continued physical activity in persons with this disease can contribute to a prolonged convalescent period.

Treatment is symptomatic, with medication for fever and pain such as the non-Rx Percogesic or ibuprofen, each given 1 or 2 tablets every 4 to 6 hours. A mild form of hepatitis frequently occurs with mononucleosis that causes nausea and loss of appetite. This requires no specific treatment other than rest. If severe ear pain begins, add a decongestant (or just use the Percogesic), 2 tablets every 6 hours, to promote relief of eustachian tube pressure. Due to the uncertainty of diagnosis, treat the severe sore throat as if it were a strep infection, with an antibiotic for 10 days or with Zithromax, as indicated above.

MOUTH SORES

When mouth sores develop, patients frequently believe they either have cancer or infection, especially herpes. A common reason for a lesion is the sore called a papilloma, caused from rubbing against a sharp tooth or dental work. They may look serious but are not. They are raised, normally orange in color. One can usually find an obvious rough area causing the irritation. Treatment is to avoid chewing at the lesion and to apply 1% hydrocortisone cream from the Topical Bandaging Kit every 3 hours. If the Rx Oral/Topical Medication Kit is available, use the Topicort 0.25% ointment every 4 hours. An alternative therapy, which can be used simultaneously, is to apply oil of cloves (eugenol).

A canker sore, also called an aphthous ulcer, can appear anywhere in the mouth and be any size. It has a distinctive appearance of a white crater with a red, swollen border. Treatment is as indicated earlier.

If there is generalized tissue swelling, possibly with drainage or whitish cover on the gums, foul-smelling breath, and gums and mouth tissue that bleed easily when scraped, it is possible that the victim has trench mouth or Vincent's infection. This is caused by poor hygiene, which is unfortunately common on long expeditions under adverse circumstances. If the white exudate is located over the tonsils, one has to be concerned about strep throat (see page 72), mononucleosis (page 72), and diphtheria. Treat trench mouth with warm water rinses, swishing the crud off as well as possible. If the Rx Oral/ Topical Kit is available, give the full dose regimen of Zithromax, 500 mg tablets for 3 days, or treat with Levaquin, 750 mg, once daily for 5 days.

The mouth lesions of herpes simplex begin as small blisters and leave a raw area once they have broken open. The ulceration from a herpes is red rather than the white of the canker sore. They are very painful. From the Rx Oral/Topical Kit, apply the Denavir® cream every 2 hours. This is not approved for use inside of the mouth, but it is perfectly safe, and it works.

Fever blisters are sores that break out on the vermilion border of the lips, generally as a result of herpes simplex virus eruptions. These lesions can be activated by fevers (hence the name "fever blister") or other trauma, even mental stress. UV light will frequently cause flares of fever blisters. This can be a common problem of mountain travel due to the more intense UV radiation encountered at higher altitudes. Treat as above for the herpes simplex inner mouth lesions. These lesions can be prevented with adequate sunscreen and/or by taking an antiviral prescription medication.

DENTAL CARE

If your potential time on a sea voyage may be substantial, then planning for dental emergencies is critical. Keep your preventative dental care up to date. When traveling, brush twice daily. If you run out of toothpaste, use baking soda or salt as a substitute. Flossing and brushing can prevent needless pain and suffering.

Gum Pain or Swelling

Pain with swelling high on the gum at the base of the tooth usually indicates an infection and a tooth that may require extraction, or root canal therapy. In the meantime, have the patient use warm water mouth rinses. Start the victim on antibiotics such as amoxicillin/clavulanate (Augmentin) 875 twice daily for 7 to 10 days. The doxycycline and levofloxacin are alternative medications. If a bulging area can be identified in the mouth, an incision into the swollen gum made with a sharp blade may promote drainage. If the pain is severe and not relieved with any pain medication that you have, the tooth may have to be pulled.

Swelling at the gum line, rather than at the base of the tooth, may indicate a periodontal abscess. The gingiva (or gums) are red, swollen, foul smelling, and oozing. Frequently this represents food particle entrapment and abscess formation along the surface of the tooth with the gums, the so-called gingival cuff. Considerable relief can often be obtained by probing directly into the abscess area through the gingival cuff, using any thin, blunt instrument. Probe along the length of the tooth to break up and drain the abscess. Have the patient use frequent hot mouth rinses to continue the drainage process. If a foreign object, such as a piece of food, is causing the swelling, irrigate with warm salt solution or warm water, with sufficient force to dislodge the particle. Probe it loose if necessary. Dental floss may be very helpful. Acute pain and swelling of the tissue behind the third molar usually is caused by an erupting wisdom tooth. Technically this is called pericoronitis. A little flap of tissue lies over the erupting wisdom tooth called the operculum. Biting on this causes it to swell, then it becomes much easier to bite on it again, and so on. The result is considerable pain. This can be relieved by surgically removing the operculum. If local anesthetic is available, such as lidocaine, inject it directly into the operculum, and then cut it out with a sharp blade using the outline of the erupting tooth as a guideline. The bleeding can soon be stopped by biting down on a gauze or other cloth after the procedure is over. Stitching this wound is not required. If no lidocaine is available, swab the area with alcohol, as this helps provide some slight anesthesia. Application of powder from a crushed diphenhydramine tablet from the Non-Rx Oral Medication Kit might provide some anesthesia.

Swelling of the entire side of the face will occur with dental infections that spread. This condition should ideally be treated in a hospital with intravenous (IV) antibiotics. Apply warm compresses to the face. Do not lance the infection from the skin side, but a peaked, bulging area on the inside of the mouth may be lanced to promote drainage. Abscess extension into surrounding facial tissues generally means that lancing will do little good. This patient is very ill and rest is mandatory. Provide antibiotic coverage from the Rx Oral/Topical Medication Kit, with levofloxacin, 750 mg once daily, or the amoxicillin/clavulanate 875/125 twice daily. Other alternative drugs listed in the Ship's Medicine Chest are azithromycin 500 mg daily for 3 days, or, from the Rx Injectable Medication Kit, Rocephin®, giving 500 mg by IM injection every 12 hours until the infection resolves (probably a minimum of 7 days). Urgent evacuation is mandatory.

Mouth Lacerations

Any significant trauma to the mouth causes considerable bleeding and concern. The bleeding initially always seems worse than it is. Rinse the mouth with warm water to clear away the clots so that you can identify the source of the bleeding.

Laceration of the piece of tissue that seems to join the bottom lip or upper lip to the gum line is a common result of trauma to the mouth and need not be repaired, even though it initially looks horrible and may bleed considerably. This is called the labial frenum. Simply stuff some gauze into the area until the bleeding stops.

A laceration of the tongue will not require stitching (suturing), unless an edge is deeply involved. Fairly deep cuts along the top surface and the bottom can be ignored in a remote setting. If suturing is to be accomplished and you have injectable lidocaine from the Rx Injectable Kit, inject into the lower gum behind the teeth on the side of the gum facing the tongue. Technically this area is called the median raphe distal to the posterior teeth. This will block the side of the tongue and be much less painful than directly injecting into the tongue. Use the 3–0 gut sutures. These sutures will dissolve within a few days. Sutures in the tongue frequently come out within a few hours, even when they are well tied, much to the victim's and surgeon's annoyance. If this happens and the tongue is not bleeding badly, just leave it alone. Minor cuts along the edge of the tongue can also be ignored.

Make sure that cuts on the inside of the mouth do not have foreign bodies, such as pieces of tooth, inside of them. These must be removed. Inject the lidocaine into the wound before probing, if you have the Rx Injectable Medication Kit. Irrigate thoroughly with water. Even without the lidocaine, the inside of the mouth can be stitched with minimal pain. Use the 3–0 gut sutures, removing them in 4 days if they have not fallen out already. Refer to page 140 for discussion of suturing the face and the outside portion of the lips.

Dental Pain

Cavities may be identified by visual examination of the mouth in most cases. At times the pain is so severe that the patient cannot tell exactly which tooth is the offender. It helps to know that a painful tooth will not refer pain to the opposite side of the mouth and painful back teeth normally do not refer pain to front teeth and vice versa. With the painful area narrowed down, look for an obvious cavity. If none is found, tap each tooth in turn until the offending one is reached—a tap on it will elicit strong pain.

For years, oil of cloves (eugenol) has been used to deaden dental pain. Avoid trying to apply an aspirin directly to a painful tooth; it will only make a worse mess of things. Many excellent dental kits are now available without prescription that contain topical anesthetic agents and temporary fillings. A daub of topical anesthetic will work. In your Topical Bandaging Kit, you have triple antibiotic with pramoxine that you can use. It's the pramoxine component that provides the pain relief. Before applying the anesthetic, dry the tooth and try to clean out any cavity found. From the Non-Rx Oral Medication Kit, give Percogesic, 2 tablets every 4 hours, or ibuprofen, 200 mg, 2 to 4 tablets every 6 hours, for pain. When on a long voyage and a toothache begins, I would also start treating with an antibiotic if the Rx kit is available. Use the amoxicillin/clavulanate, 875/125 twice daily, or alternatively, use Levaquin, 750 mg once daily, until swelling or pain resolves, which indicates the infection is under control.

Lost Filling

This could turn into a real disaster. An old-fashioned remedy uses powdered zinc oxide (not the ointment) and eugenol. Starting with the two in equal parts, mix until a putty is formed by adding more zinc oxide powder as necessary. This always takes considerably more of the zinc oxide than at first would seem necessary. Pack this putty into the cavity and allow to set over the next 24 hours.

The Cavit® dental filling paste in the Rx Oral/Topical Kit provides a strong temporary filling. Dry the cavity bed thoroughly with a gauze square. Place several drops of anesthetic, such as oil of cloves (eugenol), to deaden the nerve endings and kill bacteria.

The triple antibiotic with pramoxine ointment from the Non-Rx Oral Kit can also be used for this purpose. Plain triple antibiotic ointment will not work. You will have to pack the ointment into the cavity area and allow it to melt. Dry the cavity carefully once again. The Cavit paste should be applied to the dry cavity and packed firmly into place. Obviously, avoid biting on the side of the filling, regardless of the materials used to make your temporary filling. The loss of a filling may indicate extension of decay in the underlying tooth and an underlying cavity.

Cavity

In the event a tooth becomes painful, you may note the formation of a cavity. While in normal dental practice the cavity area would be drilled out, in your situation if on an extended leg of a sea voyage, you may be able to handle this problem quite well without drilling. Using a dental spoon, you can scrape the edges of the decay area clean. Be careful not to go too deep as you will hit the nerve in the pulp at the core of the tooth. As long as you seal the area with your filling, you should prevent further decay. Of course, if an abscess has formed, it is too late to fill the tooth and it should be extracted. Fill with a temporary filling as mentioned earlier under lost filling. A more permanent filling can be achieved with a glass ionomer compound (in the United States, an Rx item which requires mixing just before using and allowing to harden to an appropriate stiffness) or something like Prevest DenPro Fusion Flo Dental-Cured Nano Hybrid (available without prescription from Amazon which required an UV light to cure or harden it).

When placing a permanent filling, you have to be particular about your technique. After scraping the decay out of the cavity, dry out the hole or the cement will not stick. Practice with the cement until you become used to achieve the right consistency prior to inserting or in managing the UV light to harden the material when it is in place. The UV source can be a blue cobalt pen light. If the cavity extends to the side of the tooth, protect the space between the teeth by placing something thin between the teeth, such as a tooth from a comb. It is also critical to remove extra cement from around the tooth, from between the tooth, and to make sure that the filling does not extend too high that the tooth biting down on it encounters the filling.

An excellent description of performing this procedure using the glass ionomer is found in *Where There Is No Dentist* by Murray Dickson, Hesperian Health Guides (2018). You will find it much easier to use the UV-cured Nano Hybrid. You can purchase a simple dental tool kit from Amazon, as well as any of the products mentioned in this section.

Loose or Dislodged Tooth

When you examine a traumatized mouth and find a tooth that is rotated, or dislocated in any direction, do not push the tooth back into place. Further movement may disrupt the tooth's blood and nerve supply. If the tooth is all secured, leave it alone. The musculature of the lips and tongue will generally gently push the tooth back into place and keep it there.

A fractured tooth with an exposed pink substance that is bleeding shows the exposed nerve. This tooth will need protection with eugenol and temporary filling as indicated earlier. This is a dental emergency that should be treated by a dentist immediately.

If a tooth is knocked out, replace it into the socket immediately. If this cannot be done, have the victim hold the tooth under their tongue or in their lower lip until it can be implanted. In any case speed is a matter of great importance. A tooth left out too long will be rejected by the body as a foreign substance. A delay of greater than 72 hours for professional insertion and management will generally not be successful.

All of the aforementioned problems mean a soft diet and avoidance of chewing with the affected tooth for many days will be necessary. On a prolonged sea leg of a voyage, start the patient on an antibiotic such as doxycycline, 100 mg, 1 daily, for any of the earlier problems.

Trauma that can cause any of the above may also result in fractures of the tooth below the gum line, and of the alveolar ridge affecting several teeth. If this is suspected, start the patient on an antibiotic as mentioned in the previous paragraph. Oral surgical help must be obtained as soon as possible. A soft diet is essential until healing takes place, possibly a matter of 6 to 8 weeks.

Pulling a Tooth

It is best not to pull a tooth from an infected gum, as this might spread the infection. If an abscess is forming, place the patient on an antibiotic such as levofloxacin, 750 mg daily, or doxycycline, 100 mg twice daily, or amoxicillin/clavulanate, 875/125 mg twice daily, and use warm mouth rinses to promote drainage. After the infection has subsided, it is safer to pull the tooth. Opening the abscess as described in Gum Pain or Swelling on page 74 will be helpful at times. If it appears necessary to pull an infected tooth, give the patient one of the above antibiotics about 2 hours before pulling the tooth to provide some protection against spreading the infection.

Pull a tooth by obtaining a secure hold with either a dental forceps or, even better, a side-cutting bone rongeur. You will have to obtain one from a surgical supply house or a friendly orthopedic surgeon. Slowly apply pressure in a back-and-forth, side-to-side motion to rock the tooth free. This loosens the tooth in its socket and will permit its removal. Avoid jerking or pulling the tooth with a straight outward force; it can resist all of the strength that you have in this direction. Jerking may break off the root. The rongeur will grip the tooth surface by cutting into the enamel, holding better than even dental extraction forceps. The Murray book described earlier also indicates an alternative method of dental extraction using different equipment.

If the root breaks off, you may leave it alone rather than trying to dig it out. If the root section is obviously loose, then you can pick it out with some suitable instrument. Thin fragments of bone may fracture off during the extraction. These will work their way to the surface during healing. Do not attempt to replace them but pick them free as they surface.

If you do not have the side-cutting dental rongeur or dental forceps, it is best not to attempt to pull the tooth with another instrument. Pliers may crush the tooth and the tooth can slip in your grasp. However, even a large, solid tooth can be removed by using your finger to rock it back and forth. This may take days to accomplish, but it will eventually loosen sufficiently to remove.

CHAPTER 10

CHEST

One of the most common reasons for a visit to a physician's office or emergency department is a problem with the chest. Chest pain and shortness of breath can be symptoms of serious disorders and cannot be taken lightly. Fortunately, most times the chest pain is benign, generally due to muscle spasm or chest wall inflammation. It can be very difficult to evaluate, even at the emergency department. Chest problems are best evaluated by a physician, but in a remote area, try to sort out your options with the table on page 12. In case of trauma, the patient may have suffered torn muscles between the ribs or broken ribs (see page 200).

BRONCHITIS/PNEUMONIA

Infection of the airways in the lung (bronchitis) or infection in the air sacs of the lung (pneumonia) will cause very high fever, persistent cough frequently producing phlegm stained with blood, and prostration of the victim. From the Non-Rx Oral Medication Kit treat the fever with Percogesic, 2 tablets every 4 hours, or ibuprofen 200 mg, 2 tablets every 4 hours, and the cough with diphenhydramine, 25 mg every 4 hours (see page 289).

Cool with a wet cloth over the forehead as needed. Do not bundle the patient with a very high fever, as this will drive the temperature only higher. The shivering cold feeling that the patient has is only proof that his or her thermal control mechanism is out of adjustment; trust the thermometer or the back of your hand to follow the patient's temperature. Encourage the patient to drink fluids, as fever and coughing lead to dehydration. This causes the mucus in the bronchioles to become thick and tenacious. Force fluid to prevent this sputum from plugging up sections of the lung.

Provide antibiotic. From the Rx Oral/Topical Medication Kit give the Levaquin, 750 mg daily, until the fever is broken and for an additional 4 days. Alternately, give the Zithromax as directed on page 291. Or from the Rx Injectable Medication Kit, you may give Rocephin, 500 mg twice daily.

Prepare a sheltered camp for the victim as best as circumstances permit. Rest until the fever is broken is essential with or without the availability of antibiotic. Encourage the patient to eat. Even though they are very ill, people lose their appetites.

PNEUMOTHORAX

Even in healthy young adults and teenagers, it is possible for an air cell of the lung to break for no apparent reason and fill a portion of the chest cavity with air, thus collapsing part of one lung. A minor pneumothorax will spontaneously take care of itself, with the air being reabsorbed and the lung re-expanding over 3 to 5 days. The classic sign of decreased breath sounds over the area of the collapse will be very difficult for an examiner to detect, even with a stethoscope. But listen first to one side of the chest and then the other to see if there is a difference. Part of the difficulty lies in the fact that patients with chest pain do not breathe deeply and all breath sounds are decreased. Other parts of the physical exam are even more subtle. In unexplained severe chest pain in an otherwise healthy individual, pneumothorax might be the cause.

Severe pneumothorax will have to be treated by a physician or trained medic with removal of the trapped air with a large syringe or flutter valve, or by other methods currently employed in a hospital setting. If pain is severe and breathing difficult, the only choice is evacuation of the victim.

From the Non-Rx Oral Medication Kit, you may give 2 Percogesic for pain every 4 hours, or 2 to 4 ibuprofen 200 mg tablets every 6 hours. This can be augmented with Atarax, 25 mg every 6 hours. It is possible for the pain to be so severe that the use of injectable Nubain or inhaled Stadol will be necessary (see page 297).

PULMONARY EMBOLUS

A pulmonary embolus is a blood clot breaking loose from its point of origin, normally from a leg or pelvic vein, which then lodges in the lung after passing through the heart. When serious, this condition appears as shortness of breath and rapid breathing, with a dull substernal chest pain. There may be cough, bloody sputum, fever, and sharp chest pain. A pulmonary embolus can mimic pneumonia (page 83). It can be fatal if an embolus large enough to block off more than 50% of the lung circulation occurs at once. This condition generally resolves within a matter of days. Increased risk is found in older people who have been sitting a long time (such as on plane flights) or anyone immobilized after injury.

The only medication in the suggested ship's medicine chest that would be of any help would be ibuprofen, 200 mg given 4 times daily. Stronger doses of this product (up to 800 mg given 4 times daily) or additional pain medication can be given to help with the discomfort. The use of Plavix from the Rx Cardiac Medication Kit is not supported by the literature, but giving a loading dose of 300 mg, and then 75 mg daily, is a possible field technique. Due to the uncertainty of the diagnosis, treat with an antibiotic such as Zithromax, as described on page 291, or Levaquin, 750 mg once daily, until the pain and/or fever resolves, and then for an additional 4 days. This would not help a pulmonary embolus, but it would properly treat pneumonia.

CHAPTER 11

ABDOMEN

Even with years of clinical experience and unlimited laboratory and X-ray facilities, abdominal pain can be a diagnostic dilemma. How serious is it? Should evacuation be started, or can it be waited out or safely treated at sea? Or what treatment protocol can be followed when there is no evacuation possible or the return to port will be lengthy?

ABDOMINAL PAIN

Any abdominal pain that lasts longer than 24 hours is a cause for concern and professional help should be sought if possible. Diagnosis will be determined from the history (type and severity of pain, location, radiation, when it started), as well as certain aspects of the physical examination and the clinical course that develops. Some of these aspects are summarized in table 11.1 on page 87 and in the discussion that follows.

A burning sensation in the middle of the upper part of the abdomen (mid-epigastrium) is probably gastritis or stomach irritation. If allowed to persist, this can develop into an ulcer, a crater eaten into the stomach or duodenal wall. In the latter case, the pain may be most notable in the right upper quadrant. For some reason ulcers will sometimes feel better if you press against them with your hand. This supposedly was why Napoleon is seen with his hand inside his jacket in his favorite pose—he was pressing against his abdomen to relieve the pain of an ulcer.

Severe, persistent mid-epigastric pain that is also frequently burning in nature can be pancreatitis, an inflammation of the pancreas.

This is a serious problem, but rare. Alcohol consumption can cause pancreatitis, as well as gastritis and ulcer formation. Avoid alcohol if pain in this area develops. In fact, any food that seems to increase the symptoms should be avoided. Reflux of stomach acid up the esophagus, caused by a hiatal hernia—protrusion of a part of the stomach through a hole in the diaphragm through which the esophagus passes—will cause the same symptoms. The reflux also causes the burning pain to radiate up the center of the chest.

Treatment for all of the above is aggressive antacid therapy. These conditions can be made worse by eating spicy food, tomato products, and other foods high in acid content. Milk may temporarily help the burning of an ulcer or gastritis but may increase the burning sensation later. Avoid any medications containing aspirin and ibuprofen. Acid suppression medication such as cimetidine (Tagamet®), famotidine (Pepcid®), nizatidine (Axid®), lansoprazole (Prevacid®), esomeprazole (Nexium®), rabeprazole (AcipHex®), dexlansoprazole (Dexilant®), and omeprazole (Prilosec®) help greatly, and anyone with a history of these disorders should consider adding such items to the medical kit. There is a concern that these medications can make the user more vulnerable to traveler's diarrhea, cholera, and other infectious disease from which a normal or high stomach acid level might otherwise provide some protection. A safer medication for persons afflicted with heartburn not responsive to antacids, who must travel in a third world situation, would be Carafate taken 1 g 4 times daily. This is a prescription medication.

Mild nausea may be associated with the above problems, but intense nausea could indicate gastroenteritis, food poisoning (generally these cause significant diarrhea also), hepatitis, or gall bladder disorder.

Gall Bladder Problems and Appendicitis

Nausea associated with pain in the right upper quadrant of the abdomen may be from a gall bladder problem. No burning is associated with gall bladder pain, and this discomfort is typically made worse by eating, and sometimes even by smelling, greasy foods. While drinking cream or milk would initially help the pain of gastritis or an ulcer, it causes an immediate increase in symptoms if the gall bladder is

Table 11.1 Symptoms and Signs of Abdominal Pathology

	BURNING	NAUSEA*	FOOD RELATED	DIARRHEA	FEVER
Gastritis/Ulcer (pages 85–86)	n	l	n		
Pancreatitis (page 86)	n	l	l		l
Hiatal Hernia (pages 94–95)	n		l		
Gall Bladder (page 86)		n	n		l
Appendicitis (page 86)		l			l
Gastroenteritis (page 86)		n	l	n	l
Diverticulitis (pages 90–93)			l	l	l
Colitis (page 91)				n	
Hepatitis (pages 223–224)			n	l	l
Food Poisoning (page 107)			n	n	n l

Legend	n	Frequent or intense
	l	Usual or less intense
	Blank	Less likely to be associated

*See also Vomiting, page 90.

involved. Treatment is avoidance of fatty foods. Nausea and vomiting can be treated as indicated on page 90. Treat for pain as described on page 89.

The onset of fever is an important indication of infection of the blocked gall bladder. This is a surgical emergency. Treat with the strongest antibiotic available. If the Rx Injectable Medication Kit is available, give Rocephin, 500 mg, 2 doses, IM immediately, repeated with 2 doses every 12 hours. Lacking that medication, give Levaquin, 750 mg daily. Continue to treat the pain and nausea as required for relief. Offer as much fluid as the patient can tolerate.

Gall bladder disease is more common in overweight people over the age of 30. It is also more common in women.

The possibility of appendicitis is a major concern, as it can occur in any age group, and that includes healthy sailors. It is fortunately rare. While surgery is the treatment of choice, probably as many as 70% of people not treated with surgery or antibiotics can survive this problem. The survival rate is over 80% with appropriate IV therapy. Of course, timely surgery provides 100% survival. A 2018 Finnish study confirmed the above statement, but unfortunately also showed that within 5 years 40% of those not having surgery will have a recurrence.

The classic presentation of this illness is a vague feeling of discomfort around the umbilicus (navel). Temperature may be low grade, 99.6°F to 100°F (or 37°C) at first. Within a matter of 12 hours, the discomfort turns to pain and localizes in the right lower quadrant, most frequently at a point two-thirds of the way between the navel and the very top of the right pelvic bone (anterior-superior iliac crest). Ask the patient two questions: Where did you first start hurting? (Belly button.) Now where do you hurt? (Right lower quadrant as described.) Those answers mean appendicitis until it is ruled out.

It is possible but unusual to have diarrhea with appendicitis. Diarrhea usually means that the patient does not have appendicitis. I find it helpful to ask the patient to walk and to watch how he does it. A person with appendicitis will walk with rather careful, short steps, bent slightly forward in pain. They certainly do not bounce off the examining table and walk down the hall to the bathroom. Anyone with springy steps most likely does not have appendicitis.

Sometimes full laboratory and X-ray facilities can do no better in making this diagnosis. The ultimate answer will come from surgical exploration. If a surgeon has doubts, he might wait, with the patient safely in a hospital or at home under close supervision. But the patient with those symptoms should certainly be taken to a surgeon as soon as possible.

In the examination of the painful abdomen, several maneuvers can indicate the seriousness of the situation. The first is to determine how guarded the area is to palpation. If the patient's stomach is rigid to gentle pushing, this can mean that extreme tenderness and irritation of the peritoneum, or abdominal wall lining, exists. Use only gentle pushing. If there is an area of the abdomen where it does not hurt to push, apply pressure rather deeply. Now, suddenly take your hand away! If pain flares over the area of suspect tenderness, this is called referred rebound tenderness and means that the irritation has reached an advanced stage. This person should be evacuated to surgical help at once.

What can you do if you are far at sea, without hope of evacuation? Move the patient as little as possible. No further prodding of the abdomen should be done, as his or her only hope is that the appendix will form an abscess that will be walled-off by the bodily defense mechanisms. Give no food. Provide small amounts of water, Gatorade, and fruit drinks as tolerated. With advanced disease, the intestines will stop working and the patient will vomit any excess. This will obviously cause a disturbance to the gut and possibly rupture the appendix or the abscess.

Treat for pain, nausea, and with antibiotics as indicated in the previous paragraph on gall bladder infection.

The abscess should form 24 to 72 hours following onset of the illness. Many surgeons would elect to open and drain this abscess as soon as the patient is brought to them. Other surgeons feel it is best to leave the patient alone at this time and allow the abscess to continue the walling-off process. They feel that there is so much inflammation present, surgery only complicates the situation further. Even without surgery, within 2 to 3 weeks the patient may be able to move with minimal discomfort.

One form of therapy never to be employed when there is a suspicion of appendicitis is a laxative. The action of the laxative may cause disruption of the appendix abscess with resultant generalized peritonitis (massive abdominal infection).

It is currently thought that there is no justification for the prophylactic removal of an appendix in an individual, unless he or she is planning to move to a very remote area without medical help for an extended period of time and it is known from X-ray that he or she has a fecalith (or stone) in the colon at the mouth of the appendix. Otherwise, the possible later complications of surgical adhesions may well outweigh the "benefit" of such a procedure.

VOMITING

Nausea and vomiting are frequently caused by infections known as gastroenteritis. Many times these are viral, so antibiotics are of no value. These infections will usually resolve without treatment in 24 to 48 hours. Fever is seldom high but may briefly be high in some cases. Fever should not persist above 100°F (38°C) longer than 12 hours. Nausea may be treated with diphenhydramine, 25 mg every 8 hours, from the Non-Rx Oral Medication Kit, or with Atarax, 25 mg every 6 hours, from the Rx Oral/Topical Medication Kit. If the Rx Injectable Medication Kit is available, severe nausea and vomiting may be treated with Vistaril, 25 to 50 mg every 6 hours given IM. Vomiting without diarrhea will not require the use of an antibiotic. If the vomiting is caused by severe illness, such as an ear infection, then use of an antibiotic to treat the underlying cause is justified.

Nausea associated with jaundice, see hepatitis, pages 222–225. Nausea from ingestion of seafood, see paralytic shellfish poisoning, page 109; scombroid poisoning, pages 108–109; and ciguatera poisoning, page 108.

See also plant or food poisoning, page 107; and petroleum products poisoning, pages 107–108.

Nausea and vomiting induced by motion, see chapter 5, Seasickness.

DIARRHEA

Diarrhea is the expulsion of watery stool. This malady is usually self-limited but can be a threat to life, depending upon its cause and extent. Diarrhea can be the result of bowel disorders such as diverticulitis or colitis; infectious diseases such as cholera, campylobacter, shigella, or salmonella; and the presence of many other creatures hiding in contaminated food or water; it is seen rarely with appendicitis and gall bladder disease. The serious infectious disease malaria can have diarrhea as a presenting complaint. Obviously, diagnosing the cause of diarrhea can be of importance both in regard to treating and in estimating the danger to the patient.

Diverticulitis is usually found in people over the age of 40 and is generally only a condition of the elderly. Diverticula are little pouches that form on the large intestine, or colon, from a weakness that develops over time in the muscles of its wall. These are of no trouble unless they become infected. Infection causes diarrhea, fever, and painful cramping. Pain is usually located along the left side of the abdomen. It tends to be at a constant location, unlike many conditions with diarrhea where the pain migrates around. Appendicitis pain is in the right lower quadrant of the abdomen (see pages 86–89). Treatment for diverticulitis is with antibiotics such as Levaquin, 750 mg daily, or Rocephin, 500 mg, given by injection twice daily.

Colitis and other inflammations of the bowel cause repeated bouts of diarrhea. At times, a fever may be present. These cases are chronic, and like diverticulitis, the diagnosis must be made with CT scan using contrast or colonoscopy. If in doubt, treat with antibiotics as indicated under diverticulitis. Both conditions require specific drugs for treatment, such as the steroids included with the Rx Oral/ Topical and Injectable Kits, but unless the person has a prior history of these diseases, the use of such drugs when at sea without physician advice is inappropriate.

Traveler's diarrhea is caused by infections, so prevention seems an appropriate priority. Prevention equates to staying alert. Water sources must be known to be pure or should be treated, as indicated on pages 113–114. Once dehydrated or freeze-dried food has been reconstituted, it should be stored as carefully as any fresh, unprocessed food. Certain animal products are tainted in various parts of the world, particularly at specific times of the year. Know the flora and fauna that your survival plans to utilize from local sources! The primary prevention that has been classically stressed concerning food safety is: "Peel it, boil it, or forget it." But this has not been proven to be practical or even accurate. The proven method of reducing diarrhea in travelers has been to improve the hygiene of food handlers preparing the food. Simple measures such as washing hands appropriately, using clean utensils, and reasonable food preparation techniques apply at sea as well.

Diarrhea is diagnosed when an individual has 2 to 3 times the number of customary bowel movements for that individual. These stools can be either soft, meaning that they will take the shape of a container, or watery, meaning that they can be poured. By definition at least one associated symptom of fever, chills, abdominal cramps, nausea, or vomiting must be present. This will generally mean 4 unformed stools in a day, or 3 unformed stools in an 8-hour period, when accompanied by at least one other symptom listed earlier.

While the disease is generally self-limiting, lasting 2 to 3 days, this illness can result in chronic bowel problems in many patients. Initially, as many as 75% of people will have abdominal pain and cramps, 50% will have nausea, and 25% will have vomiting and fever. An acute onset of watery diarrhea usually means that an enterotoxigenic *E. coli* is the cause, but shigellosis will also first present in this manner. Symptoms of bloody diarrhea or mucoid stools are frequently seen with invasive pathogens such as *Shigella*, *Campylobacter*, or *Salmonella*. The presence of chronic diarrhea with malabsorption and gas indicates possible giardia. Rotavirus disease starts with vomiting in 80% of cases.

In a study of U.S. students in Mexico, the cause of diarrhea was found to be: enterotoxigenic *E. coli* 40%; enteroadherent *E. coli* 5%; *Giardia lamblia* and *Entamoeba histolytica* 2%; rotavirus 10%; aeromonas 1%; *Shigella* 15%; *Salmonella* 7%; *Campylobacter* 3%; and unknown 17%. Studies of traveler's diarrhea show different frequencies from the above in various other locations of the world, but the cause is always due to infection.

Various medications have been shown effective in prevention of traveler's diarrhea, but experts discourage their use due to cost, exposing people to drug side effects, and the possible development of resistant germs due to antibiotic overuse. Pepto-Bismol, 2 ounces (4 tablespoons) or 2 tablets taken 4 times daily, can prevent this problem. Ugh! About 8 aspirin tablets worth of salicylate are in that quantity of Pepto-Bismol. Prevention with antibiotics is effective, although not usually indicated. Prevention of diarrhea-causing illness is best accomplished in a survival situation with good hygiene.

Treating diarrhea with Pepto-Bismol requires 2 tablespoons every 30 minutes for 8 doses. As most diarrhea in developing countries is from bacterial causes, the use of antibiotics can be very effective. A single dose of the antibiotic Levaquin, 750 mg, can eliminate diarrhea instantly. loperamide, 2 mg, from the Non-Rx Oral Medication

Kit, may not be required if you have access to Levaquin. A dose of loperamide may be given simultaneously with the Levaquin. When using loperamide, give 2 tablets at once, followed by 1 tablet after each loose stool, with a maximum adult dose of 8 tablets per day. One tablet of the pain medication Norco-10/325 can also stop diarrhea, but it would be best to use the loperamide and/or Levaquin if they are available. In parts of the world where Levaquin is losing its effectiveness, such as the Indian subcontinent, Southeast Asia, and Africa, Zithromax is a better choice. Since diarrhea in North America is seldom caused by bacteria, antibiotics should be used there only after stool cultures.

CONSTIPATION

One of the popular wilderness medical texts has instructions on how to break up a fecal impaction digitally, that is, using your finger to break up a hard stool stuck in the rectum. Don't let it get that far. In healthy young adults (especially teenagers), there may be a reluctance to defecate in unusual circumstances due to the unusual surroundings, dehydration and the possibility of fecal hoarding failing to defecate in a reasonable length of time. Certainly, one should be concerned after 3 days of no bowel movements.

To prevent this problem, you might want to include a stewed fruit at breakfast on your ship's menu. The use of hot and cold food and water in the morning will frequently wake up the "gastric-colic reflex" and get things moving perfectly well.

If the 5-day mark is approaching, especially if the patient—and the person has become a patient at about this point—is obviously uncomfortable, it will become necessary to use a laxative. From the medical kit (Non-Rx Oral Medication Kit), give one 5 mg bisacodyl laxative tablet at bedtime. If that fails, the next morning take 2 tablets. Any laxative will cause abdominal cramping, depending upon how strong it is. Expect this.

HEMORRHOIDS

Also called piles, this painful swelling is a cluster of varicose veins around the rectum. External hemorrhoids are small, rounded, purplish masses that enlarge when straining at stool. Unless a clot forms in them, they are soft and not tender. When clots form, they can become very painful, actually excruciating. Hemorrhoids are the most common cause of rectal bleeding, with blood usually appearing on the toilet tissue. The condition can be very painful for about 5 days, after which the clots start to absorb, the pain decreases, and the mass regresses, leaving only small skin tags.

Provide the patient with pain medication (non-Rx item) Percogesic, 2 tablets every 4 hours. The application of heat is helpful during the acute phase. Heat a cloth in water and apply for 15 minutes 4 times a day if possible. Avoid constipation, as mentioned in that section. If you are carrying the Rx Oral/Topical Kit, Topicort 0.25% ointment will provide the anti-inflammation ability from the steroid and some local pain relief.

HERNIA

The most common hernia in a male is the inguinal hernia, an outpouching of the intestines through a weak area in the abdominal wall located above and on either side of the groin. It is through this area that the spermatic cord connects the testes to the back of the penis. A hernia can be produced while straining or lifting, even coughing or sneezing, when the bowel pushes along the spermatic cord. There will be a sharp pain at the location of the hernia and the patient will note a bulge. This bulge may disappear when he lies on his back and relaxes (i.e., the hernia has reduced).

If the intestine in the hernia is squeezed by the abdominal wall to the point that the blood supply is cut off, the hernia is termed a strangulated hernia. This is a medical emergency, as the loop of gut in the hernia will die, turn gangrenous, and lead to a generalized peritonitis or abdominal infection (peritonitis is discussed under Gall Bladder Problems and under Appendicitis). This condition is much worse than appendicitis. Death will result if not treated surgically.

The hernia that fails to reduce or disappear when the victim relaxes in a recumbent position is termed incarcerated. While this may turn into an emergency, it is not one at that point.

Most hernias caused by straining in adults will not strangulate. Further straining should be avoided. If lifting items is necessary, or coughing cannot be prevented, and so forth, the victim should protect himself or herself from further tissue damage by pressing against the area with one hand, thus holding the hernia in reduction.

BLADDER INFECTION

The hallmarks of bladder infection (cystitis) are the urge to urinate frequently, burning upon urination, small amounts of urine being voided with each passage, and discomfort in the suprapubic region— the lowest area of the abdomen. Frequently the victim has fever, with its attendant chills and muscle ache. In fact, people can become quite ill with a generalized infection caused by numerous bacteria entering their bloodstream. At times the urine becomes cloudy and even bloody. Cloudy urine without the above symptoms does not mean an infection is present and is frequently normal. The infection can extend to the kidney, at which time the patient also has considerable flank pain, centered at the bottom edge of the ribs along the lateral aspect of the back on the involved side (often both sides). While bladder infections are more common in women than men, they are not an uncommon problem in either sex. One suffering from recurrent infections should be thoroughly evaluated by a physician prior to an extended voyage.

There have been many drugs developed for treating infections of the genitourinary system. Doxycycline, 100 mg, 1 tablet taken twice daily, is very effective. Levaquin, 750 mg tablet once daily, is ideal to use if the doxycycline seems ineffective. Generally, 3 days is a sufficient length of time for treatment, unless flank pain is involved, in which case provide 10 days of antibiotic. Symptoms should disappear within 24 to 48 hours, or it may mean that the bacteria is resistant to one antibiotic and the other should be substituted.

For severe infections with high fever that has not responded within 48 hours to oral antibiotic use, the injectable Rocephin, 500 mg IM given twice daily, given in place of the oral antibiotic, would be a superior choice.

Additional treatment should consist of drinking copious amounts of fluid, at least 8 quarts (7.5 liters) per day! At times, this simple rinsing action may even cure a cystitis, but I wouldn't want to count on it. Use an antibiotic, if it is available. Percogesic or ibuprofen may be needed to treat the fever and pain that accompanies this diagnosis during the early stages of therapy.

URINARY RETENTION

No problem can be so acute or such an emergency as the patient suddenly being unable to urinate. Sometimes this problem can be temporary, but it will be hard to identify the various causes or know how long this emergency will last. If the patient literally cannot urinate, and they are not dehydrated as evidenced by a history of appropriate water intake and not having signs of dehydration (poor skin turgor, elevated heart rate, low BP) and have distension of the lower abdomen with discomfort, their story of urinary obstruction and desperation to urinate is probably correct and they will need help.

Any ship leaving port for a multi-day voyage should carry a Foley catheter set in its medicine chest.

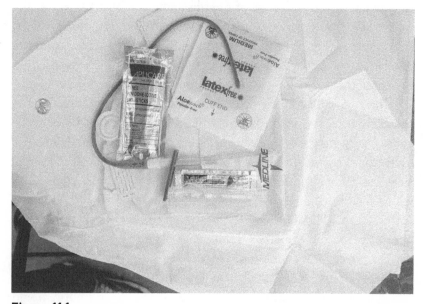

Figure 11.1
An open pre-packaged Foley catheter kit. This kit has the cleansing solution, a catheter, and a syringe with fluid that will properly inflate the catheter to hold it in place within the bladder.

How to Insert a Foley Catheter

Using an indwelling Foley catheter tray, collect all needed supplies.

1. Discuss all aspects of the procedure with the patient before proceeding.

2. Thoroughly wash your hands.

3. Help the patient rest on his or her back and spread the legs for easy access to insert the catheter.

4. Carefully open the catheterization kit, removing the sterile drape and placing it in the procedure area. Before proceeding, place an absorbent pad under the patient to catch any excess fluid during the procedure.

5. Apply sterile gloves, open the Betadine®, and pour it over the cotton balls included in the Betadine kit. Remove the plastic that covers the catheter without touching the tube and squirt the jelly on the catheter to lubricate it. Remove the rubber cap on the syringe that contains water.

6. It is no longer recommended to inflate or pre-test the balloon prior to insertion.

7. Clean the urinary opening of the female patient. Using the nondominant hand, gently separate her labia. Do not touch anything after this with the unclean, nondominant hand. For a male patient, gently clean the periurethral mucosa with a cleaning solution. Clean the area using one swipe per swab. Make sure to discard the swab from the sterile area immediately.

8. Using the sterile dominant hand, pick up the catheter with a gloved hand. Holding the catheter loosely, insert it into the urethral opening of a female patient. For a male patient, lift his penis to a perpendicular position and lightly apply traction in an upward position using the nondominant hand. Gently insert the catheter one to two inches past where the patient's urine is located.

9. Using the correct amount of liquid, inflate the balloon (check the balloon size for the correct amount). After

inflating the balloon properly, carefully pull the catheter until it is snug against the neck of the bladder. Connect the drainage system to the catheter. Make sure that the drainage bag in lower than bladder level but not on the floor. Carefully inspect the function of the catheter before ending the process.

The catheter will need to be drained into a receptacle, either a premade leg bag or a larger bag for non-ambulatory use, or frankly into any container if the drainage is to be left open. The catheter may be bent and clamped off and used intermittently, but best be left inserted until return to port and proper medical care for the underlying condition is identified and treated (see figure 11.1) on page 96.

CHAPTER 12

REPRODUCTIVE ORGANS

VENEREAL DISEASES

Venereal infections are totally preventable by abstention; any other technique falls short of being foolproof. Most venereal infections cause symptoms in the male and frequently do not in the female. Either may note increased discomfort with urination, the development of sores or unusual growths around the genitalia, and discharge from the portions of the anatomy used in sex (pharynx, penis, vagina, anus). Some venereal diseases can be very difficult to detect, such as syphilis, hepatitis B, and AIDS. Hepatitis B is rampant in many parts of the world, with high carrier rates in local population groups. It can be prevented with a vaccine. There are no vaccines against the other venereal diseases except human papillomavirus (HPV).

Gonorrhea is common and easy to detect in the male. The appearance of symptoms is from 2 to 8 days from time of contact and basically consists of a copious greenish-yellow discharge. The female will frequently not have symptoms. From the Rx kit, provide ceftriaxone 250 mg IM as a single dose to cure gonorrhea. Also give Zithromax, 1 g at once (4 of the 250 mg tablets), to cure chlamydia, which frequently is a coinfection.

Syphilis has an incubation period of 2 to 6 weeks before the characteristic sore appears. The development of a painless ulcer (1/4 to 1/2 inch, or 0.6 to 1.2 cm in size), generally with enlarged, nontender lymph nodes in the region, is a hallmark of this disease. A painful ulcer formation is more characteristic of herpes simplex. The lesion may not appear in a syphilis victim, making the early detection of this disease very difficult. A second stage consisting of a generalized skin rash (which usually does not itch, does not produce blisters, and frequently appears on the soles of the feet and palms of the hands) appears about 6 weeks after the lesions mentioned above. The third phase of the disease may develop in several years, during which nearly any organ system in the body may be affected. The overall study of syphilis is so complicated that a great medical instructor (Sir William Osler) once said, "To know syphilis is to know medicine." Treatment of primary-stage syphilis is 15 days of antibiotics, as mentioned earlier. Development of a clear, scanty discharge in the male may be due to chlamydia or other nonspecific urethral infections. Symptoms appear 7 to 28 days after contact. Women may have no symptoms. Treat with doxycycline, 100 mg twice daily, for 15 days. The preferred treatment for syphilis is penicillin G benzathine 2.4 million units IM, but this has not been recommended in this book's standard Ship's Medicine Chest. If you do carry it, it must be refrigerated. Blood tests for syphilis should be performed now (ideally) and again in 3 months. Since 20% of victims with nonspecific urethritis will have a relapse, adequate medical follow up after the trip is essential.

Herpes lesions can respond to penciclovir (Denavir) 1% cream applied frequently during the day until they disappear in 8 to 10 days. Famciclovir (Famvir®) capsules, 250 mg taken 3 times daily for 7 to 10 days, are effective during the acute phase. If it is a recurrent problem, then provide 4 capsules (total 1,000 mg), twice per day for 2 days.

Upon returning home, members who may have experienced a sexual disease should be seen by their physician for serology tests for syphilis, hepatitis B tests, chlamydia smears, gonorrheal cultures, herpes simplex titers, and possibly HIV studies for AIDS. Lesions or growths should be examined as possible molluscum contagiosum, and venereal warts should be treated.

VAGINAL DISCHARGE AND ITCHING

Vaginal discharge and/or itching are frequently not indicators for venereal disease. The most common cause is a fungal or monilia (candida) infection. This condition is more common in conditions of high humidity or with the wearing of tight clothes such as pants or panty hose.

A typical monilia infection has a copious white discharge with curds like cottage cheese. From the Non-Rx Oral Kit, one can use the clotrimazole 1% cream. This formulation has been designed for foot and other skin fungal problems, but it will work vaginally as well. From the Rx Oral Medication Kit, use 1 fluconazole (Diflucan®) 150 mg tablet for treatment.

A frothy, greenish-yellow, irritating discharge may be due to trichomonas infection. This can be spread by sexual encounters. The male infected with this organism generally has no symptoms, or a slight mucoid discharge early in the morning, noted before urinating. The treatment of choice is Flagyl metronidazole (Flagyl®), 250 mg capsule 3 times a day for 10 days, or 8 capsules given as 1 dose. This drug cannot be taken with alcohol. Sexual abstention is important until medication is finished, and a cure is evident clinically. Generic metronidazole is frequently available in third world countries at pharmacies without a prescription.

A copious yellow-green discharge may indicate gonorrhea (see treatment discussion above).

Any irritating discharge that is not thick and white of unknown cause is best treated with Levaquin, 750 mg once daily. If sexual contact may have been the source of the problem, treat for 15 days to also kill any syphilis that may have been caught simultaneously. A douche of very dilute Hibiclens® surgical scrub, or very dilute detergent solution, can be prepared and may be helpful. Very dilute is better than too strong. Frequent douching is not required, but it may be done for a few days as required for comfort and hygiene.

MENSTRUAL PROBLEMS

Rolling several Nu-Gauze® pads from the Topical Bandaging Kit will substitute as an outer sanitary napkin, if none is available. Menstrual cramping can generally be controlled with ibuprofen, 200 mg, 1 or 2 tablets every 4 to 6 hours, from the Non-Rx Oral Medication Kit. While this medication is used as an antiarthritic, its anti-prostaglandin activities make it an ideal medication for the treatment of menstrual pain.

Menorrhagia, either excessive flow or long period of flowage, should be evaluated by a physician to determine if there is an underlying pathology that could or should be corrected. If the problem is simply one of hormone imbalance, this can frequently be corrected with the use of birth control pills with higher amounts of estrogen and lower progestogen content. Consult a physician well in advance of the voyage so that these symptoms can be brought under control by the time of the expedition. It takes at least 3 cycles of the "correct" hormone dose to comfortably predict adequate management.

SPONTANEOUS ABORTION

Bleeding during pregnancy is not unusual—20% to 30% of women bleed or cramp during the first 20 weeks of their pregnancies. This is termed threatened abortion and is treated with bed rest, since this usually decreases the bleeding and cramping. About 10% to 15% of pregnant women will go on to abort. As long as all products of the abortion pass—a "complete abortion"—the bleeding and pain stop and the uterus shrinks back to its normal size.

An incomplete abortion—the expulsion of only a portion of the fetus or the rupture of the membranes only—will often require a surgeon's care to perform a D&C (dilation and curettage). However, urgent evacuation is always mandatory. Watch for signs of sepsis, such as elevated temperature, and start an antibiotic if possible. Give Rocephin, 1 g IM, followed by 500 mg IM every 12 hours. The best oral antibiotic recommended from your kit would be Levaquin, 750 mg given daily. Give pain medication as necessary.

ECTOPIC PREGNANCY

In an ectopic pregnancy, spotting and cramping usually begin shortly after the first missed period. If a pregnancy test is positive and the woman has severe lower abdominal pain lasting more than 24 hours, you probably have a surgical emergency on your hands. A rupture of the uterine tube usually occurs at 6 to 8 weeks of pregnancy, while a rupture of a cornual pregnancy occurs at 12 to 16 weeks. The rupture causes massive blood loss with a rapid onset of shock and death when it occurs.

While other causes of spotting during pregnancy are possible, you are in no position to handle any of them while at sea. Evacuate this woman urgently.

If a woman is having spotting and lower abdominal pain, and the pregnancy test is negative, you are in no position to bet her life that she is not pregnant. Ectopic pregnancies have lower blood levels of ß subunit HCG hormone to detect and the test may, therefore, be falsely negative.

PREGNANCY

In case you are planning a voyage and a member of your team is in advanced pregnancy, you will need to have the supplies and basic knowledge of delivery. During the second trimester she should receive an additional 340 kCal and during the third trimester 450 additional kCal of food per day. She should also have a multivitamin that includes: 400 to 600 mcg of folic acid, 400 IU vitamin D, 300 mg of calcium, 70 mg of vitamin C, 3 mf of thiamine, 2 mf of riboflavin, 20 mg of niacin, 6 mg of vitamin B-12, 290 mcg of iodine (but not more than a total daily amount of 1,100 mcg), and trace amounts of zinc and copper.,

Over 94% deliveries are uncomplicated. But about 10% to 20% of pregnancies end with a spontaneous abortion before the 20th week, but this amount might be much higher as many miscarriages occur so early in pregnancy that the woman might not realize she was even pregnant. Once pregnancy is advanced and obvious (generally beyond the 12th to 16th weeks), care must be taken to make sure that the lady's diet is appropriate as mentioned earlier and that she does not develop hypertension (not usual before week 20). This hypertension is best controlled with reduced sodium intake and the possible use of a diuretic BP medication. Gestational diabetes can occur between weeks 24 and 28, and one should ideally check blood sugar level at that time. If the person develops signs of diabetes (frequency of urination matched with thirst), diet and exercise usually manages 80% of these cases, while some ladies will require insulin. Frequency and burning while urinating small amounts may mean a urinary tract infection. Obstetricians would treat a urinary tract infection usually with nitrofurantoin 100 mg twice daily, but the Rx Oral/Topical Medication Kit suggestion of levofloxacin, 750 mg once daily for 3 days, is safe. This antibiotic's safety in pregnancy has not been established. Edema in late pregnancy is a serious sign of a condition called pre-eclampsia (hypertension, protein in urine, and edema). It must be treated as a medical emergency, return to the shore if possible. Otherwise, bedrest, salt restriction, and diuretic are recommended. Ashore, frequently the baby is delivered early to prevent this condition from progressing, which can lead to death of both the mother and child otherwise. Seizures from eclampsia are difficult to treat and are rare in places like the United States, but relatively common in areas where I volunteer, like Haiti. This is a deadly situation without help.

In general, delivery progresses through various stages without danger to mother or child. However, even basic training for the birthing assistant will provide a safer birth and management of the newborn and identify issues requiring sometimes very basic maneuvers, or some very desperate ones, to save lives in the 10% of situations that require help. There is an ideal chapter on birthing in Buck Tilton's book *Wilderness First Responder* (Falcon Guides, 2010), covering basic principles in detail, including immediate care of the newborn.

Keep the new mother on her prenatal vitamins, encouraging breastfeeding, exclusively for 6 months, then continue combining breast feeding with solid food for 2 years. Hopefully, this is not being managed exclusively without professional care while afloat!

PAINFUL TESTICLE

If pain is severe, provide support by having the victim lie on the insulated ground with a cloth draped over both thighs, forming a sling or cradle on which the painful scrotum may rest. If ambulatory, provide support to prevent movement of the scrotum. Cold packs would help initially and providing adequate pain and nausea medication as available is certainly appropriate. An antibiotic is not required unless a fever ensues.

Spontaneous pain in the scrotum, with enlargement of a testicle, can be due to an infection of the testicle (orchitis) or more commonly to an infection of the sperm-collecting system called the epididymis (epididymitis). Treatment of choice would be to provide an antibiotic such as doxycycline, 100 mg, 1 tablet twice daily, or levofloxacin

(Levaquin), 750 mg once daily. Pain medication should be provided as necessary.

The problem may not be due to an infection at all. It is possible for the testicle to become twisted, due to a slight congenital defect, with severe pain resulting. This testicular torsion, as it is called, is a surgical emergency. It can be almost impossible to distinguish from orchitis. In a suspected case of torsion, it is helpful to try to reduce the torsion. Since the testicle always seems to rotate "inward," one need only rotate the affected testicle "outward." This will often result in immediate relief of the pain. If you cannot achieve this, or if you are dealing with an orchitis, no harm is done; but if it is a torsion, you have saved the testicle and the trip. A person with severe testicular pain should be evacuated as soon as possible, as infection or torsion can result in sterility of the involved side. An unreduced testicular torsion can become gangrenous, with life-threatening infection resulting.

CHAPTER 13
POISONING

PLANT OR FOOD POISONING

The ideal treatment after poison plant ingestion would be to give the patient activated charcoal. If all fails, induce vomiting by gagging the throat with a finger or spoon. This latter technique may well be the only method available at sea. If it is not immediately identified that the food was contaminated, the ship's master, and everyone else on board, may want to consult the section of this book specific to nausea, vomiting, and diarrhea!

PETROLEUM PRODUCTS

The danger from accidentally drinking various petroleum products—while siphoning from one container to another—is the possibility of accidentally inhaling or aspirating this liquid into the lungs. That will kill. The substances are not toxic enough in the gastrointestinal (GI) tract to warrant the danger of inducing vomiting. Do not worry about swallowing several mouthfuls of any petroleum product. If the person vomits, there is nothing you can do about it, except position him or her so that there is less chance of aspiration into the lungs—sitting, bending forward is probably ideal. The more volatile the substance, the more the danger of aspiration. In other words, kerosene is less dangerous than Coleman fuel.

If organic phosphorous pesticides are dissolved in the fuel, you have a more complex problem. These substances are potentially toxic and must be removed. In the emergency room this would be accomplished by gastric lavage, or stomach pumping. At sea, if you cannot evacuate the person within 12 hours, you will have to take a chance of inducing vomiting, with possible lethal aspiration—to eliminate the poison. Treat by inducing gagging as described under Plant or Food Poisoning. After vomiting, administer a slurry of activated charcoal, if available. This helps bind non-regurgitated toxins. Charcoal powder, to which you add water to form a slurry, is available at pharmacies. In the field, you might consider tearing apart a charcoal water filter and crushing the charcoal granules.

CIGUATERA POISONING

Ciguatera poisoning is caused by a toxin released by a small ocean organism called a dinoflagellate. As various species of fish eat this small plant, they acquire the toxin. Larger fish that in turn prey on the smaller fish acquire larger and larger amounts of the toxin and thus result in more severe cases of ciguatera toxin poisoning in humans. Over 400 species of fish from the tropical reefs of Florida, the West Indies, and the Pacific have been implicated, but most often it has been barracuda, grouper, and amberjack that are contaminated. No deep-sea fish such as tuna, dolphin, or wahoo have been found contaminated.

There is no way to detect contamination—no change in flavor, texture, or color of the fish flesh. Worse yet, no method of preserving, cooking, or treating fish can destroy this toxin. One must rely on local knowledge to avoid potentially polluted species.

Symptoms usually start with numbness and tingling of the lips and tongue, and then progress to dry mouth, abdominal cramping, vomiting, and diarrhea that lasts 6 to 17 hours. Muscle and joint pain, muscle weakness, facial pain, and unusual sensory phenomena such as reversal of hot and cold sensations develop. Occasionally low BP, respiratory depression, and coma can result. Neurological symptoms are made worse by alcohol and exercise. Start rescue breathing if necessary (see page 17). This type of poisoning does not result in death.

Please also pay attention to the following sections on scombroid poisoning and paralytic shellfish poisoning.

SCOMBROID POISONING

The flesh of dark meat fish, such as tuna, mackerel, albacore, bonito, amberjack, and mahi-mahi (dolphin), contain large amounts of histidine. Improper storage after catching these fish allows bacterial enzymatic changes of this meat, releasing large amounts of histamine and other toxic byproducts that are not destroyed by cooking.

Symptoms of scombroid poisoning include flushing, dizziness, headache, burning of the mouth and throat, nausea, vomiting, and diarrhea. Severe poisoning can cause significant respiratory distress. Diphenhydramine has been reported to cause an increase in symptoms at times, which is surprising since it is an excellent antihistamine. Cimetidine (Tagamet), 400 mg every 12 hours, from the Non-Rx Oral Medication Kit may block the effects of scombroid poisoning. While normally used to control stomach acid formation, its mode of action is known as a histamine-2 receptor blocker and can block some of the effects of the histidine.

PUFFERFISH POISONING

Incorrectly prepared pufferfish (*fugu*) contain tetrodotoxin, which can be lethal as it leads to respiratory failure and cardiac collapse. Symptoms may be slow in onset. Provide CPR as necessary (see pages 18–22). More people are probably killed by ingesting poisonous marine creatures than are killed by any other form of encounter with them, such as trauma by them biting, stinging, or shocking. There is certainly a tragedy when the predator becomes the victim, especially when it is us!

PARALYTIC SHELLFISH POISONING

Mussels, clams, oysters, and scallops may ingest the poison saxitoxin from dinoflagellates known as the "red tide," which occurs from June to October along the New England and Pacific coasts. Numbness around the mouth may occur within 5 to 30 minutes after eating. Other symptoms are similar to ciguatera poisoning. These include GI illness, loss of coordination, and paralysis progressing to complete respiratory paralysis within 12 hours in 8% of cases. No specific treatments or antidotes are available but purging of stomach contents should be encouraged. Artificial support of respirations is potentially lifesaving.

CHAPTER 14
MANAGING DIABETES

Diabetic children or adults can have an active sailing life, but learning to control their diabetes must first be worked on with their physicians. The increased caloric requirement of significant exercise may range above an extra 2,000 calories per day, yet insulin dosage requirements may drop as much as 50%.

The diabetic, as well as the trip partners, must be able to identify the signs of low blood sugar (hypoglycemia)—staggering gait, slurred speech, moist skin, clumsy movements—and know the proper treatment, that is, oral carbohydrates or sugar candies and, if the patient becomes unconscious, the use of injectable glucagon. Urine of diabetic travelers should be tested twice daily to confirm control of sugar.

This testing should preclude a gradual accumulation of too much blood sugar, which can result in unconsciousness in its far advanced stage. This gradual accumulation would have resulted in massive sugar spill in the urine, and finally the spill of ketone bodies, providing the patient ample opportunity to increase insulin dosage to prevent hyperglycemia (too high a blood sugar level). Battery-powered, point-of-care blood sugar test devices (glucometers) must be included in personal property of anyone taking insulin.

Storage of insulin on a sail of less than 1 month, when it must forgo recommended refrigeration, is not a major problem so long as the supply is fresh and direct sunlight and excessive heat is avoided. Unopened insulin usually has an expiration date of 1 year. With proper storage this might be extended several years, but there is an unknown finite point when it will not be viable. Biologicals such as insulin will not have long, extended storage times.

Syringes, alcohol prep pads, Keto-Diastix urine test strips, insulin, and glucagon are light additions to the ship's medical chest. Adults, whose diabetes started later in life, might do adequately with oral medications, but need to have an ideal body mass index and eat no more calories than they are expending. They also need to have diabetes in good control before departure.

Any ship sailing away from port with a crewmember on the roster with a history of diabetes must have a glucometer aboard.

CHAPTER 15

WATER SAFETY, FLUID REPLACEMENT

ORAL FLUID REPLACEMENT

Replacement of fluid loss is required for three different circumstances: diarrhea, heat stress sweat formation, and insensible moisture loss from breathing and skin respiration (yes, skin must breathe also). The ideal fluid replacement for each of these losses differs in electrolyte and sugar content. In general, diarrhea replacement fluids should not have a greater sugar content than 2.5%, as a higher concentration might cause additional diarrhea. A higher sugar concentration is not a problem in a person who is not ill; however, sweat replacement solutions should not have a sugar concentration greater than 8.5%; this slows the emptying of the fluid from the stomach. The uptake of water by the body is decreased, as this occurs in the intestines and not the stomach. The ideal electrolyte composition for these circumstances also differs dramatically.

Profound diarrhea from any source may cause severe dehydration and electrolyte imbalance. The non-vomiting patient must receive adequate fluid replacement, equaling his stool loss plus about 2 liters (2 quarts) per day. For a couple of days, an adult can replace these losses by drinking enough plain water. A child, or less healthy adult, will require electrolyte replacement in addition to the water. The Centers for Disease Control and Prevention recommends the oral replacement cocktails for fluid losses caused by profound diarrhea, as seen in table 15.1. Drink alternately from each glass. Supplement with carbonated beverages, or water and tea made with boiled or carbonated water as desired. Avoid solid foods and milk until recovery.

Table 15.1 Oral Replacement Cocktails

Prepare two separate glasses of the following:

Glass 1)	Orange, apple, or other fruit juice (rich in potassium)	8 ounces
	Honey or corn syrup (glucose necessary for absorption of essential salts)	½ teaspoon
	Table salt (rich in sodium and chloride)	1 pinch
Glass 2)	Water (carbonated or boiled)	8 ounces
	Soda, baking (sodium bicarbonate)	¼ teaspoon

Throughout the world, UNICEF and WHO distribute an electrolyte replacement product called Oralyte. It must be reconstituted with adequately purified water.

If the patient is maintaining fluid balance with an effective oral rehydration therapy, such as with the packets as indicated earlier, the additional glass of carbonated or bicarbonate water is not necessary. Other products that are considered safe for rehydration due to diarrheal losses are Naturalyte, Pedialyte, Infalyte, and Pediatric. Gatorade is too high in carbohydrate and too low in sodium, potassium, and base to be considered a safe substitute, even with modification.

Water Purification

Your ship requires adequate water storage to last between ports. This system must be cleaned and replenished appropriately to its specifications. If you must rely on any but certified refilling, then here are suggestions for producing potable water:

Water can be purified adequately for drinking by mechanical, physical, and chemical means.

The clearest water possible should be chosen or attempts made to clarify the water prior to starting any disinfectant process. Water with high particulate counts of clay or organic debris allows high bacterial counts and tends to be more heavily contaminated. In preparing potable, or drinkable, water, we attempt to lower the germ counts to the point that the body can defend itself against the remaining numbers. We are not trying to produce sterile water—that would generally be impractical.

The use of chlorine-based systems has been effectively used by municipal water supply systems for years. There are two forms of chlorine readily available to the outdoors traveler. One is liquid chlorine laundry bleach and the other is halazone tablets.

Laundry bleach that is 4% to 6% sodium hypochlorite can make clear water safe to drink if 2 drops are added to 1 quart (liter) of water. Avoid brands of bleach that contain soap or surfactant. This water must be mixed thoroughly and let stand for 30 minutes before drinking. The resulting blend should have a slight chlorine odor. If not, the original laundry bleach may have lost some of its strength and you should repeat the dose and let stand an additional 15 minutes prior to drinking.

Halazone tablets from Abbott Laboratories are also effective. They are quite stable, with a shelf life of 5 years, even when exposed to temperatures over 100°F (38°C) occasionally. Recent articles in outdoor literature have stated that halazone has a short shelf life and that it loses 75% of its activity when exposed to air for 2 days. Abbott Labs refutes this and has proven the efficacy of use for halazone sufficiently to receive FDA approval. A clue to the stability of the tablets is that they turn yellow and have an objectionable odor when they decompose. Check for this before use. Five tablets should be added to a quart (liter) of clear water for adequate chlorination.

Chlorine-based systems are very effective against viruses and bacteria. They work best in neutral or slightly acid waters. As the active form of the chlorine, namely hypochlorous acid ($HClO$), readily reacts with nitrogen-containing compounds such as ammonia, high levels of organic debris decrease its effectiveness. The amount of chlorine bleach or halazone added must be increased if the water is alkaline or contaminated with organic debris.

Iodine is a fairly effective agent against protozoan contamination such as *Giardia lamblia* and *Entamoeba histolytica*, both of which tend to be resistant to chlorine. Further, iodine is not as reactive to ammonia or other organic debris, thus working better in cloudy water. It is relatively ineffective against Cryptosporidium, which must be destroyed by either filtration or heat. Tincture of iodine, as found in the home medicine chest, may be used as the source of the iodine. Using the commonly available 2% solution, 5 drops should be added to clear water or 10 drops to cloudy water, and the resultant mix should be allowed to stand 30 minutes prior to drinking.

An elemental iodine concentration of 3 to 5 ppm (parts per million) is necessary to kill amoeba and their cysts, algae, bacteria and their spores, and enterovirus. Crystals of iodine can also be used to prepare a saturated iodine water solution for use in disinfecting drinking water. About 4 to 8 g of USP-grade iodine crystals can be placed in a 1-ounce glass bottle. Water added to this bottle will dissolve an amount of iodine based on its temperature. This saturated iodine water solution is then added to the quart (liter) of water. The amount added to produce a final concentration of 4 ppm will vary according to temperature, as indicated in table 15.2.

This water should be stored for 15 minutes before drinking. If the water is turbid, or otherwise contaminated, the amounts of saturated iodine solution indicated in table 15.2 should be doubled and the resultant water stored 20 minutes before using. This product is now commercially available as Polar Pure through many outdoor stores and catalog houses.

Mechanical filtration methods are also useful in preparing drinking water. They normally consist of a screen with sizes down to 6 microns, which are useful in removing tapeworm eggs (25 microns) or *Giardia lamblia* (7 to 15 microns). These screens enclose an activated charcoal filter element, which removes many disagreeable tastes. As

Table 15.2 Iodine Concentrations for Water Disinfection*

TEMPERATURE	VOLUME (CC)	CAPFULS
37°F (3°C)	20.0	8
68°F (20°C)	13.0	5+
77°F (25°C)	12.5	5
104°F (40°C)	10.0	4

*Assuming 2.5 cc capacity for a standard 1-ounce glass bottle cap.

most bacteria have a diameter smaller than 1 micron, bacteria and the even smaller viral species are not removed by filtration using these units. For water to be safe after using one of these devices, it must be pretreated with chlorine or iodine exactly as indicated earlier prior to passage through the device. While these filters remove clay and organic debris, they will plug easily if the water is very turbid. A concern with the charcoal filter usage is that the filters may become contaminated with bacteria when they are used the next time. Pretreating the water helps prevent this. I have frequently used a charcoal filter system to ensure safe, good-tasting water after chemical treatment.

Another filtration method is perhaps one of the oldest, namely filtering through unglazed ceramic material. This was done in large crocks, a slow filtration method popular in tropical countries many years ago. A modern version of this old system is the development of a pressurized pump method. Made in Switzerland, the Katadyn Pocket Filter has a ceramic core enclosed in a tough plastic housing, fitted with an aluminum pump. The built-in pump forces water through the ceramic filter at a rate of approximately 3/4 quart (0.7 liter) per minute. Turbid water will plug the filter, but a brush is provided to easily restore full flow rates. This filter has a 0.2-micron size, which eliminates all bacteria and larger pathogens. Pretreating of the water is not required. There is evidence that viral particles are also killed by this unit, as the ceramic material is silver-impregnated, which appears to denature viruses as they pass through the filter. The European Union did not approve this claim and, subsequently, the manufacturer no longer makes this statement in their literature. I have worked with many groups using this device, and they have had many favorable comments. These units are not cheap, costing about $370 retail. They weigh 23 ounces. There are several less expensive ceramic units now available but be sure to pretreat the water chemically when using these systems, as they may be ineffective against viral disease without the silver impregnation.

Using the same technology as kidney dialysis systems, Sawyer Products produces a microtubule filter with a 0.1-micron absolute size. Normally a filter with such a small diameter would be very difficult to pump water through, but the microtubules have an effective large surface area allowing one to suck water or to gravity-feed water through the system easily. I prefer the Sawyer personal water bottle filter, as the oral opening is protected by a closing flap mechanism. In dusty areas, especially those with possible fecal contamination, such as trails in developing countries, this is ideal. Sawyer also makes an attachment using this filter system that screws into common commercial disposable water bottles.

A quality water filter not only removes virus and bacteria but also protects against chemical contaminates and waterborne parasites if it has an absorption mechanism to remove chemicals. This may require prefiltering to remove large particle, charcoal, or similar filtering to remove chemicals, then a microfilter to remove bacteria. Sawyer also produces a microtubule system with an absolute pore size of 0.02 microns, thus also effective against hepatitis C virus particles.

SteriPEN and similar devices use UV C rays to kill virus, bacterial, and protozoan cysts. The water should be prefiltered if it is turbid, as shadows in the water from particles potentially shield these germs from destruction. Of course, agitation or swirling the wand in the water helps overcome this problem, and the light must be kept on longer. Loss of battery power ends the device's usefulness.

Another method of water purification has been with us a long time, namely using our old friend fire. Bringing water to a boil will

Figure 15.1
Cutaway photograph of the Sawyer microtubule system. The microtubules are folded into the filter apparatus that effectively give this filter a large surface area through which water can drain with minimal squeezing pressure or sucking vacuum.

effectively kill pathogens and make water safe to drink. One reads variously to boil water 5, 10, even 20 minutes. But simply bringing the water temperature to 150°F (65.5°C) is adequate to kill the pathogens discussed earlier, and all others besides. It will never be necessary to boil water longer than 5 minutes, and the shortest time mentioned (just bringing the water to a boil) will suffice for a safe drinking water. This water will not be sterile, but it will be safe to drink.

DRINKING SEAWATER

In case of a shortage of freshwater aboard the craft, is it ok to drink seawater?

If the seawater were to be diluted to no more than 0.9% salinity, it would not dehydrate you. Seawater is generally 4 times that concentration, but the surface salinity varies greatly. For a map depicting the varying salinity of surface seawater taken from the NASA Aquarius Project, go to https://www.gislounge.com/access-6-years-sea-surface-salinity-maps-data/.

The only reason to ever consider doing this would be in an emergency when you were hoping to extend your freshwater stores. Thus, in a severe water shortage when you need to extend your freshwater stores, it would be possible to use seawater in a ratio of 1:4 to freshwater to extend your supply. Many other issues remain such as the possibility of microbiological contamination of the water, which must be dealt with, of course.

Seawater is problematic, as the surface water has varying amounts of salt concentrations, depending upon currents, melting ice, and the like, and even river influxes, which are sometimes hundreds of miles away.

Figure 15.2

Dr. Lorenzo Marcolongo using a refractometer to determine the concentration of seawater. The model shown is the $18.00 Brix device, using seawater taken offshore of English Harbor, Antigua.

As long as sea spray mixing into fresh rainwater has a concentration below 0.9%, it will not dehydrate you. The best way to determine the concentration of a seawater/water mixture is to check its specific gravity, which would be 1.0046 if the salt water is at a concentration of 0.9%. Thus, a mixture with a specific gravity lower than that has less than 0.9% salt concentration, which would indicate a safely diluted level of salt. The specific gravity of your mixture of seawater and freshwater can be determined by using a hydrometer, or more conveniently with the use of a refractometer.

Surprisingly, it is possible to survive quite a long time drinking only urine. For an historic example of that, please read *Skeletons on the Zahara: A True Adventure of Survival* by Dean King, or other accounts of the story of Captain James Riley and crew of the U.S. ship *Commerce*, shipwrecked off the coast of Africa in August of 1815. While concentrated urine has a specific gravity of over 1.030, the salt concentration is not higher than a safe amount and represents a small fraction of the solute concentration causing this high of a reading.

CHAPTER 16
SOFT TISSUE CARE AND TRAUMA MANAGEMENT

Understanding risk and developing skills to avoid injury and death are skill sets any endeavor requires. By evaluating the risks as described earlier, we can understand the skills we require to avoid or prepare to manage those issues. Discussing how to manage accidents means we are trying to manage some sort of a failure. The great explorer Roald Amundsen once said: "Adventure is just bad planning." I have never agreed with that. In my opinion, adventures develop from planning a great trip, calculating risks, and then acquiring skills and equipment to minimize the risk.

A fundamental understanding of the types of fatal and nonfatal injuries and their causation due to sailing accidents can help you with your risk assessment.

USCG data of all sailing injuries collected from 2000 through 2011 provided the following insights to injury incident and fatalities sailing.

Table 16.1 Nonfatal Injuries USCG Data (2000–2011) (16.9 Million Sailor Person/Days)

PRIMARY ACCIDENT TYPE	MOTORIZED SAILBOATS	NONMOTORIZED ONLY	TOTAL
Collision with vessel or fixed, submerged or floating object	184	73	257 (30.6%)
Capsizing	64	163	227 (27.0%)
Fall in vessel	57	17	74 (8.8%)

Other	41	21	62 (7.4%)
Grounding	57	4	61 (7.3$)
Falls overboard or ejected from vessel	35	21	56 (6.7%)
Fire/explosion	33	5	38 (4.5%)
Struck by boat or propeller	19	9	28 (3.3%)
Flooding/swamping/sinking	17	7	24 (2.9%)
Unknown	7	2	9 (1.1%)
Carbon monoxide exposure	3	0	3 (0.4%)
Departure from vessel	1	0	1 (0.1%)
Skier mishap	1	0	1 (0.1%)
TOTAL	519	322	841

Table 16.2 Fatal Injuries USCG Data (2000–2011) (16.9 Million Sailor Person/Days)

PRIMARY ACCIDENT TYPE	MOTORIZED SAILBOATS	NONMOTORIZED ONLY	TOTAL
Falls overboard or ejected from vessel	64	48	112 (41.3%)
Capsizing	29	49	78 (28%)
Departure from vessel	17	4	21 (7.8%)
Flooding/swamping or sinking	8	11	19 (7.0%)
Collision with vessel or fixed or submerged object	9	4	13 (4.8%)
Unknown	3	6	9 (3.3%)
Other	2	4	6 (2.2%)
Fire/explosion	3	1	4 (1.5%)
Carbon monoxide exposure	3	0	3 (1.1%)
Grounding	3	0	3 (1.1%)
Electrocution	1	0	1 (0.4%)
Fall in vessel	1	0	1 (0.4%)
Struck by propeller	1	0	1 (0.4%)
TOTAL	144	127	271

Table 16.3 Contributing Factors to Fatal and Nonfatal Injuries USCG Data (2000–2011)

CONTRIBUTING FACTOR	NONFATAL INJURY	DEATHS
Operator/passenger-preventable		
Improper lookout or operator inattention	182 (21.6%)	20 (7.4%)
Operator inexperience	96 (11.4%)	21 (7.8%)
Careless/reckless operation or excessive speed or sharp turn	55 (6.5%)	6 (2.2%)
Passenger behavior	40 (4.8%)	7 (2.6%)
Alcohol use	27 (3.2%)	33 (12.2%)
Rules of road infraction	22 (2.6%)	1 (0.4%)
Improper loading or overloading	11 (1.3%)	6 (2.2%)
Lack of or improper lights	7 (0.8%)	2 (0.7%)
Standing/sitting on gunwales, bow, transom	2 (0.2%)	2 (0.7%)
Improper anchoring	1 (0.1%)	2 (0.7%)
Other factors		
Weather	165 (19.6%)	51 (18.8%)
Equipment or machinery failure	64 (7.6%)	12 (4.4%)
Unknown	53 (6.3%)	57 (21.0%)
Other	38 (4.5%)	18 (6.6%)
Hazardous waters (tidal flow or current related)	34 (4.0%)	25 (9.2%)
Restricted vision	11 (1.3%)	2 (0.7%)
Hull failure	10 (1.2%)	1 (0.4%)
Force of wave/wake	9 (1.1%)	
Congested waters	5 (0.6%)	
Ignitions of spiller fuel or vapor	5 (0.6%)	
Failure to vent	4 (0.5%)	1 (0.4%)
Sudden medical condition		3 (1.1%)
Dam/lock		1 (0.4%)

Table 16.4 Source of injury Dinghy versus Keelboat

PARTS OF DINGHY ASSOCIATED WITH INJURY	PART OF KEELBOAT ASSOCIATED WITH INJURY
Mask 2%	Mask 2%
Sail <1%	Sail 3%
Spinnaker pole 1%	Spinnaker pole 5%
Boom 6%	Book 12%
Deck 18%	Deck 18%
Sheets/lines 12%	Sheets/lines 22%
Cleat 8%	Cleat 5%
Trapeze 3%	Winches 8%
Tiller 2%	Lifelines/stanchions 4%
Center/dagger Board 6%	Hatch/companionway 8%

Table 16.5 Type of Injury—Dinghy versus Keelboat Sailing

TYPE OF INJURY	DINGHY	KEELBOAT
Lacerations/abrasions	31%	12%
Fracture	2%	12%
Sprain/strain	16%	10%
Contusion	41%	36%
Dislocation	2%	1%
Concussion	2%	7%
Burns	4%	16%
Other	8%	6%

*Multiple injuries possible

Thus, soft tissue injuries, then orthopedic problems, are the major results of accidents on smaller boats specifically. Most large vessel accidents reported are major events involving the mechanism of injury reported in tables 16.1 page 121 to 16.3 on page 123.

Probably no issue will distress the sailor more than worrying about managing wounds. And with good reason. This chapter will provide guidance in your approach to managing soft issue injuries. Bites and stings are covered in chapter 18, orthopedics in chapter 17, poisoning symptoms in chapter 13, and overexertion in chapter 20.

The first aid approach to a bleeding wound is to stop the bleeding, treat for shock, and transport the victim (with appropriate assessments) for definitive care. At sea, it will be very appropriate for the party to provide its own definitive care.

Table 16.6 Skin Injuries and Management Techniques

The bleeding wound	126
Stop the bleeding	126–127
Clean the wound	131–134
Antibiotic guidelines	134–135
Wound closure techniques	135
Tape closure techniques	135
Stapling	135–136
Suturing	136–137
Special wound considerations	139
Shaving the wound area	139
Bleeding from suture or staple use	139
Scalp wounds	139
Eyebrow and lip closure	140
Mouth and tongue lacerations	140
Control of pain	140–141
Dressings	141–142
Other types of wounds	
Abrasions	142
Puncture wounds	143
Splinter removal	143
Fishhook removal	144
Friction blisters	147–148
Thermal burns	149–152
Human bites	152
Animal bites	152–153
Finger and toe problems	153
Ingrown nail	153–154

Paronychia (nail base infection)	154
Felon	154–155
Blood under the nail (Subungual Hematoma)	155–156
Wound infection and inflammation	156
Abscess	156–157
Cellulitis	157–158
Skin rash	158–159
Fungal infection	159
Allergic dermatitis	159–160
Bacterial skin rash	160–161
Seabather's eruption	161–162

STOP THE BLEEDING

Wound care can be broken into chronological phases. The first phase consists of saving the victim's life—by stopping the bleeding and treating for shock. Even if the victim is not bleeding, you will want to treat for shock. Shock has many medical definitions, but bottom line, it amounts to an inadequate oxygenated blood supply getting to the brain. Lie the patient down, elevate feet above the head, and provide protection from the environment—from both the ground and the atmosphere. Grab anything that you can find for this at first—use jackets, coiled rope, unfurled sails, whatever. Eventually you will be able to put up a rain fly or sun shield, perhaps even move the victim to shelter below deck, and prepare materials for further wound care. See also Shock, page 15.

Direct pressure is the first and frequently the best method of stopping bleeding. In fact, pressure alone can stop bleeding from some amputated limbs! When the accident first occurs, you may even have to use your bare hand to stem the flow of blood. Ideally, you will have something to protect yourself from direct contact with blood and to protect the wound from your dirty hand. The best item to carry would be a pair of nitrile gloves. These can withstand long-term storage as well as heat and cold better than latex gloves. In their absence, grab a piece of cloth (bandanna, clothing article) or other barrier substance (plastic food wrapper) and press. My book *Basic Illustrated Wilderness*

First Aid, 2nd Edition (FalconGuide, 2016, page 20) describes the various glove materials and their suitability for long-term storage. In general, nitrile gloves will prove to be the best solution.

HEMOSTATIC DRESSINGS
There are now five hemostatic dressings approved by the military. Since the addition of Combat Gauze™ (ZMedica LLC, Wallingford, CT, USA; www.quikclot.com) in April 2008 to the TCCC Guidelines, based on the recent battlefield success, the addition of Celox™ Gauze (Medtrade Products Ltd., Crewe, UK; www.celoxmedical. com) and ChitoGauze® (HemCon Medical Technologies, Portland, OR, USA; http://www.tricolbiomedical.com) have been added. To use, place into the wound on top of the bleeding vessel, and not on top of other bandage material. Direct pressure must be applied continuously for a minimum of 5 minutes or as per the manufacturer's recommendation. As of August 2019, the following are the TCCC recommended hemostatic dressings:

Common Name / Brand Name	DLA Nomenclature	NSN
Combat Gauze (CG) Z-Fold	Bandage Gauze Impregnated 3" W X 4 YDS L Kaolin Hemostatic Quik	6510-01-562-3325
Celox Gauze, Z-fold 5'	Dressing Hemostatic Celox Gauze 3"X5' Z-folded	6510-01-623-9910
ChitoGauze	Dressing Hemostatic 144" length 3" width coated with Chitosan	6510-01-591-7740
X-Stat, Single Applicator	Applicator Hemostatic Sponges and Dispenser Xstat-30 Each	6510-01-644-7335
ITClamp	Clamp hemorrhage Control Sterile Medical Grade Polycarbonate	6515-01-629-7044

X-Stat has an applicator syringe with little pellets of expanding gauze that shoot into a deeper wound—but these require surgical removal and are not appropriate on a long ship voyage unless surgical assistance can be obtained within hours.

Junctional tourniquets are new devices designed to stop bleeding in groin or armpit deep vessel damage and requires special training for use.

The other items are straightforward to use, pull and replace, but it is essential to follow the protocol to place it directly into the bleeding wound and not above other dressings, to pack tightly, and to maintain pressure. Any of these dressings are temporary and are meant to buy time until surgical care can be obtained.

Control of blood loss is a priority. This makes the "tourniquet first" approach appropriate if blood loss cannot be controlled by direct pressure on an extremity wound. The military initially approved two commercial strap and windlass-style tourniquets: the Combat Action Tourniquet and the Special Operations Forces Tactical Tourniquet Wide (SOFTT-W), which are specially constructed to give a true 1 and 1/2 inch circumference without pinching when tightened using the windlass.

Figure 16.1
Pictured is the latest model called the SOFTT-W, which is specially constructed to give a true 1 and 1/2 inch circumference without pinching when tightened using the windlass.

Due to the interest in "Stop the Bleed" programs caused in the United States by active shooter incidents, the American Red Cross is also comarketing the SOFTT-W. A number of additional tourniquets have been approved by the TCCC folks. Their latest approved list may be found at www.deployedmedicine. com. Deployed medicine is part of an ongoing research and development activity sponsored by the Defense Health Agency in partnership with the Joint Trauma System and Committee on TCCC.

TOURNIQUETS, LIMB NON-PNEUMATIC		
Common Name / Brand Name	DLA Nomenclature	NSN
Combat Application Tourniquet (CAT) Gen 7	Tourniquet Nonpneumatic Combat Application One-Handed 37.5" LG 1	6515-01-521-7976
Combat Application Tourniquet (CAT) Gen 6	Tourniquet Nonpneumatic Combat Application One-Handed 37.5" LG 1	Until Replaced by Gen 7
Ratcheting Medical Tourniquet (RMT) Tactical	Tourniquet, One Handed Burke Device Tactical	6515-01-527-3841
SAM Extremity Tourniquet (SAM-XT)	Tourniquet Nonpneumatic 25S	6515-01-670-2240
SOF-Tactical Tourniquet-Wide (SOFTT-W)	Tourniquet Nonpneumatic Nylon Strap 1.5" Wide Nylon Strap for Br	6515-01-587-9943
Tactical Mechanical Tourniquet (TMT)	Tourniquet Nonpneumatic Tactical Mechanical Tourniquet	6515-01-656-8191
TX2 Tourniquet (TX2)	Tourniquet Nonpneumatic TX2 Ratcheting One-Hand Coyote	6515-01-667-6027
TX3 Tourniquet (TX3)	Tourniquet Nonpneumatic Tx3 Ratcheting OD Green One Hand	6515-01-667-6208

TOURNIQUETS, LIMB PNEUMATIC		
Common Name / Brand Name	DLA Nomenclature	NSN
Emergency Medical Tourniquet (EMT)	Tourniquet Pneumatic Single-hand application fits upper and lower	6515-01-580-1645
Tactical Pneumatic Tourniquet 2" (TPT2)	Tourniquet Pneumatic Slide Fastener	6515-01-656-4831

Once applied, keep the tourniquet in place until definitive care has been reached. A careful exception might be made for a remote situation. To quote from the current Boy Scouts of America Wilderness First Aid doctrine:

In a very remote area where care might not be reached for days, continuous application will result in loss of the limb. It is more important to save a life than a limb. In all situations, it is better to apply a tourniquet prior to seeing the signs and symptoms of shock. A rule of thumb is to leave a tourniquet on an extremity with severe arterial bleeding, not venous bleeding, no longer than 2 hours, and attempt to transition to wound packing and a pressure dressing to control severe bleeding. If a tourniquet is left on an extremity longer than 6 hours then it is recommended to leave on until definitive care can be reached. Tourniquets should not be released periodically just to resupply the limb with blood. The control of blood loss is a critical step in a remote care situation. Only remove the tourniquet if it seems feasible to apply adequate direct pressure to fully control the bleeding.

If direct pressure does not stop the bleeding, immediately apply a tourniquet. Extensive military experience has indicated that even temporary removal of a tourniquet results in a higher loss of life. Additionally, placement of an effective tourniquet can be difficult. Ineffective placement allows continued bleeding. Continue applying direct pressure while the tourniquet is on to facilitate the clotting process. If an inadequate result is obtained, immediately place a second tourniquet about an inch from the first one.

If the patient has lost a massive amount of blood, do not attempt to remove the tourniquet. Sometimes bleeding control with direct pressure may require hours of direct pressure, but this is unusual.

There are three main lessons to remember concerning a tourniquet: first, applying it sooner rather than later is critical. If bleeding is not controlled by pressure in an extremity, apply the tourniquet immediately. Second, a wide tourniquet is better than a narrow one. Third, don't remove the tourniquet if you need it in the first place.

Improvising an adequate tourniquet is difficult to achieve. Belts seldom work, cords and surgical tubing will not adequately, and an appropriate fastening technique is not easy to maintain. The minimal width for a tourniquet is 1 1/2 inches. Tie a short stick or another rigid object into the material to create a windlass technique, and twist it, tightening the tourniquet until bleeding stops—and no more. Attached the stick to the windless by incorporating it into the knot and fasten one end of the windless when it has been adequately tightened by tying a square knot over it and the limb.

In areas where a tourniquet cannot be applied, plunge two fingers into the bleeding wound. This always stops bleeding and works anywhere on the body, shy of a massive explosive injury. Use your index and middle fingers held together. This is the technique used over and over again during surgery when something cuts loose and blood wells up in the surgical field.

A third technique is an internal pressure packing using a moist piece of sterile or clean cloth. Wet the cloth with sterile or at least drinkable water, wringing it out until it's practically dry. Then stuff this cloth into the wound firmly, continuing to pack more cloth into the wound until the bleeding is stopped by the tamponade or compression. If bleeding continues, do not remove the material, but firmly stuff in more. This dressing is covered with a dry clean cloth. It should be replaced in 24 hours.

With the bleeding stopped, even with your hand, and the victim on the ground in the shock treatment position, the actual emergency is over. His or Her life is safe. And you have bought time to gather together various items you need to perform the definitive job of caring for this wound. You have also treated for psychogenic shock—the shock of "fear." Obviously, someone knows what to do: he or she has taken charge, he or she has stopped the bleeding, he or she is giving orders to gather materials together.

In the first aid management of this wound, the next step is simply bandaging and then transporting the victim to professional medical care. For those at sea who must provide long-term care for wounds, further management will go through several more phases: cleaning, closing, dressing, and treating the possible complications of infection.

WOUND CLEANING

Adequate cleansing is the most important aspect of wound management. Especially when in an isolated or survival situation, the prevention of infection is of critical importance and can be assured only by aggressive irrigation techniques.

There is an adage in nature: "The solution to pollution is dilution." In wound care, this means copious irrigation. The whole purpose of scrubbing a wound is to reduce the total number of potentially harmful bacteria. You won't get them all out, but if the total number is sufficiently small, the body's own defense mechanisms can take over and finish the job for the patient.

To best provide water for irrigation, prepare sterile water. This can be done by boiling the water for 5 minutes. Lacking the ability to do this, try to use water that is fit for drinking (see page 114 for techniques

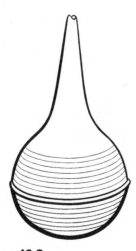

Figure 16.2

The irrigating bulb syringe.

Figure 16.3

The Zerowet Splashield™ attached to a syringe.

of water purification). In a pinch, clean water from a stream or lake can be used as long as you are not downstream from the sewage pipe of a third world village, or the bloated, rotting carcass of a moose.

To provide adequate force to the irrigation stream, there are two items of potential importance. One is the bulb syringe (see figure 16.2). The 1-ounce model is adequate for most wounds. The other approach is to use a syringe (10 to 35 ml size) with a device attached called a Zerowet Supershield® (see figure 16.3). With either technique, one can increase the velocity of the water to aid in dislodging debris and those all-important germs.

Forceful water irrigation is the mainstay of wound cleaning. The use of a "bota" bag, a squeezable plastic water cube, or simply a Ziplock baggy with a small hole poked in it to bring a stream of water to the wound is very helpful, but the stream generated using them is not fully adequate to provide the irrigation force required. Adding mild surgical scrub solution to the initial batch of irrigation water is a good step but does not make up for the lack of adequate forceful irrigation. Adding mechanical abrasion can be helpful and probably is the only hope of adequate wound cleansing. Several products can be particularly useful for this technique. The most effective is Hibiclens surgical scrub.

Another is povidone iodine (Betadine) diluted to a 1% solution (the stock solution is 10%). Another approach is to use a very dilute soap solution. Err on the side of making the soap solution too weak, because strong soap solutions can damage healthy tissue. Make the solution weak enough that you could drink it without purging yourself.

Many cleaning techniques and compounds should not be used: Tincture of iodine, Mercurochrome, or alcohol are very harsh; hydrogen peroxide destroys good flesh as well as germs. Red-hot branding irons and pouring gun powder into a wound and lighting it, while effective in killing germs and among Rambo's favorite techniques, also destroy good tissue. And destroyed tissue is not something you want when you are providing care.

When stuck with a weak irrigation stream, perhaps only being able to pour water into the wound from a container, the mechanical abrasion technique saves the day. Besides irrigation, a technique of cleaning used by physicians in the operating room is called debridement. This amounts to cutting away destroyed tissue. Of course, there is no way a person can do this at sea—especially with inadequate lighting, equipment, and training. But we can safely approximate it by vigorously rubbing the area with a piece of sterile gauze or clean cloth. The rigorous scrubbing action will remove blood clots, torn bits of tissue, pieces of foreign bodies—all items that generally result in higher bacteria counts or foci for bacterial growth. This scrubbing process has to be accomplished quickly—it is painful and the victim will not tolerate it for long. Have everything ready: clean, dry dressing to apply afterward; the water supply; an instrument to spread the wound open (a pair of tweezers or the needle holder are ideal); and sterile gauze to use for scrubbing this wound.

To sterilize cloth and any instruments, boil for 5 minutes, if necessary in the water you are preparing to use for irrigation. While having adequate sterile dressings would be ideal, you may find yourself slicing and dicing your wool shirt or Polarguard jacket into bandaging material. A rough cloth works better at wound cleaning than a smooth cloth, such as cotton.

Once everything is ready, and assistance is at hand (perhaps someone to squirt the jet of water into the wound and another to assist shooing the black flies away or comforting the victim), go to it! If this job is performed well, the final outcome will be great. This part of wound care is far more important than wound closure technique. It will be messy. And it will hurt. But spread the wound apart, blast that water in there the best you can, and scrub briskly with the gauze pad. This whole process will have to be completed in 20 to 30 seconds. In the operating room, or under local anesthesia in the emergency room, we might take 15 minutes or longer. You won't be able to take that much time, but you must be thorough and vigorous. You should use at least 1 cup of water for a very small wound and 1 quart (1 liter) for most wounds. When in doubt, you must do more—if the patient can tolerate it within reason.

Once the irrigation is completed, the wound will bleed vigorously again, since the blood clots have been knocked off during the cleansing process. Apply a sterile dressing and use direct pressure as long as necessary to stop bleeding. About 5 to 10 minutes usually suffice, but if an hour or more is required, keep at it or use the pressure dressing technique described earlier. If you fail to adequately clean a wound, the resulting infection could cost the patient his or her life. It would simply be a slower and more painful death than bleeding to death.

Antibiotic Guidelines

It is always tempting to place a person on antibiotics after a laceration, but I would advise against doing this unless the wound was from an animal or human bite (page 152), the wound occurred in contaminated water, or there was an open fracture (page 172). Bacteria are jealous creatures and do not like to share their food source with other species. If an infection develops, it will generally be a pure culture, the other species originally contaminating the wound having been killed off by the body's defense mechanisms and the winning bacterium. If the patient is on an antibiotic from the beginning, the winning bacterium is guaranteed to resist your medication. If no antibiotic is used initially, there is hope that the emergent bacterium will be sensitive to the antibiotic that you are about to employ.

If it is necessary to start a prophylactic antibiotic, from the Rx Oral/Topical Medication Kit, use Levaquin, 750 mg once daily for 3 days. In case of infection, see page 291.

WOUND CLOSURE TECHNIQUES

With direct pressure still applied, dry around the wound. We are ready to now enter the wound closure phase of wound care. Perhaps more worry and concern exist about this phase of wound care than the others, but it is really the easiest—and much less important than the first two phases just discussed.

Tape Closure Techniques

If the laceration can be held together with tape, then by all means use tape as the definitive treatment. Butterfly bandages are universally available, and generally work very well. The commercial butterflies are superior to homemade in that they are packaged sterile with a no-stick center portion. They can be made in the field by cutting and folding the center edges in to cover the adhesive in the very center of short tape strips, thus avoiding adhesive contact with the wound. Of course, such homemade strips will not be sterile, but in general, they will be very adequate. Steri-Strips and their generic equivalents are now commercially available in neighborhood pharmacies. These are ideal wound closures, and are lightweight, inexpensive, and easy to apply.

When using a tape method of closure, adhere the strips next to each other to opposite sides of the wound, then use them to pull the wound together as you proceed down the wound length, closing it as you go. Even with very sticky tape, there may be times when they cannot hold a wound closed and the wound will have to be stapled or sutured (stitched).

Stapling

A fast, strong method of holding skin edges together is with the use of stainless steel staples. A special disposable device will contain a certain number of sterile staples that rapidly staple the wound edges while pinching the wound together. This obviously stings while being used, but the pain is brief and the wound is secure. A very useful device is the Motrix Wizard skin stapler, containing 55 preloaded staples. A special disposable staple remover is provided with any purchase of their kit, which is very handy for taking staples out virtually painlessly. The skin stapler and staple remover are nonprescription and shown in figure 16.4. They come packaged in sterile, waterproof containers.

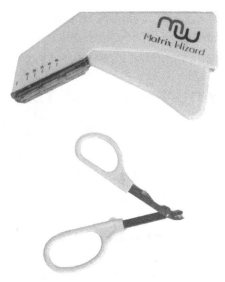

Figure 16.4
The Motrix Wizard skin stapler.

Suturing

Suture (stitching) material is available in many forms and with many types of needles. For the expedition medical kit, I would recommend using 3–0 nylon suture with a curved pre-attached needle, shown in figure 16.5. This comes in a sterile packet ready for use. It will be necessary to use a needle holder to properly hold this suture. The needle holder looks like a pair of scissors, but it has a flat surface with grooves that grab the needle and a lock device that holds the needle

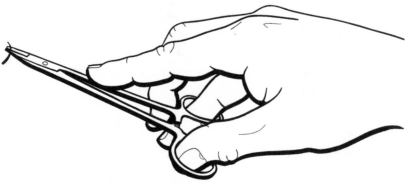

Figure 16.5
Grasping the needle holder; this technique decreases hand tremor.

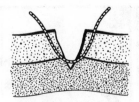

Figure 16.6a

Proper placement of suture, showing passage of the suture material at an equal depth on both sides of the cut.

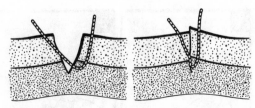

Figure 16.6b

Improper placement of suture, showing that different depths of penetration result in tissue puckering.

firmly. It is held as illustrated to steady the hand. All fly-tying stores sell needle holders.

Apply pressure in the direction of the needle, twisting your wrist is such a manner that the needle will pass directly into the skin and cleanly penetrate, following through with the motion to allow the needle to curve through the subcutaneous tissue and sweep upward and through the skin on the other side of the wound (see figure 16.6a).

DEPTH OF SUTURES

Suture through the skin surface only and avoid important structures underneath. If tendon or nerve damage has occurred, irrigate the wound thoroughly as previously described and repair the skin with either tape or sutures as necessary. The tendon, and the like, can be repaired by a surgeon upon return to the outside—weeks later if necessary.

It is important to have the needle enter both sides of the wound at the same depth or the wound will not pull together evenly, and there will be a pucker if the needle took a deep bite on one side and a shallow bite on the other (see figure 16.6b).

A square knot is tied with the use of the needle holder in an amazingly easy manner, as in figure 16.7 on page 138. Frankly, a knot tied in any fashion will do perfectly well.

SPACING OF STAPLES AND SUTURES

These stitches should not be placed too closely together. Usually, on the limbs and body, 4 stitches per inch will suffice. On the face,

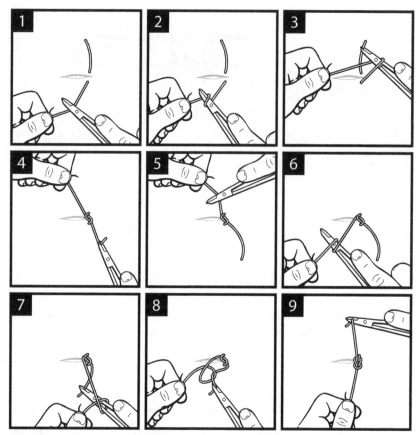

Figure 16.7
How to tie a square knot: Loop the suture around the needle holder once, using the long end of the thread. Grasp the short end and pull the wound together. Loop the long end around the needle holder again the opposite way. This will form a square knot. Repeat this process a third time in the original direction to ensure a firm knot. Do not pull too tightly, as this will pucker the skin; just an approximation is required.

however, use 6 per inch. Here it is best to use 5–0 nylon, as it will minimize scar formation from the needle and suture. I use a 6–0 suture on the face, but it is considerably more difficult to use than the 5–0.

These stitches can be combined with tape strips or butterfly bandages to help hold the wound together and to cut down on the number of stitches required.

Once they are in, leave stitches in the limbs for 10 days, in the trunk and scalp for 7 days, and in the face for 4 days. A wound that tends to break open due to tension, such as over the knee, can be stabilized by splinting the joint so that it cannot move while the wound is healing.

SPECIAL WOUND CONSIDERATIONS

Shaving the Wound Area

It has been found that shaving an area increases the chance of wound infection. Scalp lacerations are hard to suture when unshaven due to the matting of hair with blood and accidental incorporation of hair into the wound. However, catching hair in the wound is not detrimental. Just pull it loose from the wound with a pair of forceps or tweezers when you are through suturing.

Bleeding from Suture or Staple Use

Anywhere on the body you will note that entrance and exit points of the needle puncture will bleed quite freely. A little pressure always stops the bleeding—it is not necessary to delay your sewing to even worry about it. Just complete your stitching of the wound, then apply pressure until the bleeding from the needle punctures stops, cleanse the skin when you are done to remove dried blood, and dress the wound.

SCALP WOUNDS

Scalp wounds bleed excessively—expect this. Spurting blood vessels can be clamped with the needle holder and tied off with a piece of the 3–0 gut suture in the surgical kit of the Topical Bandaging Module. To tie, simply place a knot in the flesh to fall beneath the tip of the needle holder. Someone may have to remove the needle holder while you are cinching the first loop of the knot. Or you may simply suture the scalp wound closed and apply pressure between each suture to minimize intraoperative bleeding. Apply firm direct pressure after suturing to minimize hematoma (blood pocket formation) from bleeding within the wound.

I have read many times that a scalp laceration can be closed by tying the hair on either side into a knot, thus holding the wound together. I have sutured a lot of scalp lacerations and I doubt this technique would work very well. A scalp laceration bleeds so profusely, blood is so sticky and slippery at the same time, and the hair would have to be long enough and of the right texture. See the discussion on head injuries on page 174.

EYEBROW AND LIP CLOSURE

When sewing an eyebrow or the vermilion border of the lip, approximate the edges first with a suture before sewing the ends or other portion of the laceration. Never shave an eyebrow. Use the 5–0 nylon suture on the face and remove these sutures in 4 days, replacing them with strips of tape at that time.

MOUTH AND TONGUE LACERATIONS

When sewing the inside of the mouth, use the 3–0 gut suture. These sutures tend to unwind very easily, especially if the patient cannot resist touching them with his or her tongue. When making the knot, tie it over and over. As the mouth heals rapidly, if the sutures come out within a day, the laceration has generally stopped bleeding and may heal without further help. These mouth sutures will generally dissolve on their own, but remaining ones can be removed within 4 days.

Lacerations on the tongue can almost always be left alone. The wound may appear ugly for a few days, but within a week or two there will be remarkable healing. Infections in the tongue or mouth from cuts are very rare. If the edge of the tongue is badly lacerated, so that the tongue is cut one-quarter of the way across or more, sewing the edge together is warranted. Use the 3–0 gut suture.

Control of Pain

For anesthesia, you will require a prescription to obtain injectable lidocaine 1% and a syringe with needle. Inject into the wound, just under the skin on both sides of the cut. Cleansing and suturing soon after a cut may help minimize the pain, due to tissue "shock" in the immediate post-trauma period. Ice applied to the wound area can help numb the pain, but local topical anesthetic agents are of no help in pain control. Two Percogesic, or 2 or 3 ibuprofen, 200 mg, given about 1 hour prior to surgery may help minimize pain.

DRESSINGS

Most sutured lacerations leak a little blood during the first 24 hours. Increased pain or apparent swelling is a reason to remove the dressing to check for signs of infection (see page 153). The dressing should be removed, and replaced, when it is time to remove staples or sutures as indicated earlier. When using a hydrogel dressing system, it is not necessary to remove the dressing, as it facilitates more rapid healing and provides protection from the environment while in place. There are many brands of these dressings at local drug stores. Look for a bandage that has a gel pad construction.

Alternative dressings in the Topical Bandaging Kit are the NuGauze pads and the Tegaderm and Spenco 2nd Skin dressings. An initial covering that can soak up leaking wounds is the NuGauze pads. After the wound becomes dry, the Tegaderm dressing will keep the sutures visible and the wound protected even if it must get submersed in water. Wounds that continue to leak considerable serum and/or blood should be covered by Spenco 2nd Skin and managed as discussed on page 282.

The latest development in wound dressings is a real game changer—namely, the silver-impregnated dressings made by Argentum Medical, LLC, Geneva, Illinois. Silverlon® is a nylon material coated with 99% pure silver and 1% silver oxide. When silver ions are activated with moisture, the ions kill a wide range of pathogens held within the material. Silverlon has been tested effective against many pathogens, including drug-resistant pathogens such as methicillin-resistant *Staphylococcus aureus* (MRSA).

Silverlon Wound Dressings have been used for years in the military and in hospitals around the world. This technology is battle-tested and has received sixteen 510(k) clearances from the FDA for use as an antimicrobial dressing in surgery, burn, trauma, and wound care. The bandages come in a variety of sizes for packing and direct wound covering and are also incorporated into adhesive strips of various sizes. The bandages can be left on a wound for 7 days at a time. If the dressing becomes pussy, it can be washed off and reused. It works best when damp, so what better place to think of its use than while afloat. I have had person success in treating many nasty bullet and dog bite wounds with this material. I am a fervent believer in their products.

ABRASIONS

An abrasion is the loss of surface skin due to a scraping injury. The best treatment is cleansing with Hibiclens surgical scrub, application of triple antibiotic ointment, and the use of gel pad dressing, all components of the Topical Bandaging Module. This type of wound leaks profusely, but the above bandaging allows rapid healing, excellent protection, and considerable pain relief. Avoid the use of alcohol on these wounds as it tends to damage the tissue, to say nothing of causing excessive pain. Lacking first aid supplies, cleanse gently with mild detergent and protect from dirt, bugs, and the like, the best that you can. Tetanus immunization should be within 10 years.

A significant question on the mind of the victim and the medic is how aggressively ground-in cinder and dirt should be removed from a road rash. Having raced bicycles for several years on a cinder track (the Indiana University Little 500), I have had personal experience with this—which perhaps clouds my perspective. In the early 1960s, team doctors aggressively cleaned these wounds with a wire brush. During my racing years, luckily, the approach changed to simply coating the wound with a layer of the antibiotic ointment and allowing the resultant scab formation to lift the cinders out of the wound when it fell off. A recent publication has shown that antibiotic salve, if applied within 3 hours of a surface wound, significantly decreases wound infection in animal studies. I have not experienced problems with cinder tattoos or wound infection using gentle scrub with soft cloth (Hibiclens surgical scrub), removal of deeply embedded debris carefully with tweezers, and a liberal coating of triple antibiotic ointment, reapplied daily or as necessary until the wound heals. I like to avoid a bandage, leaving the wound open to the air, or using a gel pad dressing when a covering is required over the ointment. Another dressing that would be ideal for these wounds is the recently developed Silverlon dressings described earlier.

PUNCTURE WOUNDS
Briefly allow a puncture wound to bleed, thus hoping to effect some irrigation of bacteria from the wound. Cleanse the wound area with surgical scrub or soapy water and apply triple antibiotic ointment to the surrounding skin surface. Do not tape shut, but rather start warm compress applications for 20 minutes, every 2 hours for the next 1 to 2 days, or until it is apparent that no subsurface infection has started. These soaks should be as warm as the patient can tolerate without danger of burning the skin. Larger pieces of cloth, such as undershirts, work best for compresses, as they hold the heat longer. Infection can be prevented, or treated, with antibiotics as described in the section on cellulitis, pages 157–158. Dressing should be with a clean cloth. If sterile items are in short supply, they need not be used on this type of wound. Tetanus immunization should be current (see chapter 19).

SPLINTER REMOVAL
Prepare the wound with Hibiclens surgical scrub or other solution that does not discolor the skin. Minute splinters are hard to see. If the splinter is shallow, or the point buried, use a sharp blade to tease the tissue over the splinter to remove this top layer. The splinter can then be pried out better.

It is best to be aggressive in removing this top layer and obtaining a substantial bite on the splinter with the tweezers, rather than nibbling off the end when making futile attempts to remove with inadequate exposure. When using tweezers, grasp the instrument between the thumb and forefinger, resting the instrument on the middle finger and further resting the entire hand against the victim's skin, if necessary, to prevent tremor. Approach the splinter from the side, if exposed, grasping it as low as possible (see figure 16.8 page 144). Apply triple antibiotic after removal.

Tetanus immunization should be current. If the wound was dirty, scrub afterward with Hibiclens or soapy water. If deep, treat as indicated earlier for Puncture Wounds, with hot soaks and antibiotics.

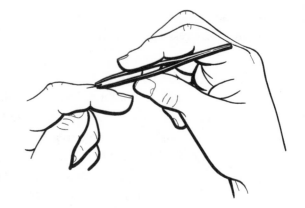

Figure 16.8
Hold tweezers parallel to the skin surface and grasp only after obtaining adequate exposure of the splinter.

FISHHOOK REMOVAL

The first aid approach to an impaled fishhook is to tape it in place and not try to remove it if there is any danger of causing damage to nearby or underlying structures, or if the patient is uncooperative. Cut the fish line off the hook. Destroy triple hooks, but do not cut the hook close to the skin with your wire cutters. This makes subsequent manipulation by the surgeon more difficult. Anyone fishing with barbed hooks needs to include side-cutting wire cutters in their tackle equipment.

If you will be longer than 2 days from help, it is important to remove any impaled object, including a fishhook, as such objects are a high risk for infection. And, since fishhooks are relatively easy to remove anyway, you may wish to do it yourself to prevent a long trip back to port and the doctor's waiting room.

There are three basic methods for removing a fishhook, which I refer to as "the good, the bad, and the ugly" techniques. I will let you decide which is which:

Push Through, Snip Off Method

While the technique seems straightforward, consider a few points:

(1) Pushing the hook should not endanger underlying or adjacent structures. This limits the technique's usefulness, but it is still frequently an easy, quick method to employ.

(2) Skin is not easy to push through. It is very elastic and will tent up over the barb as you try to push it through. Place

the side-cutting wire cutters, with jaws spread apart, over the point on the surface where you expect the hook point to punch through to hold the skin down while the barbed point punches to the surface.

(3)   This is a painful process and skin hurts when being poked from the bottom up, as much as from the top down. Once committed, get the push through portion of this project over with in a hurry.

(4)   This adds a second puncture wound to the victim's anatomy. Cleanse the skin at the anticipated penetration site before shoving the hook through, using soap or a surgical scrub.

(5)   When snipping the protruding point off, cover the wound area with your free hand to protect yourself and others from the flying hook point. Otherwise, you may need to refer to the section on removing foreign bodies from the eye on pages 47–49.

The steps are simple: (1) Push the hook through; (2) Snip it off; (3) Back the barbless hook out; (4) Treat the puncture wounds. If you do not have wire cutters, you may still use this technique but be able to crush the barb flat enough that you will be able to back the hook out.

The String Jerk Method

This is the most elegant of the methods. Fingers are loaded with fibrous tissue that tends to hinder a smooth hook removal. This technique works best for the back of the head, the shoulder, and most aspects of the torso, arms, and legs. It is highly useful and can be virtually painless, causing minimal trauma.

See figure 16.9: (A) Loop a line, such as the fish line, around the hook, ensuring that this line is held flush against the skin. Pushing down on the eye portion of the hook helps disengage the hook barb, so that the quick pull (B) will jerk the hook free with minimal trauma. Many times a victim will ask "When are you going to pull it out?" after the job has been completed.

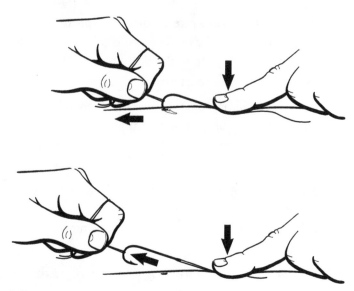

Figure 16.9
Press the shank of the hook against the skin surface. Vigorously jerk the hook along the skin surface.

The Dissection Method

At times it just seems we are not to be so lucky and we must resort to what will probably be a difficult experience for the victim and surgeon alike. This is the case with embedded triple hooks, a hook near the eye, or other situations when the aforementioned methods cannot be used. No person in his or her right mind would attempt this on his or her own if evacuation to a physician was at all possible. It is tedious, and without a local anesthetic, such as injectable lidocaine, extremely painful.

The technique employs the use of either a sharp, thin blade or an 18-gauge or larger bore hypodermic needle. Examine a hook similar to the one that is embedded in the victim to note the bend in the shank and the location of the barb. You will need to slide the blade along the hook shank, cutting the strands of connective tissue so that the hook can be backed out. If using the needle, you will need to slide it along the hook and attempt to cover the barb with a hollow tube, thus shielding connective tissue strands from the barb, allowing the hook to be similarly backed out. This is an elegant method and can result in minimal tissue damage, with only the entry hole left. But it can take time and without local anesthesia the victim would have to be stoic. If available, inject a little 1% lidocaine from the Rx Injectable Medication Module. Practice using a piece of closed-cell foam sleeping pad, rather than human skin, prior to your trip at sea.

FRICTION BLISTERS

Blisters can be prevented if immediate care is taken of any hot spot as soon as it develops. Generally, a simple piece of tape placed directly over the hot spot will eliminate any friction causing the problem. An easily obtainable substance has revolutionized the prevention and care of friction blisters. The substance is Spenco 2nd Skin, available at most athletic supply and drug stores. Made from an inert, breathable gel consisting of 4% polyethylene oxide and 96% water, it has the feel and consistency of, well, most people would say, snot. It comes in various sized sheets and is sterile and sealed in watertight packages. It is very cool to the touch; in fact, large sheets are sold to cover infants to reduce a fever. Three valuable properties make it so useful: It will remove all friction between two moving surfaces (hence its use in prevention); it cleans and deodorizes wounds by absorbing blood, serum, or pus; and its cooling effect is very soothing, which aids in pain relief.

The 2nd Skin comes between two sheets of cellophane. It must be held against the wound, and for that purpose the same company produces an adhesive knit bandage. For prevention, 2nd Skin can be applied with the cellophane attached and secured with the knit bandaging. For treatment of a hot spot, remove the cellophane from one side and apply this gooey side against the wound, again securing it with the knit bandaging.

If a friction blister has developed, it will have to be lanced. Cleanse with soap or surgical scrub and open along an edge with a sharp blade. There is no advantage to making a small hole as opposed to a wide incision. Allow the skin covering to collapse by expressing the fluid, and then apply a fully stripped piece of 2nd Skin. This is best done by removing the cellophane from one side, then applying it to the wound. Once it adheres to the skin surface, remove the cellophane from the outside edge. Over this you will need to place the adhesive knit. The bandage must be kept moist with clean water. The 2nd Skin should be replaced daily. If the skin cover is still covering the wound, it should be cut off after 2 days, as the skin underneath is now less raw and the dead skin will start to decompose. Until you use it on a friction blister, you'll find it hard to believe how well 2nd Skin works!

It makes good sense to coat all open blisters with triple antibiotic ointment. This acts as a barrier to prevent infection. An alternative is to cover the raw wound with Silverlon dressing.

The old technique of blister care with rings of moleskin is seldom effective. Moleskin should be relegated to the Dark Ages of Medicine. But it is cheap, and for that reason most commercial first aid kits include it rather than Spenco 2nd Skin or Silverlon.

THERMAL BURNS

As soon as possible, remove the source of the burn. Quick immersion into cool water will help eliminate additional heat from scalding water or burning fuels and clothing. Do not overcool the victim and cause hypothermia. If water is not available, suffocate the flames with clothing, sand, and the like. Do not allow a victim to panic and run, as this will fan the flames and increase the injury.

Treatment of burns depends upon the extent (percentage of the body covered) and the severity (degree) of the injury. The percentage of the body covered is estimated by referring to the "Rule of Nines," as indicated in figure 16.10. An entire arm equals 9% of the body surface area; therefore the burn of just one side of the forearm would equal about 2%. The chest and back equal 18%, and the abdomen and back equal 18%. The proportions are slightly different for small children, the head representing a larger percentage (18%) and the legs a smaller percentage (13.5%). Severity of burns is indicated by degree. First degree (superficial) will have redness and be dry and painful. Second degree (partial skin thickness) will be moist, painful, and have blister formation with reddened bases. Third degree (deep) involves the full thickness of the skin and extends into the subcutaneous tissue with char, loss of substance, or discoloration.

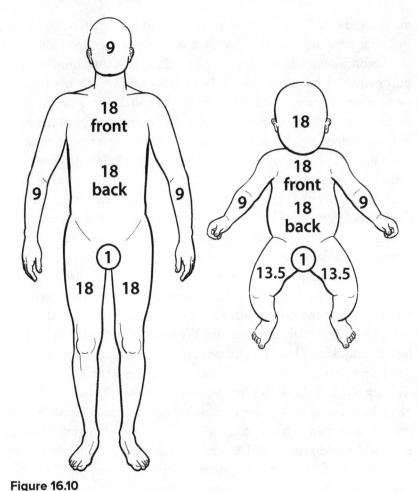

Figure 16.10

The "Rule of Nines" burn chart helps determine the percentage of a body covered by burns. Note the differences between an adult and an infant.

For purposes of field management, victims can be divided into three groups depending upon a combination of the extent and severity of the burn.

First-degree burns, regardless of the extent, rarely require evacuation. The severe pain initially encountered in a first-degree burn usually disappears within 24 hours. The patient's requirement for pain medication can range from ibuprofen, 200 mg, 4 tablets every 4 to 6 hours, to Percogesic, 2 tablets every 3 to 4 hours. After a few doses, further pain medication is generally not required. Surface dressings are not indicated, but soothing relief of small burns can be obtained by either applying a Spenco 2nd Skin dressing or a damp cloth.

Second-degree burns covering less than 15% and third-degree burns covering less than 10% of the body surface area do not require rapid evacuation but should receive professional care. Provide pain medication as above. Cleanse the area with either a surgical scrub or nonmedicated soap. Do not attempt to remove debris that is stuck to the burn site. Gently pat dry. The general consensus is to remove skin from blisters that have ruptured or that are blood-filled. I find it best to initially leave the skin covering on the blister, removing it after 3 days. People generally feel better when you open turgid blisters with a long cut using a sharp blade. Apply Spenco 2nd Skin dressing and change twice daily. Second-degree burns will slough the skin after 3 to 4 days. An unopened or covered blister surface will turn white in 3 days, and frequently an ooze of pus may develop in the underlying blister fluid. If the underlying skin does not become red and swollen, this is a normal development. White, moist, dead skin should be cut away. If you have no ointment or dressings, leave a second- or third-degree burn alone. The surface of the blister, if it is drained, will dry out and slough off on its own. Either way, healing will take place in 2 weeks or less for a second-degree burn. A third-degree burn greater than half a square inch will require a skin graft to heal. Red swollen skin under and around the burn site probably indicates an infection. If this develops, provide antibiotics from the Rx Oral/Topical Medication Module, such as Levaquin, 750 mg once daily, or from the Rx Injectable Kit give Rocephin, 500 mg IM twice daily. Elevate the burned area to minimize the swelling.

A third-degree burns greater than 10% and second-degree burns greater than 15% of the total body surface area; any serious burn to the face; and any third-degree burns of hands, feet, or genitals, require urgent evacuation of the patient. Wound management is the least important part of the care of these patients. Burn wounds are sterile for the first 24 to 48 hours. Burn management is aimed at keeping the wound clean, reducing pain, and treating for shock.

An important aspect of treating for shock will be maintaining adequate fluid replacement. Generally, patients with less than 20%

of their body surface area burned can tolerate oral fluids very well. If they are not vomiting, those with between 20% and 30% of their body surface area involved can be resuscitated by drinking adequate fluids. This individual will be prone to go into shock. If the victim is vomiting, he or she will fall behind in fluid replacement.

The replacement fluid should initially consist of Gatorade diluted 1:1 with water, or a mixture consisting of 1/3 teaspoon of salt and 1/3 teaspoon of baking soda in 1 quart (1 liter) of flavored, lightly sweetened water. Avoid the use of potassium-rich solutions (orange juice, apple juice), as serum potassium can rise to high levels during the first 24 hours. During the second day, the oral fluids should be diluted Gatorade and lightly sweetened, flavored water (such as Wyler's or dilute Tang). Push as much fluid during these 2 days as the patient can tolerate without becoming nauseous. Attempt to keep urine flow 50 to 100 ml (12/3 to 31/3 ounces) per hour. Nausea can be suppressed with adequate pain management and the use of Atarax, 25 to 50 mg every 6 hours, from the Rx Oral/Topical Medication Module, or Vistaril, 25 to 50 mg by IM injection every 4 hours as needed, from the Rx Injectable Module. Pain relief will require Nubain, 10 to 20 mg IM, or the nasally inhaled Stadol (see page 297), or the oral medications as tolerated. Patients who lapse into a coma during the first 48 hours will require IV fluids to save their lives. Physicians equipped with IV fluids are aware of the massive doses that are required to succeed at this point.

Starting on the third day, the patient should be given a moderately high carbohydrate diet, rich in protein. Approximately 200 mg of vitamin C and substantial vitamin B complex should be started daily. This would equal about 4 each One-A-Day multiple vitamin (Miles Laboratories) or equivalent. Continue to push fluids.

Spenco 2nd Skin is the ideal dressing for these severe burns. It provides a breathable cover that is sterile and will exclude bacteria from the environment. It is also easily removed with whirlpool or gentle cleansing. Otherwise, apply a topical dressing such as triple antibiotic ointment. Occlusive dressings must not be used. The ointment may be placed on thick gauze held against the wound with a single layer of gauze roll dressing. The wound should be cleaned daily, removing obviously dead tissue. This can be done with gentle scraping using a sterile gauze and clean water with a little Hibiclens surgical scrub added, about half an hour after proper pain medication has been provided. Lacking Hibiclens, use a very dilute soap solution. Elevate the burned area, if practical. Have the victim gently and regularly move the burned area as much as possible to minimize contraction of burn tissue across joints. This will only be a concern with long-term care lasting many weeks.

Avoid the use of oral or injectable antibiotics to prevent wound infection. If you suspect an infection has developed because the underlying tissue is becoming red and swollen, red streaks are traveling from the burn toward the heart, or the burn was grossly contaminated (such as from an explosion), use antibiotics as described earlier.

HUMAN BITES

Unless group discipline has really degenerated, human bites are due to accidents such as falling and puncturing flesh with teeth. Bites within the victim's own mouth seldom become infected and are discussed in the section on mouth lacerations (see pages 75–76). Human bites to any other location of the body have the highest infection rate of any wound. Scrub vigorously with Hibiclens surgical scrub, soapy water, or any other antiseptic that you can find. Pick out broken teeth or other debris. Coat the wound area with triple antibiotic ointment. Start the application of hot, wet compresses as described under Puncture Wounds. Start antibiotics with Rocephin, 500 mg IM every 12 hours, or from the Rx Oral/Topical Kit use Levaquin, 750 mg once daily. Bite wounds to the hand are extremely serious and should be seen by a qualified hand surgeon as soon as possible.

ANIMAL BITES

Animal bites tend to be either tearing or crushing injuries. Animal bite lacerations must be vigorously cleaned, but hot soaks need not be started initially. Some authorities state that bite lacerations should not be taped or sutured closed due to an increased incidence of wound infection. This has not been my personal experience nor that of many emergency department physicians with whom I have discussed this problem. After vigorous wound cleansing, I would close gaping wounds as described under Wound Closure Techniques (page 135). Puncture wounds should not be closed, only gaping wounds. Start antibiotic coverage immediately, as described in the section on Human Bites.

The massive lacerations from a large animal bite, such as bear or puma injuries, are another matter. The entire goal of treatment is to stop the bleeding, treat for shock, and evacuate. You may need to close these massive lacerations to help control bleeding.

If an infection seems to start, treat as indicated in the section on wound infection on page 153 by removing the closures and starting hot soaks and antibiotics.

Treat crush injuries with cold packs and compressive dressings. Large lacerations can also be treated with compressive dressings. The ideal item would be a 6-inch elastic bandage. Cold sources can be chemical cold packs or the coldest water available, safely packaged in poly bottles or similar containers.

Refer to Rabies, page 241.

FINGER AND TOE PROBLEMS

Ingrown Nail

This painful infection along the edge of a nail can, at times, be relieved with warm soaks. There are several maneuvers that can hasten healing, however. One technique is a taping procedure, shown in figure 16.11. A piece of strong tape (such as waterproof tape) is taped to the inflamed skin edge next to—but not touching—the nail. The tape

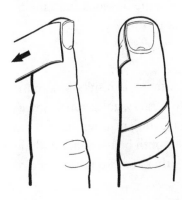

Figure 16.11
Apply tape to the skin edge next to the nail and tug the skin away from the nail, fastening the tape down under the toe or finger.

is fastened tightly to this skin edge with gentle but firm pressure. By running the tape under the toe or finger, the skin edge can be tugged away from the painful nail and thus relieve the pressure.

Another method is to shave the top of the nail by scraping it with a sharp blade until it is thin enough that it buckles upward. This "breaks the arch" of the nail and allows the ingrown edge to be forced out of the inflamed groove along the side.

The above techniques should be implemented at the first sign of irritation rather than once infection has developed, though even then they are effective. Provide antibiotics such as doxycycline, 100 mg twice daily, or Levaquin, 750 mg once daily.

Paronychia (nail base infection)

Paronychia, an infection of the nail base, is a very painful condition that should initially be treated with warm soaks, 15 minutes every 2 hours, and the use of oral antibiotics such as doxycycline, 100 mg twice daily, or Levaquin, 750 mg daily. Oral pain medication will also be necessary. If the lesion does not respond within 2 days, or if it seems to be getting dramatically worse, an aggressive incision with a sharp blade will be necessary,

Figure 16.12
Paronychia, showing the incision required to drain the abscess.

as shown in figure 16.12. This wound will bleed freely. Allow it to do so. Change bandages as necessary and continue the soaks and medications as described under Abscess (pages 156–157).

Felon

A deep infection of a fingertip is called a felon. It results in a tense, tender finger pad. Soaking a felon prior to surgery, unlike other infections, does not help and only increases the pain. Treatment is effected by a very aggressive incision, called a fish-mouth incision, made along the tip of the finger from one side to the other and extending deep to the bone (see figure 16.13 on page 155).

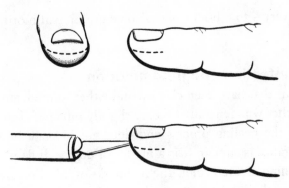

Figure 16.13
Felon, showing the incision required to drain the abscess.

An alternate incision is a through and through stab wound going under the finger bone, from one side to the other. A gauze or sterile plastic strip is then inserted through the wound to promote drainage of the pus from the felon.

The pain is severe and not helped by local injection of lidocaine. But relief is quick as pressure from the pus buildup is alleviated. Allow this wound to bleed freely. Soak in warm water for 15 minutes every 2 hours until drainage ceases (about 3 days). Give pain medication about 1 hour prior to your surgical procedure, using the strongest that you have in your kit. Simultaneously start the victim on an antibiotic such as Levaquin, 750 once daily, doxycycline, 100 mg twice daily, or Rocephin, 500 mg IM twice daily.

Blood under Nail (Subungual Hematoma)

Blood under a fingernail or toenail, called a subungual hematoma, is generally caused by a blow to the digit involved. The accumulation of blood under a nail can be very painful. Relieve this pressure by twirling the sharp point of a blade through the nail (using the lightest pressure possible) until a hole is produced and draining effected. This is a painless procedure and the tip of the blade should not enter the nail bed, only the pocket of blood under the nail. Soak in cool water to promote continual drainage of this blood. The finger may still hurt from the contusion, however, so additional pain treatment with Percogesic, 1 or 2 tablets every 4 hours, or Norco-10/325,

1 tablet every 4 to 6 hours, may also be useful. Antibiotic use is not necessary.

Wound Infection and Inflammation

Lacerations that have been cleaned and either sutured, taped, or stapled together will generally become slightly inflamed. Inflammation is part of the healing process and does not indicate infection, yet the appearance is similar. It is a matter of degree. Inflammation has slight swelling and red color. The hallmarks of infection are swelling, warm to touch, reddish color, and pain. Pus oozing out of a wound is another clue. If the cut has a red swelling that extends beyond 1/4 inch from the wound edge, infection has probably started.

The method of treatment of wound infection is quite simple. Remove some of the tapes (sutures or staples) and allow the wound to open and drain. Apply warm, moist compresses for 15 to 20 minutes every 2 hours. This will promote drainage of the wound and increase the local circulation, thus bringing large numbers of friendly white blood cells and fibroblasts into the area. The fibroblast tries to wall off the infection and prevent the further spread of germs. Once an infection has obviously started, the use of an antibiotic will be helpful but is not always essential. From the Rx Oral/Topical Kit use Levaquin, 750 mg once daily. If the Rx Injectable Kit is available, use Rocephin, 500 mg twice daily IM or 1,000 mg once daily IM.

Abscess

An abscess (boil, furuncle) is a pocket of pus (white blood cells), germs, and red blood cells that have been contained by an envelope of scar tissue produced by fibroblasts. This protects the body from the further spread of germs. It is part of the body's strong natural defense against invasion by bacteria. Conversely, many antibiotics cannot penetrate into the abscess cavity very well. The cure for an abscess is surgical. It must be opened and drained.

There are two basic ways in which this can happen. First, moist warm soaks will not only aid in abscess formation but will also aid in bringing the infection to the surface and cause the infection to "ripen," even open and drain on its own. An abscess can be very painful and this opening period very prolonged. Once the abscess is on the surface, it is generally better to open it using a technique called incision and drainage, or I&D. The ideal instrument for an I&D is a thin, sharp blade. Use the blade to penetrate the surface skin and open the cavity with minimal pressure on the wound.

Abscesses are very painful, primarily because of the pressure within them. A person coming into a doctor's office with a painful abscess would expect to have it anesthetized before opening. Injections into these areas only add to the pain. The best anesthesia is to cool the wound area. In the field an ice cube or application of an instant cold pack will help provide some anesthesia. A person with a painful abscess will usually let you try the knife, as they can become desperate for pain relief. The relief that they get when the pressure is removed is immediate, even without cooling.

Coat the skin surface around the abscess with triple antibiotic ointment from the Non-Rx Topical Bandaging Kit to protect the skin from the bacteria that are draining from the wound. Spread of infection from these bacteria is unlikely, however, unless the skin is abraded or otherwise broken.

Cellulitis

Cellulitis is a very dangerous and rapidly progressive skin infection that results in red, painful swelling of the skin without pus or blister formation. The lesion spreads by the hour, with streaks of red progressing ahead of the swelling toward the heart. This represents the travel of infection along the lymphatic system and is frequently called blood poisoning in the vernacular. While lymphatic spread is not strictly blood poisoning, cellulitis does frequently lead to generalized blood poisoning (septicemia) and can cause the development of chills, fever, and other symptoms of generalized profound infection, such as lethargy and even shock. Very dangerous and virulent germs are responsible. Strong antibiotics are necessary, and the application of local heat is very helpful.

Old time remedies included the use of various "drawing salves," but nothing works better than local hot compresses. Local heat increases the circulation of blood into the infected area, bringing white cells that will kill the bacteria directly and produce antibodies to aid in killing the germs. The infection fighters, and the walling-off process of the fibroblasts, will hopefully contain and destroy the infection. When this walling-off process succeeds, an abscess is formed (see preceding section). If the Rx Injectable Kit is available, give Rocephin, 500 mg IM twice daily. Or, if only the Rx Oral/Topical Kit is available, give doxycycline, 100 mg twice daily, or Levaquin, 750 mg once daily.

Skin Rash

A rash is a frequent outdoor problem. At times, a rash is associated with certain diseases and can help in the diagnosis. If the patient is feverish, or obviously ill, review the sections on Lyme disease, Rocky Mountain spotted fever, typhoid fever, syphilis, meningococcal meningitis, strep throat, measles, and mononucleosis.

Many infections that cause rash are viral and will not respond to antibiotics. But in the isolation, after a foreign port of call with no professional medical help available, rash associated with symptoms of illness, particularly fever and aching, should be empirically treated with an antibiotic such as doxycycline, 100 mg twice daily, for at least 2 days beyond the defervescence (loss of fever). Some of the above infections require longer antibiotic treatment, so it should be continued as indicated if there is a probability that you are dealing with one of them.

Localized rashes without fever are usually due to superficial skin infections, fungal infections, or allergic reactions. Itch can be treated with antihistamine or any pain medication. The Non-Rx Oral Medication Kit has diphenhydramine, 25 mg, as an antihistamine. One capsule (2 in severe cases) every 6 hours will help with itch from nearly any cause.

As itch travels over the same nerves that carry the sensation of pain, any pain medication can also help with itch. Warm soaks generally make itch and rash worse and should be avoided, unless there is evidence of deep infection (see Abscess and Cellulitis above). It is hard to do better than diphenhydramine with regard to oral antihistamine effect, but it should be noted that Atarax (in the Rx Oral/Topical Module), and the same medication in injectable form, Vistaril (in the Rx Injectable Module), also have antihistamine action and can be used for itch. Also soothing to either a non-weeping lesion or a blistered and weeping lesion is the application of a piece of Spenco 2nd Skin from the Topical Bandaging Module. Cool compresses will also soothe a rash.

For a moist, weeping lesion, wet soaks of dilute Epsom salts, boric acid, or even table salt will help dry the lesion (this includes poison ivy, poison oak, and poison sumac). If it is a dry, scaly rash, an ointment works the best, much better than a gel, lotion, or cream. Blistered rashes are treated best with creams, lotions, or gels. Specific types of rashes require specific types of topical medications, however.

Fungal Infection

A fungal infection is commonly encountered in the groin, in the armpit, in skinfolds, on the scrotum, under a woman's breasts, and around the rectum. Rashes can range from bright red to almost colorless, but are generally at least dull red, and frequently have small satellite spots near the major portion of confluent rash. Fungal infections are very slow in spreading, with the lesions becoming larger over a period of weeks to months. Body ringworm is a circular rash with a less intense center area (caution: see Lyme Disease, pages 236–238).

Fungal rashes should be treated with a specific antifungal, such as clotrimazole 2% cream from the Non-Rx Topical Bandaging Module. Apply a thin coat twice daily. Good results should be obtained within 2 weeks for "jock itch," but athlete's foot and body ringworm may take 4 weeks, and need to have continued treatment until all evidence of rash is gone, then treatment continued once daily for an additional 3 weeks. If no improvement has been made, the diagnosis may have been wrong, or the fungus is refractory to your medication. From the Rx Oral Medication Module, Diflucan, 150 mg daily, will destroy most body surface fungal infections, but it is included in only a small quantity for primary use in the treatment of vaginitis.

Allergic Dermatitis

The hallmarks of an allergic dermatitis are vesicles, or small blisters, on red, swollen, and very itchy skin. A line of these blisters clinches the diagnosis of allergic, or contact, dermatitis. The most common reasons are poison ivy, poison sumac, and poison oak. Contact with caterpillars, millipedes, and many plants—even such innocent species as various evergreens—can induce allergic or toxic skin reactions.

A toxic reaction to a noxious substance, such as from certain insects and plants, is treated like an allergic dermatitis. First aid treatment is a thorough cleansing with soap and water. Further treatment is with diphenhydramine, 25 mg every 6 hours, from the Non-Rx Oral Medication Module, and twice daily applications of hydrocortisone cream 1% from the Topical Bandaging Unit. Weeping lesions can be treated with wet soaks as mentioned earlier. An occlusive plastic dressing will allow the rather weak 1% hydrocortisone to work much better.

The Rx Oral/Topical Medication Kit has two very effective medications to treat this problem. Continue use of the diphenhydramine, but add Decadron, 4 mg tablets, 1 daily for 5 to 7 days, and apply Topicort 0.25% ointment in place of the hydrocortisone cream. A thin coat twice daily without an occlusive plastic dressing should work rapidly.

Stinging nettle causes a severe irritation that can be instantly eliminated by the application of "GI jungle juice," a mixture of 75% DEET insect repellent and 25% isopropyl (rubbing) alcohol. I discovered this neat trick the hard way (accidentally) while camping in fields of the stuff along the Cape Fear River in North Carolina. Since mentioning this in the first edition of my book *Wilderness Medicine* in 1979, many others in contact with this plant have confirmed the treatment's instantaneous effectiveness.

Bacterial Skin Rash

A common bacterial superficial skin infection causing a rash is impetigo. The normal appearance of this condition is reddish areas around pus-filled blisters, which are frequently crusty and scabbed. The lesions spread rapidly over a period of days. The skin is generally not swollen underneath the lesions. It often starts around the nose and on the buttocks, spreads rapidly from scratching, and can soon appear anywhere on the body. Early lesions appear as small pimples, which form crusts within 12 to 24 hours. Lesions should be cleaned with surgical soap (or hydrogen peroxide), and then covered with an application of triple antibiotic ointment. Avoid placing bandages on these lesions, as the germs can spread under the tape.

Bacterial skin infections generally must be treated with prescription antibiotics. From the Rx Oral/Topical Medication Module, give Levaquin, 750 mg once daily. The Rx Injectable Medication Kit contains Rocephin, which would be ideal for this condition. Give 500 mg IM once daily.

Treatment of abscess and cellulitis, forms of deep skin infections, are discussed on pages 156 through 158.

See page 72 for treatment of cold sores and lip or mouth lesions.

Seabather's Eruption

"Seabather's eruption" is the term used for the sudden onset of a very itchy rash associated with swimming. In South Florida and the Caribbean, it is caused by larvae of the thimble jellyfish (*Linuche unguiculata*) or by the larvae of the sea anemone (*Edwardsiella lineata*). The latter was shown to be responsible for thousands of cases on Long Island, New York. Global warming will probably cause this condition to become a problem much farther north than that.

Welts (urticaria) or a fine red rash or pimply rash appears within 24 hours of exposure to ocean water, normally in areas covered by bathing suits. The tiny larvae are trapped next to the skin within the bathing suit and discharge nematocysts that cause the disease. Additional symptoms frequently associated with this rash include fever, chills, weakness, and headache, as the larvae penetrate the skin and cause illness. In South Florida, the occurrence is from March to August, with a peak of outbreaks in May. In Long Island waters, the outbreaks occur from mid-August until the end of the swimming season in early September. These outbreaks are episodic, with very few cases some years and thousands of cases during peak years.

Treatment consists of topical corticosteroid (1% hydrocortisone cream from the Non-Rx Topical Bandaging Kit applied 4 times daily, or 0.25% Topicort ointment from the Rx Oral/Topical Kit applied twice daily) and antihistamine (diphenhydramine, 25 mg, from the Non-Rx Oral Medication Kit taken 4 times a day). Swimmers should remove bathing suits and shower as soon as possible after leaving the water. And swimming at a nude beach doesn't protect you just because you are not wearing a bathing suit.

CHAPTER 17
ORTHOPEDICS

Orthopedics includes the study of bone, joint, and muscle function and disorders. This section establishes basic protocols for the assessment and care of orthopedic disorders. General concepts of care will be followed by a systematic evaluation by anatomical region with suggested care plans. No condition can be more debilitating or interfere with operations more than an injury or simply the development of pain that interferes with your ability to survive or function in the challenging circumstances of traveling on the high seas.

While diagnosis and management can be complex, this chapter will provide you an approach caring for these concerns in a reasonable and often definitive manner, even in the case of the inability to make radio contact for advice or direct contact with advanced care.

Table 17.1 Concepts of Orthopedic Care

Muscle Pain—No Acute Injury	164–165
Muscle Pain—Acute Injury	165–166
Joint Pain—No Acute Injury	167–168
Joint Pain—Acute Injury	168–169
Fractures, Broken Bones	170–172
Open Fracture	172–173
Diagnosis and Care Protocols	173–174
Head	174–175
Neck	176–177
Spine	177–179
Collarbone	179–181
Shoulder	181–183

Shoulder Blade—Scapula	183–184
Upper Arm Fractures (Near the Shoulder)	184–185
Upper Arm Fractures (Below the Shoulder)	185–186
Elbow Trauma	186–188
Forearm Fractures	188–189
Wrist Fractures and Dislocations	189–191
Thumb Sprains and Fractures	192
Hand Fractures and Injuries	192
Finger Fractures and Sprains	192–193
Hip Dislocation and Fracture	194–196
Thigh (Femur) Fractures	196–197
Kneecap (Patella) Dislocation	197–198
Knee Sprains, Dislocations, and Fractures	198–199
Ankle Sprains, Dislocations, and Fractures	199
Foot Injuries	200
Chest Injuries	200–201

The above table will refer you to general management principles and to diagnosis and treatment plans by anatomical region.

MUSCLE PAIN—NO ACUTE INJURY

Muscle aches can arise from chronic inflammation disorders such as lupus and fibromyalgia, but the discussion here will be limited to those conditions that might reasonably arise when performing strenuous or repetitive activities.

When associated with a fever, consider an infectious basis for the pain. Without a reasonable method of diagnosis, it would be best to treat with both an antibiotic and appropriate anti-inflammatory pain medication such as ibuprofen. Even in North America, several serious conditions can present in this manner that require antibiotic treatment, such as Rocky Mountain spotted fever. Regardless of cause, it is appropriate to start ibuprofen, 200 mg tablets with 2 to 4 tablets each dose, repeated every 6 hours, for fever and muscle ache.

While it's best to have a physician see the patient and to draw the appropriate lab tests before commencing antibiotics (when you are in port and can obtain tests), if the pain is localized to a specific area and accompanied by swelling, redness and especially fever, start doxycycline, 100 mg twice daily. If you might be treating Lyme disease, this treatment will need to be continued for at least 2 weeks (see page 236).

Under conditions of heat stress, heavy exertion causing sweating, or diarrhea and vomiting, or the use of diuretics causing increased urine output, muscle cramping may be caused by the resulting electrolyte abnormality. Appropriate fluid and electrolyte replacement is necessary, as discussed on page 113.

Overuse syndromes cause pain in muscles that go beyond the mild ache you are accustomed to feeling after a workout at the gym. While it is possible to suddenly tear muscles with sudden movements, significant pain that starts gradually or soon after the exercise is over could be tendinitis, spasm caused by a pinched nerve, or significant inflammation in the muscle. The treatment for these conditions is the same as that employed for tendinitis, as described in that section. Additionally, the use of a muscle relaxant is of benefit. From the Non-Rx Oral Medication Kit take Percogesic, 2 tablets every 6 hours, or from the Rx Oral/Topical Kit, use Atarax, 25 mg every 6 hours. These medications can be used in addition to the others prescribed for tendinitis, unless the condition is relatively mild, when the use of ibuprofen alone should suffice.

MUSCLE PAIN—ACUTE INJURY

Pain occurs immediately after a significant muscle injury, a contusion or strain being the general cause. RICE is the acronym that applies here: Rest, Ice, Compress, and Elevate, Some authorities have recently tried to express it as Rest, Immobilize, Cold, and Elevate. An elastic bandage, cold water or cooling by evaporation of a wet cloth, elevation of a limb, and rest may not all be possible, but they comprise the initial treatment. The application of cold is most important as it decreases tissue bleeding by constricting blood vessels, though be careful not to cause freezing injury. Compression can provide stability as well as accomplishing much the same benefit.

Contusions cause bleeding into the surrounding muscle tissue through the rupture of small blood vessels. Using the RICE technique will minimize the bleeding and local swelling. Strains on muscles result in either microscopic muscle fiber tears or muscle mass tears. These are graded Grade I (microscopic) to Grade IV (total tear of a muscle). Grades II and III are partial tears of a muscle mass. A total tear would require surgical repair. All will be treated similarly in a remote setting without the ability to evacuate to surgical care. Initially use RICE, as indicated earlier. If significant swelling of the muscle occurs, consider that you are dealing with a Grade III or IV tear, and continue RICE for 2 days. Otherwise, use RICE for the first 24 hours.

The next step in treating significant muscle injury would be the application of local heat. In the case of minor injuries, apply the next day. For more serious injuries, delay the use of heat for 2 days. Continue the use of the compression dressing. Splint or sling as necessary for comfort. Decrease activity to a level where the pain is tolerable.

A full rupture of a muscle body will generally result in a bulging of the muscle mass and a loss of strength during the late recovery period. This may not be noticeable at first, as the swelling would initially be attributed to local bleeding and pain would restrict use. Once the pain is gone, continued swelling, especially after several weeks have passed, is probably due to a significant muscle tear or a ruptured tendon. This should be repaired when possible, but it is not a reason to despair if at sea and surgeons are not available. The acute pain of a muscle belly tear will subside within a few weeks, noticeable discomfort ceases after 6 weeks, and then scar tissue forms and the body will replace the primary actions of the torn muscle (if fully torn) by using accessory muscles to the extent that it can and the injured individual will have to subsequently adapt to the weakened condition that will result. It is amazing how well we can perform with some of these injuries, one of the most common being total tear of the biceps muscle or tendon. The muscle contract, which means that it will bulge, but its major action, that of pronation (turning a screw-driver), will be greatly weakened. Fortunately, accessory muscles will aid in must function of the upper arm, such as flexion of the elbow.

JOINT PAIN—NO ACUTE INJURY

Pain in the joint without a history of injury is generally due to arthritis, bursitis, or tendinitis. Without a history of previous arthritis, the latter two are the more likely diagnosis, but the treatment is the same for all three. The most common reason for tendon or joint inflammation is overuse. French trappers frequently complained of Achilles tendinitis while snowshoeing, which they appropriately termed *mal de racquette*. Persons hammering, chopping wood, or playing tennis are familiar with "tennis elbow" (lateral epicondylitis of the elbow). Tendinitis can occur in the thumb, wrist—in fact, any tendon in the body can become inflamed with overuse. Joints similarly become inflamed with repetitious activity or even unusual compression. Brick layers and others who must work kneeling will, on occasion, encounter a patellar bursitis of the knee (called commonly "housemaid's knee). Many people have developed bursitis flare-ups in a shoulder after repetitive arm actions or in the forearm due to the overuse of flexor tendons of the wrist.

Treatment of these conditions must include adjusting the technique for the activity that seems to have caused it. By changing a grip when pulling on a lanyard or working the handle of a windless, using the tool with a different pitch to the blades, or altering a movement in any fashion to avoid generating additional pain, the victim can try to alleviate the discomfort and avoid inflaming it more. Prior to an activity, the application of heat to the sore area helps with prevention. Immediately after aggravating the condition, applying cold is of benefit. Within an hour return to a local heat application and continue this during the evenings.

Applying a cream such as Aspercreme (other brand names are Myoflex and Mobisyl) with a dry heat might help a tendinitis, as the active ingredient (trolamine salicylate 10% concentration) penetrates the skin and provides local anti-inflammatory action. Sports creams that feel warm, such as Icy Hot, simply irritate the skin surface to cause an increased blood flow and thus provide warmth to the area. They do not have an anti-inflammatory effect and they do not provide any benefit over the application of heat. This does not mean that these creams do not have a potentially valuable role here. It is very difficult to apply hot soaks in an ocean setting, and these creams can serve the purpose. Topical products containing diclofenac are now widely available by prescription (brand names Voltaren 1% gel, Pennsaid, or Flector 1.3% patches). These are the most effective topical treatment possible, but the onset of relief takes a few days of application.

If hot compresses seem to aggravate the pain, switch to a cold compress technique. Avoid making any movements that seem to cause pain for 5 to 7 days. Splinting may help during this period. Avoid nonuse of the shoulder for longer than 2 weeks, as it is prone to adhesion formation and loss of function from stiffness can result.

The best medication for chronic joint pain is ibuprofen from the Non-Rx Oral Medication Kit due to its anti-inflammatory properties. Four tablets every 6 hours will aid in joint and tendon pain. From the Rx Oral/Topical Medication Kit, one could use Decadron, 4 mg, given once daily for 7 days for joint inflammation. See the warning in the discussion of the use of the antibiotic Levaquin regarding tendonitis and tendon rupture (page 292).

JOINT PAIN—ACUTE INJURY

Immediately after a joint injury, we will want to evaluate the injury, determine how serious it is, and figure out how or if the injury may affect our whole group's sailing situation. Frankly, making a precise diagnosis usually isn't possible initially, so our approach to the acute joint injury must be to look at methods of treatment and potential long-term care. The discussion on orthopedic injuries in this book considers the body by region, not by precise diagnosis of injury. Nevertheless, we must try to have some understanding of what might have happened, make an accurate prognosis early in the event, and minimize the damage while keeping the victim as functional as possible.

Unusual stress across a joint can result in damage to supporting ligaments. Ordinarily this is a temporary stretching damage, but in severe cases, rupture of ligaments or even fracture of bones or damage to the cartilage can result. These injuries are serious problems and may require surgical repair. This is best done immediately but can be safely delayed 3 weeks. Fractures entering the joint space may result in long-term joint pain and subsequent arthritis. Cartilage defects do not heal themselves, unlike ligament, tendon, and bone damage. These frequently cause so much future pain and instability that surgical correction is eventually required.

Proper care of joint injuries must be started immediately. RICE forms the basis of good first aid management. Cold should be applied for the first 2 days, as continuously as possible. Then apply heat for 20 minutes or longer, 4 times daily. Cold decreases the circulation, which lessens bleeding and swelling. Heat increases the circulation, which then aids the healing process. This technique applies to all injuries, including muscle contusions and bruises.

Elevate the involved joint, if possible. Wrap with elastic bandage or cloth tape to immobilize the joint and provide moderate support once ambulation or use of the joint begins. Take care that the wrap pings are not so tightly applied that they cut off the circulation or exacerbate swelling.

Use crutches or other support to take enough weight off an injured ankle and/or knee so that increased pain is not experienced. The patient should not use an injured joint if use causes pain, as this indicates further strain on the already stressed ligaments or fracture. Conversely, if use of the injured part does not cause pain, additional damage is not being done even if there is considerable swelling. If the victim must walk on an injured ankle or knee, and doing so causes considerable pain, then support it the best way possible (wrapping, crutches, decreased carrying load, tight boot for ankle injury) and realize that further damage is being done, but that in your opinion the situation warrants such a sacrifice.

While compression is good for an acute injury, too much could cut off circulation and must be avoided. If an ankle is injured, the boot can provide needed compression, but remove it if the pain becomes intolerable. A boot can always be put back on a swollen ankle by undoing the laces and just wrapping them around the boot circumference rather than using the eyelets.

Pain medications may be given as needed, but elevation and decreased use will provide considerable pain relief. See also Fractures below.

FRACTURES—BROKEN BONES

A fracture is a medical term meaning a broken bone. It is not true that "if you can move the part it is not broken." Pain will prevent some movement, but this does not aid in the diagnosis between a fracture and a contusion. Fractures may consist of a single crack in the bone and be rather stable, or have many cracks and pieces and be, consequently, very unstable. There may be no way of telling which is present, or even if a fracture is there at all, without an X-ray. Deformity indicates either a fracture or contusion causing swelling with soft tissue bleeding if located in the middle of a long bone area, or a possible dislocation or severe sprain with or without a fracture if located at a joint. The hallmark of a fracture is point tenderness or pain to touch over the site of the break. Swelling over the break site is further evidence of a fracture. Another way to deduce the presence of a fracture is to apply gentle torsion or longitudinal compression to the bone in question, with either technique causing increased pain at the fracture site.

Each fracture has several critical aspects in its management to consider: (1) correct loss of circulation or nerve damage due to deformity of the fracture; (2) prevent the induction of infection if the skin is broken at or near the fracture site; (3) prevent further soft tissue damage; and (4) obtain reasonable alignment of bone fragments so that adequate healing takes place. The nonskilled practitioner is limited to the first three management techniques.

The first aid approach to a fracture is to "splint them as they lie." This is not an appropriate response in remote areas. Straighten gross deformities of angulated fractures with gentle inline traction, as in figure 17.1. Before straightening, check and compare the pulses beyond the fracture site on the left and right sides of the victim and check for any abnormality of sensation. After correcting the angulation, circulation should improve. As arteries and veins are hollow tubes, their lumen will stretch and narrow if they are forced to bend around a corner, thus decreasing blood flow. When this bend is eliminated, the vessel will return to its normal size and blood flow will improve. As the person could be in shock, it might be difficult to feel the pulses on either side. It is much more accurate to evaluate the circulation by examination of both sides and comparing the results.

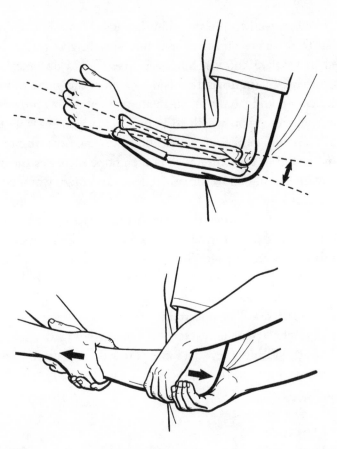

Figure 17.1
Use inline traction to straighten grossly angulated fractures. This technique is not meant to perfectly align the bone ends; it is only meant to eliminate gross deformity, improve circulation, decrease nerve damage from stretching, and, in certain cases, decrease pain.

Grossly angulated fractures also cause sharp ends of bone to project against the skin surface and create an impending open fracture. Even with careful padding, jostling along during an evacuation may cause one of these bone spicules to penetrate the skin surface, causing an open fracture and increasing the chance of serious wound and bone infection.

The chance of causing harm while straightening an angulated fracture would be extremely low. It is possible for a blood vessel or nerve to become trapped within the fracture site, but gentle repositioning into slight deformity should correct this.

Pad splints well to prevent skin damage. Pneumatic splints are available from many outfitters. Fracture splinting is generally well covered in first aid courses. Such a course should be taken before any major voyage. Improvisation is the name of the game in fracture immobilization and having an adequate first aid course provides one with information upon which to improvise. In general, splint fractures to immobilize the joint above and below the fracture site.

Any wound in the skin near a broken bone increases the chance of a bone infection. Follow the principles of thorough wound cleansing as indicated on pages 131–134.

With proper splinting the pain involved with a fracture will decrease dramatically. Provide pain medication when possible. Pain control is discussed on pages 34–35. The Rx hydroxyzine (Atarax or Vistaril) can be given to aid in muscle spasm control. Mild sedation with diphenhydramine (Benadryl) may help its sedating effects.

At times, there will be uncertainty about whether a fracture exists. When in doubt, splint and treat for pain, avoiding the use of the involved part. Within a few days, the pain will have diminished and the crisis may be over. If not, the suspicion of a fracture will loom even larger.

Open Fracture

Even a laceration or puncture wound near a broken bone is a cause for alarm. Such a wound can allow bacteria into the fracture site, causing a serious bone infection and inhibit fracture healing. The wound should not be closed, as this increases the chance of infection. Wet dressings are best over an open wound. Soak the sterile dressing in sterile water, and cover with a clean, dry dressing. Change this dressing twice daily.

If a piece of bone is protruding from the skin, the break is called an open fracture. The first aid approach is to splint in position and cover with a sterile dressing. In a remote area, this approach will not work. This wound requires aggressive irrigation with surgical scrub or soap as described on pages 131–134.

The aggressiveness of this cleansing action should be done in such a manner as to not cause further damage, but the area must be free of foreign particulate matter and as antiseptic as possible. Cover the wound with triple antibiotic ointment. Protect with sterile gauze dressings, with enough pressure to control bleeding only. Straighten the gross angulation of the fracture with gentle inline traction. This will cause the protruding bone to disappear under the skin surface, unless the fragment is loose from the main bone. Allow this wound to remain open and dress as indicated earlier. If available, use the Silverlon dressing as suggested in the Ship's Medicine Chest.

In all cases of a laceration or puncture wound near a fracture, place the victim on oral antibiotics when available. From the Rx Oral/ Topical Medication Kit, use Levaquin, 750 mg daily. However, if the Rx Injectable unit is carried, give Rocephin, 1,000 mg IM twice daily. Continue the medication until the patient is evacuated or for 72 hours or within a day after the soft tissue injuries have been closed.

Diagnosis and Care Protocols

The diagnosis of these injuries will be difficult due to lack of experience and the benefit of X-ray equipment. Uncertainties of diagnosis will exist, and therefore a systematic approach to the evaluation and treatment of the injured patient must be developed that will handle most common injuries appropriately.

The orthopedic evaluation is made easier because human beings have equal sides that can be compared. Take the clothing off both the injured and normal sides and compare, weather permitting. Look for swelling or different configuration. When examining the injured side, touch lightly. A fracture or sprain is very tender and will not require hard poking to elicit obvious pain. Swelling results from localized bleeding, which a fracture will almost always cause. Several days after the injury a bruise may appear near it, or lower on the person. Gravity, as well as various muscle groups and local anatomy, can cause this spilled blood to migrate to a place at a different location from the injury site. This does not mean that the injury is spreading; it just represents the displacement of blood and part of the reabsorption process of healing. Don't be concerned about the appearance of bruising and its spread in the days after the injury. Elevation of the injury can alleviate swelling and bruising. Prolonged immobilization, however, may lead to joint stiffness.

HEAD FRACTURES—UNCONSCIOUS

Lacerations of the scalp or face result in massive bleeding, the care of which is discussed on pages 139–140. Internal head injuries range from insignificant to lethal. Check the level of consciousness as per page 9. Urgent evacuation is necessary for anyone who has any of the following:

- Unconsciousness for more than 2 minutes
- Debilitating headache
- Loss of coordination or garbled speech
- Persistent nausea and vomiting
- Bruising behind the ears (a sign of skull fracture)
- Bruising around the eyes (a sign of skull fracture)
- Decrease in vision
- Clear fluid draining from nose and/or ears (possible spinal fluid)
- Seizures
- Relapse into unconsciousness

Suspect a neck injury in anyone with a head injury. On most trips, it is prudent to seek medical care for anyone who has been knocked unconscious for even a brief moment. The patient can walk and assist in his or her own evacuation if there is no apparent spine injury. If the patient is not thinking clearly, or has any of the above signs, immobilize the neck and entire spine. Initially this may have to be done on the deck, with the patient lying down and using hand traction to stabilize his or her head and neck.

A head-injured patient will frequently vomit. To avoid aspirating this into his lungs, place him face down with his face turned to one side, or sit the patient up with his head elevated to 30 degrees. This position may also decrease some of the headache associated with head injury.

While the patient is kept awake for neurological assessments of levels of responsiveness in civilization, if evacuation will take a long time (several days), allow the person to fall asleep. While asleep the brain has its best chance to control its own swelling.

While the use of pain and anti-nausea medication might alter the mental status and is avoided in urban first aid care, when you are at sea and responsible for long-term care, it makes sense to use these medications. It is best to use the mildest medication necessary for relief. Refer to pain management (page 33) and nausea management (page 90).

If you detect improvement in the symptoms over the next 2 days, the prognosis is very good. If symptoms increase, rapidly return the patient to the nearest port if possible. If there is no chance of reaching help, most everything you do will be of no additional help. In the past, large doses of steroid were given (such as dexamethasone 16–24 mg per day from the Rx Oral/Topical Medication kit). Recent studies indicate steroids cause more harm than good, although if all you have to offer is death in a deteriorating patient, going back to the widely used old protocol is appropriate. Improved results from that therapy may show within 1 day or take up to 8 days. When dexamethasone is used in this high of a dose, it will need to be gradually withdrawn (tapered) when concluding the treatment period in order to allow the adrenal glands to recover and produce the normal cortisol levels that will have been suppressed by this therapy. When using low-dose dexamethasone, 4 mg per day, if used less than 10 days, it can be stopped abruptly. But large doses when used as indicated earlier, must be tapered no matter how long they are used. Reduce high dose (16 to 24 mg) by halving the dose every few days, until down to 2 mg, then reduce by 0.5 to 1 mg every 5–7 days. A standard method of treating increased intracranial pressure is the use of hyperosmolar diuretics (such as mannitol) via IV infusion. This item is not in your suggested ship's medicine chest, but another item used is a "loop diuretic," which is suggested. Use furosemide (Lasix), 40 mg daily, until improvement of consciousness at which time it may be stopped abruptly. If only a milder diuretic is available, such as the hydrochlorothiazide, use 50 mg per day. It also may be stopped abruptly when symptoms improve. If the patient is conscious, you will need to insert a Foley catheter.

Neck

Examination of the neck is critical to help preserve the spinal cord from injury if the neck is unstable. Without moving the neck, gently palpate along the spinous process to elicit point tenderness in the conscious patient. No point tenderness will generally mean no significant bone damage to the neck. In an unconscious patient with head trauma, treat as if the neck is fractured. Splint carefully for maximal immobilization. If the neck is at an odd angle, it should be straightened with gentle inline traction, by pulling steadily and slowly on the head to a neutral position in a line with the spine. This is a maneuver taught by wilderness or nautical first aid classes. Practice before attempting.

Patients should not be allowed to move nor should they be lifted or transported without careful immobilization of the neck. The best technique for initial cervical immobilization is gentle but firm control by a person holding the patient's head. Remind the victim to remain still. Eventually this firm control might be replaced with a cervical collar, or a rolled Ensolite pad or other soft material. The SAM Splint® can be molded into a cervical collar, as shown in figure 17.2.

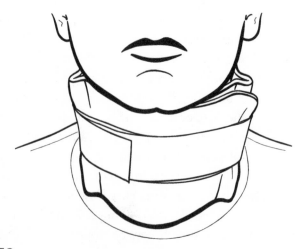

Figure 17.2
SAM Splint molded into a cervical collar. The vertical creases make the splint rigid. Generally avoid using neck splints in an acute injury (see text).

Neck injuries, when serious as described earlier, are best treated in a hospital, so arrange evacuation immediately. When stuck treating them at sea, you will have to move them onto as comfortable a bed as possible. Elevate the head to 30 degrees. Pad the neck with pillows on each side of the neck to discourage sideways movement and forward or rearward bending of the neck. The greatest challenge to be managed over the 8 weeks of healing is toilet activities. The neck must be provided adequate padding to prevent movement when the patient's position must change. Treat for pain and muscle spasm (see pages 33–34, for pain control). Numbness, radiating pain, loss of nerve or muscle function possibly could have been prevented with surgery, but lacking this, the only care you can do now is to try to relieve swelling around the spinal cord. Use the same treatments as indicated earlier for head injury regarding use of dexamethasone, furosemide, or hydrochlorothiazide.

To adequately prevent neck injury, the cervical collar will have to be augmented with total body immobilization. Current techniques are being promoted that would avoid the use of cervical collars as even attempting to put them on can cause more neck trauma than they prevent. Most cervical fractures are not unstable, so the collar adds to airway management difficulty, patient discomfort, and provides no benefit.

If no point tenderness is claimed by the conscious victim, but generalized pain and spasm of the neck muscles are present, the victim may be suffering a severe sprain. A neck brace made of a towel or other rolled cloth can help with the long-term treatment and provides adequate support. Local warmth will help relax these muscles. Pain medication and muscle relaxants are useful in curing a neck sprain and spasm. It can take weeks for this injury to cease hurting.

Spine

The neurological assessment of potential neck injury includes assessment of the entire spine. For a neurological check, ask the patient if there is any numbness or tingling anywhere on the body. Check grip strength on both sides and the ability to wiggle toes and flex feet up and down. Check the entire spine by palpating along the spinous processes, looking for any point tenderness. If the above examination is questionable, or even if the trauma seems severe, both neck and spinal immobilization are in order. Having a rescuer maintain firm hand control of the victim's neck will be necessary until the patient has been placed upon a suitable rigid stretcher. Rigid stretchers are very difficult to improvise, and moving people upon them even more difficult. While *Wilderness First Responder*, 3rd Edition (Buck Tilton; Globe Pequot Press, 2010) goes into great detail in describing this technique, these skills require practice.

Ensure that the patient has been securely tied into the litter before you secure the head. If the body shifts while the head is tied down, any damage present in the neck could increase.

When applying first responder services on shore, this is the end of the neck/spine story. The patient remains fastened rigidly to a stretcher until the emergency department physician has taken tests and made the determination that she can be removed. This may take several agonizing hours. I said agonizing, because even a normal person will hurt like crazy when attached to a rigid stretcher or backboard. If the patients don't have back trouble before being fastened down, they will now. A report in the *Annals of Emergency Medicine*, "The Effect of Spinal Immobilization on Healthy Volunteers," had 21 healthy volunteers (who had never experienced any back problems) placed in standard backboard immobilization for 30 minutes, and found that 100% had pain during that period, with 55% grading it moderate to severe, and 29% developed additional symptoms after release during the following 48 hours.

Especially in a remote location, it is important to reassess the spine to ensure that continued immobilization is necessary. This is difficult if even normal people will develop back pain after a short time on the board. You will have to use common sense. Inability to move an extremity or loss of sensation, without an orthopedic injury in that limb, must cause a high suspicion of spinal cord injury or nerve traction injury (stinger). But if these signs and symptoms are not present and you become convinced that you are dealing with only a sore muscle problem in the back, not a broken or disrupted spine, then the spine may be cleared—a term meaning let the patient out of the rigid support. Continued partial support with a soft foam pad around the neck, or even a back brace made of Ensolite foam wrapped around the patient, might make sense. Then again, it might not. It's a judgment call based upon the severity of the injury and resulting symptoms and the general situation of how far away from port you are.

Point tenderness encountered when carefully palpating the spine indicates a possible fracture. If it is a fracture of the body of the vertebrae, this very painful condition can heal with only rest—although the healing process will take 8 weeks and require continued immobilization. This is a common fracture of elderly people due to osteoporosis and is encountered when they suddenly place a compression on the spine, usually while falling. These seldom are so bad that fragments compress the spinal cord. Fractures of the vertebral process where muscles attach can be stretch injuries or blows that can be very painful, but not neurologically compromising. No numbness should result or harm endangering leg movement. Injuries causing instability of the back can result in complete paralysis below the injury. The only thing that can be done without proper X-ray evaluation is to pad the patient and prevent movement. This means feeding, toilet activities, and as much pain control as you can provide. There is no need to discuss here how tragic this injury can become without proper neurosurgical care. Eight weeks will tell the tale. Some pain relief can be attempted with the addition of oral steroid (Decadron 4 mg twice daily) as discussed under neck and head injury above.

COLLARBONE—CLAVICLE

Evaluate for pain to palpation along the collarbone (clavicle). Separations of the clavicle from the sternum (breastbone), fractures of the clavicle, and separations of the shoulder can all be treated similarly with a sling and swathe, as shown in figure 17.3 page 180.

The clavicle frequently fractures in the mid-portion. Proper reduction will occur if the shoulders are held back, like those of a Marine at attention. A figure eight (figure 17.4 page 180) will maintain this position. A stoop shoulder position will allow too much override of the fracture parts.

Figure 17.3

A sling and swathe will protect the injured shoulder and decrease pain in the recently fractured clavicle. This system can be duplicated by pinning the forearm to the front of a shirt. Use a sling without swathe if there is a danger of the person slipping off a hill or falling into water.

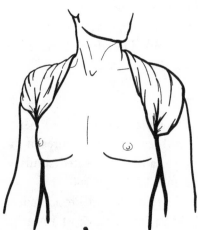
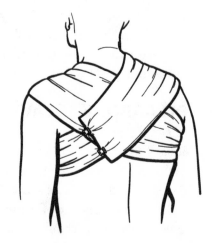

Figure 17.4

The figure-of-eight splint will hold a clavicle fracture in the proper position for healing. Add a sling for maximum pain control.

A fracture of the clavicle at the end near the shoulder may be hard to hold in proper position. In children, there is a sleeve of tissue at this location that aids in holding the proper alignment. In adults, this tissue is missing, and surgical pinning may be required for optimal healing. However, even in the adult, this fracture may be treated adequately, usually with a sling.

A fracture of the clavicle at the end near the breastbone (sternum) is best reduced and held in position with a figure-of-eight splint. In any clavicle fracture, the use of a sling will aid greatly in decreasing pain. The sling can be eliminated in 2 weeks, but the figure-of-eight splint should be kept on for 3 to 4 weeks, or until there is no pain over the fracture site with free movement of the shoulder.

A posterior dislocation of the clavicle with respect to the sternum may result in neuromuscular or respiratory compromise, which should be adequately evaluated. Nerve damage would present as electrical pain or numbness, while breathing difficulty associated with a fracture of the clavicle may indicate punctured lung or massive bleeding into the space beneath the clavicle. These obviously require immediate evacuation to shore.

SHOULDER

Shoulder separations are classified as Grade I to Grade III, depending upon the severity. Grade I has tenderness over the acromioclavicular joint, representing a strain of the ligaments but with no disruption or tear. A Grade II is a rupture of the two acromioclavicular ligaments, while a Grade III is disruption of both acromioclavicular ligaments as well as the coracoclavicular ligament. The latter case will allow elevation of the clavicle, as the entire suspension of the shoulder has been disrupted. There is no strong evidence that Grade III separations do better with surgery than without if the patient is willing to accept slight deformity at the end of the clavicle. Functionally the patient should do fine by treating with an arm sling for 3 to 6 weeks for comfort, with mobilization of the shoulder as early as possible and return to activity.

Shoulder dislocations are separations of the humerus (the long bone of the upper arm) from the shoulder and are classified as either anterior or posterior. Anterior is by far the most common, at a ratio of 10:1. Posterior dislocations are often due to electrocution and/or seizure activity resulting from unbalanced muscle contractions of the pectoralis and posterior musculature. Fractures of the head, or top part, of the humerus may be associated with dislocations. A replacement (reduction) of the dislocation should be attempted as soon as possible. Muscle spasm and pain will continue to increase the longer the dislocation is allowed to remain untreated.

Anterior dislocations may be identified by comparison to the opposite side. The normal, smooth, rounded contour of the shoulder, which is convex on the lateral (outside) side, is lost. With anterior displacement, the lateral contour is sharply rectangular and the anterior (or front) contour is unusually prominent. The arm is held away from the body and any attempted movement will cause considerable pain. See figure 17.5. A numb area located at the insertion of the deltoid muscle means that the axillary nerve has been damaged. Numbness or tingling of the little finger could mean ulnar nerve damage, while decreased sensation to the thumb, index, and middle finger

Figure 17.5

A person with an anterior shoulder dislocation holds the arm away from the body and across the chest. Note the steep shoulder contour.

may mean the radial nerve is injured. These findings increase the urgency of attempting a reduction. The best method of reducing the anterior dislocation of the shoulder is the Stimson method. While other methods exist, this technique puts less force on the shoulder, which is particularly important in case a fracture of the head of the humerus coexists with the dislocation. The technique is illustrated in figure 17.6. After reduction has been obtained, the arm is placed in a sling and a swathe is wrapped around the arm and chest to hold the arm against the body for 3 weeks. Mobilization too soon after reduction will result in a weak, unstable shoulder. In a young person, this sling and swathe may be maintained for 4 weeks prior to range-of-motion exercise. Holding the position longer than 4 weeks will not reduce the chance of recurrent dislocation, while holding it there longer may result in a frozen shoulder. In older patients, shoulder dislocations often have resulted in rotator cuff injuries. This will mean that the movement and associated pain simply will not be solved with the above instructions and will eventually require surgical correction to regain full function.

Shoulder Blade—Scapula

Fractures of the shoulder blade (scapula) are generally due to major trauma and the patient may require treatment for multiple fractures of

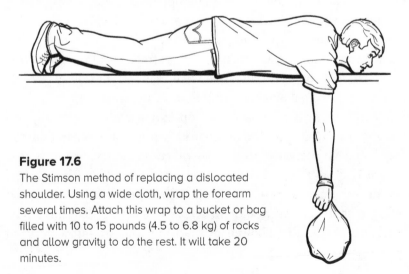

Figure 17.6
The Stimson method of replacing a dislocated shoulder. Using a wide cloth, wrap the forearm several times. Attach this wrap to a bucket or bag filled with 10 to 15 pounds (4.5 to 6.8 kg) of rocks and allow gravity to do the rest. It will take 20 minutes.

the ribs, punctured lung (pneumothorax), or heart contusion. A direct blow to the scapula may fracture it without these other injuries. Diagnosis is difficult without an X-ray, but suspicion may be high if there is point tenderness to palpation over the scapula, particularly several days after the accident. An indication of scapular fracture is Comolli's sign, which is a triangular swelling corresponding to the outline of the scapula. Treatment is with a sling and early mobilization to prevent stiffening of the shoulder.

UPPER ARM FRACTURES (NEAR THE SHOULDER)

The humerus is the upper bone of the arm. Fractures of the upper part (or head) of the humerus are most common in elderly people. Again, the shoulder will be very painful. The classification of these fractures is made with X-rays, which indicate that not only has a fracture occurred, but also shows the number of pieces in the fracture and whether angulation or displacement has transpired. Displacement or severe angulation frequently requires surgical repair, but often very conservative measures are followed by the orthopedic specialist. Without access to X-ray or an orthopedic specialist, we have to treat all injuries conservatively.

Fractures of the upper humerus are associated with swelling and eventual bruising of the shoulder and upper arm, with gravity slowly causing the swelling and bruising to appear lower and lower down the arm. Severe pain will prevent normal movement of the shoulder, but some movement is frequently possible. As fractures of the upper part of the humerus occur through bone that mends itself readily (cancellous bone), the final outcome is often more dependent upon limiting the length of time of immobilization and starting proper physical therapy than it is upon the number of pieces or the separation and angulation. Conservative treatment will consist of a sling and swathe (figure 17.3 page 180). It is important in older individuals to mobilize the shoulder as soon as possible, otherwise adhesions form, and a frozen shoulder will result. An X-ray would help determine how much time should be allowed in the sling. This would range from only a few days to 4 or even 6 weeks with a four-part fracture with marked displacement. If the patient is over 30, the best rule of thumb when treating without X-ray is to mobilize and start physical therapy at 2 weeks. A youngster's arm can be left in a sling for 4 weeks. The therapy should consist of range-of-motion movements, such as circular elephant trunk motions while bending over, and raising the arm in front, to the side, and toward the rear. Effort should be made to move the shoulder as if the patient were wiping his bottom. The patient should do this on his own, without someone forcing his arm through these motions.

UPPER ARM FRACTURES (BELOW THE SHOULDER)

Fractures in the shaft beneath the head of the humerus will result in muscle spasm, causing an overriding of the shafts of bone. This is prevented by applying a hanging cast. This amounts to a weighted cast applied to the forearm, with a loop of cloth supporting much of the weight of the cast from around the victim's neck. Mobilization and physical therapy should be started in 2 weeks. It is not practical in a setting without X-ray to properly design and follow the results of a hanging cast. Pain and apparent fracture of the humerus at the shoulder will probably have to be treated with a sling and swathe, with early mobilization as mentioned earlier.

Humeral shaft fractures take 2 to 4 months to heal. Located between the shoulder and the elbow, this is best splinted with a cast that orthopedic surgeons call a sugar tong splint. It amounts to a U-shaped plaster extending from the armpit around the elbow back up to the shoulder, molded to the arm after reduction, and wrapped with an ace bandage. A SAM Splint can be used to construct a sugar tong splint, as shown in figure 17.7 page 186. Treatment outcomes may be different between males and females. Obese patients and females with large breasts may affect immobilization and fracture apposition in humoral shaft fractures, making their care even more difficult.

Complete fractures of the shaft of the humerus will be very painful, making a crunching feel when the bone is gently stressed. Incomplete fractures will be exquisitely tender to touch. Several days after the injury, swelling and bruising will appear at the elbow and forearm.

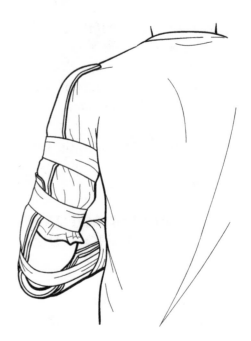

Figure 17.7
SAM Splint in sugar tong splint
for a humerus mid-shaft fracture.

Humeral shaft fractures at a point one-third of the way up from the elbow may cause damage to the radial nerve, thus causing numbness to the forearm, thumb, and index finger. This numbness generally lasts from 3 to 6 months and will commonly resolve on its own. Usually developing numbness is a serious consequence that reflects either a tear or compression on a nerve. This is a situation where the development of such a numb feeling is less cause for panic.

ELBOW TRAUMA

Fractures of the humerus above the elbow are very treacherous, as bone fragments may seriously injure the nerves or blood vessels at this location. Fractures of the elbow itself are similarly dangerous due to the possible damage to nerve, blood vessel, or articular surfaces of the bones in this joint. The immense swelling associated with fractures or sprains at the elbow causes compression that frequently does more damage than sharp pieces of broken bone.

Avoid splinting the elbow near a 90-degree angle. Allow the elbow to droop in the sling with a posterior padding. Never wrap the elbow joint at the front aspect—leave this area open to the air. It is compression in the front of the elbow joint, an area called the antecubital fossa that frequently results in serious injury to the blood vessels and nerves. Surgical intervention with X-ray assistance is required, so back to the port with you to ensure normal elbow function under many circumstances with regard to elbow fractures. Allowing the injured elbow to freeze into a 120-degree position may be the only treatment you can offer without surgical intervention if you are stranded on a desert island or for some other reason unable to get the patient to a surgeon.

Dislocation of the elbow is most common in young adults. Fractures of the tip of the elbow (the coronoid process) frequently are involved, but generally do not cause future problems. Fractures of the condyles can cause severe problems, as indicated earlier, primarily due to compression from associated bleeding on the neurovascular bundle. Reduction obviously should not be attempted if there is a chance of being treated properly by an orthopedic specialist with X-ray equipment. The appearance of the dislocated elbow would be obvious when compared to that person's other elbow. Some people have a sharper-looking elbow tip than the average individual. However, swelling and a particularly prominent, hard point behind the elbow would indicate that a dislocation has transpired.

Pain medication should be given to the victim to relax the muscles prior to attempting to reduce the dislocation. Figure 17.8 page 188 demonstrates the technique of reducing an elbow dislocation.

The ideal position after reduction of the elbow is at 90 degrees with a posterior plaster splint. A 90-degree position is potentially dangerous, as swelling may compromise the circulation. If the pulses at the wrist are decreased, then allow the elbow to droop as necessary to relieve this compression, possibly to a 120-degree position, as described earlier. The reduction of a simple elbow dislocation is best maintained in the posterior splint for 3 weeks, and then start range-of-motion exercises. Soaking the elbow in warm water about 15 minutes prior to starting a gentle exercise program is helpful. If unusual deformity has resulted, or if the elbow is frozen, this frozen position may have to be accepted under survival conditions, until definitive surgery can be accomplished. Full and proper use of this elbow will probably never again be established, even after delayed surgery.

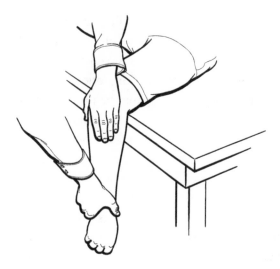

Figure 17.8
The Stimson maneuver for reducing a dislocation of the elbow. This dislocation results when the ulna is forced backward, so that the tip (olecranon) becomes very prominent. Besides traction on the wrist, pushing on the olecranon aids in the reduction.

FOREARM FRACTURES

Forearm fractures in children can generally be treated by reducing under X-ray and plaster casting, while in adults they frequently are treated surgically. Both options are not available to the isolated wilderness inhabitant if evacuation is not possible. The position of splinting of forearm fractures differs depending upon the location along the two bones, due to different forces upon these bones from tendon and muscle attachments. This positioning can be held properly only with tight-fitting plaster splints. Bone alignment can be followed only through repeated X-rays. Therefore, it is obvious that a completely fractured, unstable condyles can cause severe problems, as indicated earlier, primarily due to compression from associated bleeding on the neurovascular bundle. A fracture of the forearm will very likely not heal properly when treated by crude techniques in a nonsurgical setting.

Most fractures of the forearm are not complete and unstable, however. They will heal nicely with protective splinting being the only required therapy. A stable crack can be suspected from swelling and point tenderness to gentle finger palpation by the examiner along the radius and ulna, the two forearm bones. Under this circumstance, a splint must be manufactured that will provide stability so that this fracture can heal without danger of further trauma, as

Figure 17.9
Forearm splint technique with the SAM Splint.

in figure 17.9. The bone will weaken during the healing process and additional trauma may turn this nondisplaced fracture into an angulated mess. Pad the splint well and provide a sling for at least 3 weeks. Keep splinted for a total of 6 weeks; longer if point tenderness is still present. If point tenderness disappears within a few days or at most 2 weeks, the injury is not a fracture, but simply a contusion, and the splint may be safely removed at that time.

Fractures associated with deformity in the forearm provide the physician with two challenges: first, reducing the fracture, and second, maintaining its position with proper casting. Reduction of forearm fractures is generally done by traction, increasing the angulation to engage the fracture ends, then straightening the bones prior to casting. This is done with anesthesia. The remote sailor had best splint deformed fractures of the forearm after straightening gross angulation with inline traction. The splinted position will have to be maintained for 8 weeks or longer, depending upon the disappearance of local tenderness. A well-padded splint may generally be applied in a firm manner, immobilizing the elbow and wrist joints. Corrective surgery can be performed later. It is best to avoid a manipulation that will be extremely painful and unstable anyway.

WRIST FRACTURES AND DISLOCATIONS

Wrist fractures and dislocations are common in young adults who extend their arms and hands to help break a fall. The three most common problems are fractures of the navicular (or scaphoid) bone, dislocation of the lunate, and perilunate dislocation. See wrist anatomy in figure 17.10. Navicular fractures frequently do not heal even with appropriate casting.

Dislocations of the lunate or of the remaining carpals from the lunate would ideally be reduced, but without X-ray, experience, or at least local anesthesia, this is not possible. Symptoms of lunate dislocation would be pain in the wrist, and frequently numbness in the thumb, index, and middle fingers.

There would be pain with any attempt to move the wrist. An abnormal knob on the palm side of the wrist at the crease, when compared to the other wrist, should be obvious to palpation. The numbness described indicates pressure on the median nerve from the dislocated navicular bone, and an attempt at reduction should be made. As shown in figure 17.11 on page 191, with the wrist in extreme dorsiflexion, apply traction while attempting to push the lump back into position. The reduction often is accompanied by an obvious pop.

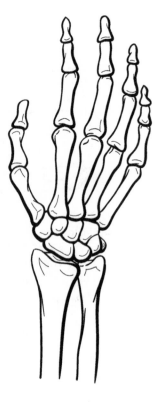

4-10

Figure 17.10
Anatomy of the wrist bones.

Perilunate dislocation will have similar symptoms and signs, with pain of attempted movement of the wrist and possible median nerve compression causing thumb, index finger, and middle finger numbness. The knob will not be present, but there will be a slight deformity of the back side of the wrist, sometimes called a modified silver fork deformity, or hump at the upper side (dorsum) of the wrist. The technique of reduction is similar; apply traction to the wrist and place your thumb firmly over the location of the lunate bone (just beyond the end of the ulna) to hold the lunate in position as the wrist is

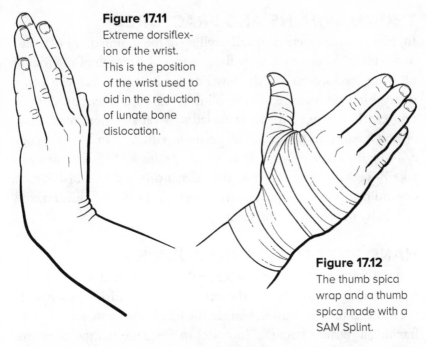

Figure 17.11
Extreme dorsiflex-
ion of the wrist.
This is the position
of the wrist used to
aid in the reduction
of lunate bone
dislocation.

Figure 17.12
The thumb spica
wrap and a thumb
spica made with a
SAM Splint.

then gradually flexed to bring the rest of the carpal bones down into proper position with the lunate and the ends of the radius and ulna. There is generally no snap when this occurs. The numb feeling should wear off within the next hour if the pressure has been removed from the median nerve.

Navicular (scaphoid) fractures will have pain on the thumb side of the wrist, and while the entire wrist will be sore to palpation, it will be particularly sore below the thumb at the wrist. This fracture seldom dislocates, but it often doesn't heal, even after being placed in a tight plaster cast for several months.

After attempting to reduce a dislocation of the wrist or treat the possible fracture of the navicular, splint the wrist and thumb so they are as immobile as possible. While it is not a rigid dressing, a thick wrap using a 2-inch Ace elastic bandage applied in the manner called a thumb spica, as illustrated in figure 17.12, can do well. Under survival conditions, fusion, arthritis, and even loss of median nerve function may have to be accepted. This is a terrible loss that proper orthopedic treatment can almost always avoid. The thumb spica wrap will also be adequate for sprains of the wrist and thumb.

THUMB SPRAINS AND FRACTURES

Injuries causing severe pain and swelling of the thumb may be sprains or fractures. A severe sprain will cause loss of strength of the thumb for many weeks, even months. Swelling can be substantial with either injury. First aid management is splinting until treatment by a physician can be arranged. In an extended survival situation, reduce any obvious deformity and hold in position with a thumb spica wrap, as in figure 17.12 on page 191. Severe sprains and all fractures will take 8 weeks to heal. There is risk of arthritis and loss of function depending upon the injury, patient's age, adequacy of reduction, and suitability of your splinting technique.

HAND FRACTURES AND INJURIES

A hand fracture of the first metacarpal can be treated with a thumb spica wrap that immobilizes the entire wrist. The fifth metacarpal is the most commonly broken bone in the hand. The name given to this fracture, a "boxer's fracture," indicates its frequent method of origin. Perfect reduction of this fracture is not required; in fact, up to 30 degrees of angulation is acceptable. Only 5 to 10 degrees of angulation is acceptable in the third and fourth metacarpals.

Measuring the amount of angulation will be impossible without an X-ray. If you are used to seeing these fractures, before and after X-rays become merely a legal maneuver and are not medically necessary. In a survival situation one may be able to tell if too much angulation has occurred by palpating the palm of the hand. If the nodular head of the metacarpal is felt where it joins the finger, there may be too much angulation. If too much angulation is allowed, a lump in the palm of the hand will make holding tools and objects uncomfortable for the rest of the patient's life. Unacceptable angulation will have to be snapped back into place. Splinting should be maintained in a position of function for 6 weeks.

Finger Fractures and Sprains

Gross lateral or sideways deviations of fingers should be corrected, and the finger splinted in the position of function. These deviations may be corrected by tugging and thus resetting the fracture, or by placing a pencil or similar object between fingers and thus getting leverage to snap a deviated finger shaft back into place. Deviations at the joints probably represent dislocations, and generally these may be easily reduced by the tugging technique. An alternate technique to tugging is to place the dislocated joint into partial flexion; it will then be easier to lever the joint into position.

Swelling associated with "jammed" fingers can become permanent if use of the finger is allowed before adequate healing has taken place. After the acute injury, splinting in the position of function is always appropriate for at least 3 weeks, followed by buddy splinting to the adjacent finger for another 2 to 3 weeks. Fingers should not be splinted straight. Buddy splinting may be used initially if the victim must use the hand immediately, as in gardening, wood cutting, or chores that require all hands on deck.

Ruptured tendons can be repaired generally by splinting in a position of function, with the exception of a rupture of the distal extensor tendon of a finger. This injury is rather common and can be caused by an object hitting the tip of the finger or catching the finger in something (often in a sheet while making a bed). While making beds may not be a problem you expect to encounter, this illustrates how easy the injury may occur. Figure 17.13 illustrates the appearance of this injury, commonly called a mallet finger deformity. The splinting technique for this injury is not the position of function, but as illustrated in figure 17.14.

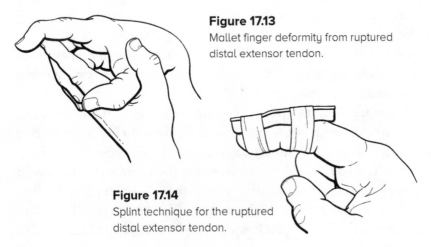

Figure 17.13
Mallet finger deformity from ruptured distal extensor tendon.

Figure 17.14
Splint technique for the ruptured distal extensor tendon.

HIP DISLOCATION AND FRACTURE

Hip injuries are very serious. Tremendous blood loss occurs internally. Fractures of the hip cause pain in the anterior medial aspect (front and side) of the thigh. Dislocations in younger people may be associated with fractures; in older people, fractures are very common and are the probable cause of the deformity. See figure 17.15 on page 195 for positions of fracture and dislocation.

Posterior dislocation of the hip is more common in healthy young adults compared to central fracture/dislocation and anterior hip dislocation. All these injuries are infrequent when compared, for instance, with dislocation of the shoulder. Posterior dislocations can cause injury to the sciatic nerve, the main nerve of the leg. This can cause shooting pains down the back of the leg and/or numbness of the lower leg. It is most important that reduction of the dislocation not be delayed longer than 24 hours. Muscle relaxants and pain medication must be given. To reduce, place the victim on her back with the knee and hip in a 90-degree position. The line of the femur should point vertically upward. The thigh should be pulled steadily upward while simultaneously rotating the femur externally, as shown in figure 17.16 on page 196, then adduct (pull outward from the base) and internally rotate the hip if required.

If possible, evacuate this patient back to the port. For evacuation purposes, pad well and buddy splint to the other leg. This victim is a litter case. Continued pressure on, or severe injury to, the sciatic nerve will cause muscle wasting and loss of sensation to practically the whole leg. This damage must be surgically repaired as soon as possible. In the extreme case of survival without possible repair, brace the affected leg to allow mobility by the victim and take care of numb skin areas to prevent sores and infection.

Central fracture/dislocations result when the head of the femur is driven through the socket into the pelvis. As in all orthopedic injuries, an X-ray is almost essential for the diagnosis. If the fragments can be replaced surgically, this is the treatment of choice. In the extreme survival situation (when there is no hope of medical care for many months), this injury can be left alone and still result in a stable and relatively painless joint. Light traction can be applied to

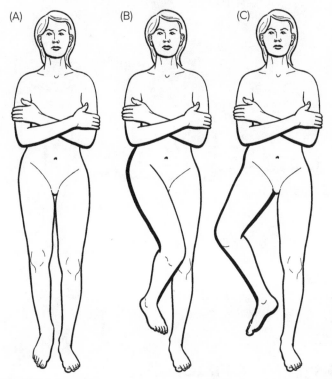

(A)   (B)   (C)

Figure 17.15

(A) Typical appearance of a fractured hip; (B) typical appearance of a posterior hip dislocation; and (C) typical appearance of an anterior hip dislocation.

the lower leg for comfort. After 3 weeks, ambulation with crutches, gradually increasing weight, can be encouraged. Range-of-motion exercises should be started from the beginning to help mold the healing fragments into a relatively smoother joint surface. Sciatic nerve injury should not occur with this injury, but an arthritic joint will result.

Anterior dislocation results from forceful injuries equal to airplane crashes and motorcycle accidents. Examination of the lower leg demonstrates considerable external rotation, or outward tilting, of the foot when the victim is lying on his back. Reduction is as described under posterior dislocation, with traction on the flexed limb but combined with medial rotation (rotating the limb inward rather than outward).

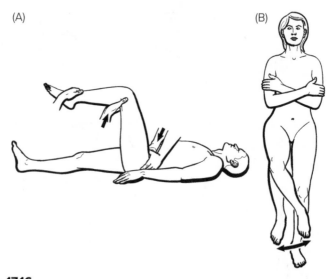

Figure 17.16

Reduction of the posterior hip dislocation, (A) providing upward traction on the hip while flexed to 90 degrees and (B) rotating externally.

THIGH (FEMUR) FRACTURES

Fractures of the thigh (femur) can, of course, occur from the hip to the knee. They are classified and treated by the orthopedic specialist differently according to the location of the break.

First aid treatment consists of treating for shock and immobilizing, initially using hand traction splinting. Start by providing pain relief with gentle hands-on inline traction. Traction splinting is initially helpful, as spasms from the powerful muscles in this region cause considerable overriding of bone fragments, increasing the extent of the injury. Traction also reestablishes the normal length and configuration of the musculature and tightens the membranes that surround the muscle (the fascia), which very importantly decreases the bleeding that occurs with this injury.

The amount of pull required is minimal due to Pascal's law of hydrodynamics. It indicates that any change in pressure applied at any point in the fluid is transmitted undiminished throughout the fluid. As the thigh is a closed cylinder, the massive bleeding that occurs with a fractured femur will have a tamponade applied by lengthening, ever so slightly, the sack of fascia or tissue covering the muscle and broken bone. This elongation of a slight sphere into more of a cylinder reduces the surface area of the sphere into that of a cylinder, but the volume of blood inside remains the same. Thus, through the magic of Pascal's law, there is a significant increase in the deep tamponade on the bleeding bone and muscle tissues with even slight traction. Partial pain relief is the guide by which you will generally know how much pull to exert. This traction is initially performed by pulling on the ankle/foot gently in line, with the patient lying on their back.

The patient should do quite well with simple buddy splinting to the other leg during litter transport. The best traction method for the person in a fixed camp situation is to have them on an adequately padded and comfortable bed with a foot board rigged to accept a sash tied around the ankle with an appropriate tug (about 2 pounds—0.9 kg—of tug). A person kept in bed with a traction splint will be at a higher risk of developing leg blood clots (thrombophlebitis). Initially, bleeding into the leg muscle is your biggest concern. Coupled with severe pain, this can lead to shock. After a few days, bleeding is less of a concern, but developing a blood clot in an immobilized patient is a concern. At that time, it is appropriate to start aspirin 81 mg per day. If you have the 325 mg aspirin, give one initially and then 1 every 2 days.

After the traction splinting period, buddy splint with non-weight-bearing ambulation. A fractured femur will take 8 to 12 weeks to firmly stabilize.

KNEECAP (PATELLA) DISLOCATION

The kneecap (patella) usually dislocates laterally, or to the outside of the knee. This dislocation results in a locking of the knee with a bump to one side, making the diagnosis obvious. Relocate the patella by flexing the hip and the knee. When straightening the knee, the patella usually snaps back into place by itself. If not, just push it back into place while straightening the knee on the next try. Splint with a tube splint (closed-cell foam sleeping pad) with the knee slightly flexed. This patient should be able to walk enough to care for themselves. No further care will be necessary in an emergency situation if professional help cannot be obtained, except physical therapy performed by attaching a light weight (4 pounds—1.8 kg) to the ankle and having the person sit with leg dangling and repeatedly extending the knee. This exercise strengthens the quadriceps muscle, providing the chance for tightening the patella when under actual use stress against the knee joint and allowing less laxity, decreasing the chance of future dislocations. An orthopedic referral for recurrent patella dislocations is appropriate to repair the torn capsule for better ensured stability.

KNEE SPRAINS, DISLOCATIONS, AND FRACTURES

The initial care of sprains, or acute joint injuries, is described on page 168. If the pain in the knee is severe, several diagnoses are possible. There may be tears of ligaments, tendon, cartilage, and/or synovial membranes. There may be associated dislocations or fractures. All you really can assess is the amount of pain that the patient is experiencing, and you have to take his word for that. You can visually assess the amount of swelling or deformity and that might tell the tale, but the most important aspect of care will be handling pain as the patient interprets it.

Have the patient lie as comfortably as possible. Apply RICE (see pages 165–166) to the knee. In case of significant pain and/or swelling, remove the boot (weather permitting) and check the pulse on top of the foot (the dorsal pedal pulse); question the victim about sensation in the feet. Check the dorsal pedal pulse on the opposite side for comparison. If the injury appears minor, this is not necessary.

Significant deformity means that a dislocation may have occurred. Serious disruption of the blood vessels and nerve damage can occur. Check the pulses and check for sensation in the foot. If these are all right, splint the knee as it lies. If not, have a helper hold the lower thigh while you grip the ankle with one hand and the calf with the other. Use inline traction while you gently flex the knee to see if you can reposition it better. If the pain is too great, you meet resistance, or you cannot do it, splint in the most comfortable position and evacuate as soon as possible back to port. If there is no port return possible, then you *must* succeed with reduction technique just described as this may become a limb-threatening situation.

Even without obvious deformity, an immediate complaint, or continuing complaint, about significant pain means that you now have a litter case, and you should make plans accordingly. If in 2 hours, the next morning, or 2 days later, the patient feels better and wishes to walk on the knee, great! Let it happen. You had best remove all weight from the patient's shoulders and provide with a cane. Have the cane used on the side opposite the injury. This places a more natural force vector on the injured joint. And continue the compressive dressing. After 2 days, begin applying heat packs during rest stops and in the evenings. The patient's perception of pain should be the key to managing these injuries, although this approach can be complicated by varying pain thresholds, from macho to wimp.

Knee dislocations are associated with multiple ligament damage, so a period of bracing is warranted and further diagnosis with an MRI should be obtained.

ANKLE SPRAINS, DISLOCATIONS, AND FRACTURES

Generally, fractures of both sides of the ankle are associated with a dislocation. The severe pain associated with the fracture is an early indication that this patient is a litter case. Splint the ankle with a single SAM Splint, or form a trough of Ensolite foam and tape it on. The latter is not a walking splint, but if the pain is significant enough, the patient isn't walking anyway. A flail ankle, caused by complete disruption of the ankle ligaments, readily slops back into position and can be held in place with a trough splint of Ensolite padding.

Allow the patient to rest after the injury, before attempting to walk on the ankle. If there is severe pain, it might be broken or badly sprained. Either way, if the pain is too severe, the patient won't be walking—at least not until it quiets down. As with the knee, if the pain diminishes enough for the victim to walk, allow him to do so without carrying equipment but let him use a cane.

FOOT INJURIES

Stubbed toes can be buddy splinted to provide pain relief. If they have been stubbed to the extent that they deviate at crazy angles sideways, they should be repositioned before buddy taping. Place a pencil (or a similar-width object) on the side opposite the bend and use it as a fulcrum to help snap the toe back into alignment. Blood under the toenail can be treated, as described on pages 155–156.

Severe pain in the arch of the foot or in the metatarsals can represent fractures or sprains. Apply RICE as described above. Allowing a little time to lapse before use might result in decreased pain in minor injuries, but it would take weeks for a fracture to decrease in severity. Reduce the patient's weight-load and provide a cane. If the foot swells to the extent that the boot cannot be placed on the foot, consider cutting it along the sides and taping the boot circumferentially around the ankle to hold it on. This provides support for the foot and ankle.

CHEST INJURIES

Broken ribs may develop after a blow to the chest. Even a severe cough or sneeze can crack ribs! Broken ribs have point tenderness or exquisite pain with the lightest touch over the fracture site. The pain at this site will be reproduced by squeezing the rib cage in such a manner as to put a stress across the fracture site. Deep breathing will also produce pain at that location.

It is not necessary to strap or band the chest, except that such a band might prevent some rib movement and make the patient more comfortable. It is very important for the patient to breathe and have some cough reflex to aid in pulmonary hygiene, namely to prevent the accumulation of fluid in the lungs, which can rapidly lead to pneumonia. For that reason, emergency departments do not discharge patients with compression rib belts. However, if I fracture a rib, I will definitely want one. Simply tying a large towel or undershirt around the victim's chest should suffice. A fractured rib will take 6 to 8 weeks to heal. A similar pain may be initially present due to a tear of the intercostal muscles or separation of cartilage from the bone of the rib near the sternum or breastbone. These problems are treated as above. They heal much more quickly, generally in 3 to 5 weeks.

If several adjacent ribs are broken in more than one location, a section of the chest wall is literally detached and held in place by the muscles and skin. This section of the chest wall can bulge out when the patient exhales instead of contracting as the chest would normally do. It can also move in when the rest of the chest expands during inhalation. This paradoxical motion of the chest wall is called a flail chest. Treatment includes placing an adequately sized rolled cloth against the flail portion to stabilize the motion. This cloth roll will have to be bound in place.

Treat all of the aforementioned conditions with pain medication, as described on page 34. Avoid unnecessary movement. Have the patient hold his hand or a soft object against his chest when coughing to prevent rib movement and decrease the pain. Allow the patient to assume the most comfortable position, which is usually sitting up. If a fever starts, treat with an antibiotic such as Levaquin, 750 mg once daily.

Broken ribs usually heal well even though considerable movement seems to occur due to breathing or even flailing of the chest. They are always so painful that patients feel like they might puncture a lung at any minute. This does not usually happen, but if it does, there is a chance that air will leak into the chest cavity, causing a pneumothorax. This can lead to significant respiratory distress, including cyanosis (blue discoloration of the skin due to inadequate oxygen in the blood). Crepitation can form in the skin. This is a crackling sensation that is very noticeable to the examiner when running the fingers over the skin (called subcutaneous emphysema in medical texts) in the upper part of the chest. It is not painful, but it indicates that air leakage and a pneumothorax have occurred. A pneumothorax can resolve on its own or it can expand, causing death. Similarly, bleeding into lung tissue can result in a hemothorax, which can either resolve on its own or progress to death. Cyanosis (bluish discoloration of the skin) with difficult breathing may be due to this condition. There is nothing you can do for this, unless you are trained in its management.

CHAPTER 18

BITES AND STINGS

Stings from bees, wasps, yellow jackets, hornets (members of the Hymenoptera family), and fire ants produce lesions that hurt instantly, and the pain lingers. The danger comes from the fact that some persons are "hypersensitive" to the venom and can go into immediate, life-threatening anaphylactic shock.

The pain of the sting can be alleviated by almost anything applied to the skin surface. Best choices are cold compresses, hydrocortisone 1% cream, or the triple antibiotic with pramoxine ointment from the Topical Bandaging Kit. Oral pain medication, or stronger injection pain medications, can be given as necessary. Delayed swelling can be prevented and/or treated with oral antihistamines such as diphenhydramine, 25 mg taken 4 times daily, from the Non-Rx Oral Medication Kit.

A generalized rash, asthmatic attack, or shock occurring within 2 hours of a sting indicates anaphylaxis, which requires special management.

ANAPHYLACTIC SHOCK

While most commonly due to insect stings, anaphylactic shock may result from a serious allergic reaction to medications, shellfish, and other foods—in fact, to anything to which one has become profoundly allergic. Some nonstinging insect bites can also produce anaphylactic shock, like bites from the cone-nosed beetle (a member of the Reduviidae family), which can be found in California and throughout Central and South America. We are not born sensitive to these things but can become allergic with repeated exposures. Those developing anaphylaxis generally have warnings of their severe sensitivity in the form of welts (urticaria) forming all over the body immediately after exposure, the development of an asthmatic attack with respiratory wheezing, or the onset of symptoms of shock.

While these symptoms normally develop within 2 hours and certainly before 12 hours, this deadly form of shock can begin within seconds of exposure. It cannot be treated as indicated in the section on "normal" shock on page 15. The antidote for anaphylactic shock is a prescription drug called epinephrine (Adrenalin). It is available for emergency use in vials or the special automatic injectable syringe called the EpiPen® (see figure 18.1 on page 205). Automatic injection syringes are quite expensive. Vials of epinephrine and multidose bottles are less expensive but will require an accurate small-barrel (1 cc) syringe to properly measure and inject. The normal dose for an adult is 0.3 cc of the 1:1000 epinephrine solution given IM (in the muscle). This is quite easy to do, and even if a dose larger than 0.3 cc is administered (even twice that dose), it will cause no harm when treating anaphylaxis or an asthma emergency. While it is not necessary to treat the itchy, generalized rash, the epinephrine should be given if the voice becomes husky (signifying swelling of the airway) and if wheezing or shock occurs. This injection may have to be repeated in 15 to 20 minutes if the symptoms return. The EpiPen Jr.® is available for use in patients weighing less than 66 pounds (30 kg) as the proper the dose is then 0.15 cc of the same solution.

Antihistamines are of no value in treating the shock or asthmatic component of anaphylaxis, but they can help prevent delayed allergic reactions. If you have oral or injectable dexamethasone Decadron, give a 4 mg tablet or 4 mg injection for long-term protection, as each dose of this medication lasts approximately 12 hours.

If possible, evacuate anyone experiencing anaphylactic reactions even though they have responded to the epinephrine. They are at risk of the condition returning, and they should be monitored carefully over the next 24 hours. People can die of anaphylaxis very quickly, even in spite of receiving aggressive medical support in a hospital emergency department. Beyond 24 hours, they are no longer at risk of an anaphylactic reaction. If the patient is still alive after that time, vital signs are stable, and there is no manifestation of anaphylaxis, the evacuation can be terminated.

Use of Epipen

The EpiPen is an auto-injection system with two injection units available per box. It is available in adult and child doses. Using the EpiPen involves the following three simple steps:

1. Pull off the blue safety cap.

2. Place the orange tip on the outer thigh, halfway between the hip and knee (lateral side), preferably against the skin, but it can be used through thin clothing.

3. Push the unit against the thigh until it clicks, and hold it in place for a count of 10.

Due to the high cost of this device, I suggest your physician prescribe vials of epinephrine and appropriate syringes for administration. Vials are sealed glass containers or runner stopper seal vials. The glass vial system will require etching the ampule neck with a glass cutter and then snapping it off. Some glass vials are marked as pre-etched, only requiring them to be carefully snapped. I always snap these vials cuddled in a thin towel. Draw the fluid up in a small-gauge needle and give the shot intramuscularly.

Figure 18.1
The EpiPen is used to treat severe allergic reactions.

Snake Bites

IDENTIFYING COMMON NORTH AMERICAN POISONOUS SNAKES

Sailors do make landfalls periodically, and often this can be on remote beaches with their own specific dangers. Encountering a poisonous snake may be one of them. With regard to the visual identification of the most common poisonous snakes in North America, pit vipers take their name from the deep pit, a heat-receptor organ, between each eye and nostril. Most of them have triangular heads and catlike vertical elliptical pupils.

Coral snakes (*Micrurus fulvius*, family Elapidae), while not pit vipers, also have vertical elliptical pupils. Some nonpoisonous snakes do as well. Color variations in coral snakes make the old saying "red-on-yellow can kill a fellow, red-on-black, venom lack" a very treacherous method of identification. This is particularly true in Central and South America. Coral snake bites should be treated as described under Neurotoxic Snake Bites, below.

The essential steps in treating snake bites are as follows: calm the victim, cause no additional harm, decide about evacuation urgency, and arrange for appropriate long-term wound care. The field first aid care of snake bites differs for nonpoisonous snakes, pit vipers (including rattlesnakes, cotton-mouth/water moccasins, and copperheads—the family Crotalidae), and neurotoxic snakes (coral snakes, cobras, green mambas, kraits, and all poisonous Australian snakes—the family Elapidae). That being said, the actual first aid care is easy to accomplish and will generally depend on where geographically the snake bite occurs. Treat North American pit viper snake bites without compression, and treat snake bites received elsewhere as neurotoxic bites requiring compression and immobilization, as indicated below.

Regardless of the type of snake bite, the first step is to calm the patient and treat for shock. How do you calm a person who has just been bitten by a snake? Not surprisingly, just telling him to remain calm won't work. In a remote area when something terrible has happened, it's only your actions and demeanor that will provide comfort. Depending on the individual, you may need to treat for shock immediately, as described on page 15.

All snake bites are puncture wounds, and nonpoisonous bites and "dry" North American pit viper bites should be treated as indicated in the puncture wound section on page 143. Studies indicate that 20% of eastern diamondback rattlesnake bites, and 30% of cotton-mouth water moccasin bites, are dry, which means no venom has been injected into the victim.

SIGNS AND SYMPTOMS OF PIT VIPER BITE

What are the signs and symptoms of envenomation from pit vipers? The first symptom noted by many is a peculiar tingling in the mouth, often associated with a rubbery or metallic taste. This symptom may develop in minutes and long before any swelling occurs at the bite site. Envenomation may produce instant burning pain. Weakness, sweating, nausea, and fainting may occur either with poisonous or nonpoisonous snake bites, due simply to the trauma of being bitten. In case of envenomation, within 1 hour there will generally be swelling, pain, tingling, and/or numbness at the bite site. As several hours pass, bruising (ecchymosis) and discoloration of the skin begin and become progressively worse. Blisters may form, which are sometimes filled with blood. Chills and fever may begin, followed by muscle tremor, decrease in BP, headache, blurred vision, and bulging eyes. The surface blood vessels may fill with blood clots (thromboses), and this can, in turn, lead to significant tissue damage after several days.

TREATMENT OF PIT VIPER BITE

For rattlesnakes, copperheads, and water moccasins (family Crotalidae), treat for shock and calm the patient as indicated earlier. Remove any constricting objects such as rings. Immobilize the injured part at heart level. And evacuate if you can.

It has been said that the best snake bite kit is a set of car keys. The reason is that envenomation can make a person very ill (on average seven people die yearly in North America from these bites), and it can cause serious tissue damage that is best treated with antivenin. There is a golden hour and a half before North American pit viper venom causes significant generalized effects that might make the victim nonambulatory. The return to port should be performed in a calm but urgent manner. If a nearby land-based facility is apparent, then walking toward that location is appropriate, but if the patient becomes ill you may have to carry him and that is obviously quite difficult. Take the shortest distance or time to help, either sailing or overland.

Do not apply compression or a tourniquet to the swelling associated with this type of bite because the venom causes considerable tissue damage from squeezing blood vessels, and further compression makes this effect worse. Do not apply ice, as this results in increased local tissue destruction. Avoid the use of a constricting band between the bite site and the heart, as this has never been shown to be effective and there is a real danger of its being applied too tightly, resulting in a tourniquet effect that increases tissue destruction.

If there is no ready access to professional help, treat as indicated earlier with immobilization with the injured part at heart level. As most bites are dry bites, or partial venom loads, this may be all that one needs to do. If locale swelling starts, slightly elevate the limb hoping to decrease pressure within the limb. Trunk and facial bites, while rare, are even more of a challenge. Treat for shock, prevent hypothermia, and provide Tylenol for pain, avoiding aspirin and anti-inflammatory medications. While the use of steroids is not required in a hospital setting, without access to care the use of steroids (Decadron 4 mg every 12 hours for 3 days) probably reduces inflammation.

NEUROTOXIC SNAKE BITES

Coral snakes, all Australian snakes, and most African, Indian, and South American snakes (most in family Elapidae) are all capable of injecting neurotoxins into their victim's system with their bite. In 1979, Australia adopted pressure/immobilization as the first aid treatment for the very dangerous snakes found on that continent and dropped their yearly death rate from snake bite to virtually zero. In Australia the wound is not washed prior to wrapping, as special "Venom Detection Kits" are available at hospitals that can identify the snake from venom in the wound. The wound is not manipulated in any way; instead, pressure/immobilization is applied immediately as indicated in figure 18.2. The pressure dressing works to slow down the venom from migrating into the main body, allowing time for the antivenom to be acquired. Without antivenom, treat the patient for shock and try to maintain breathing with respiration-assisted breathing (see page 17), but there is not anything else you can do. If you are bitten on the shores of Australia, India, or South America, poisonous animal encounters add a whole level of risk (also read below concerning neurotoxic venom). The best first aid care for a neurotoxic envenomation is the use of pressure immobilization described in figure 18.2 on page 209.

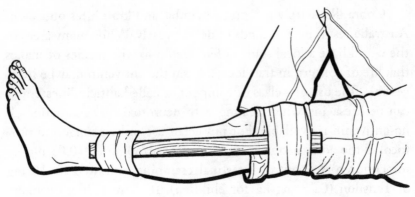

Figure 18.2
How to apply pressure/immobilization for neurotoxic snake bites:
(A) Apply a broad pressure bandage over the bite site as soon as possible. Do not take off clothing, as any movement helps the venom enter the bloodstream.
(B) The elastic bandage should be as tight as you would apply to a sprained ankle.
(C) Extend the bandage as high as possible, wrapping over clothing if necessary.
(D) Apply a splint to the leg.
(E) Bind the splint to as much of the leg as possible.
(F) Bites on hand or forearm: (1) bind to elbow with bandage; (2) splint to elbow; (3) use sling.

TREATMENT OF CORAL SNAKE BITE

North American coral snakes envenomate by a slow chewing process, so that a rapid withdrawal from the attack may result in no envenomation. For treatment: (1) treat for shock as necessary; (2) wash the bitten area promptly to possibly remove some venom; (3) make no incisions; (4) apply pressure/immobilization; and (5) evacuate to a hospital if possible. Since the coral snake is an elapid, like the cobra, signs and symptoms of envenomation take time to develop and deterioration then proceeds so rapidly that the antidote may be of no avail. Without evacuation possibility, after initial care of wound as above, allow the victim to rest with adequate protection from the environment. Just leave the compression dressing on, making sure that it is not acting as a tourniquet. If severe pulmonary symptoms develop, see paragraph below. Provide breathing assistance as long as possible.

Cobra, Russell's viper, green mamba, and krait bites outside of Australia result in thousands of deaths yearly. While many areas of the world have a local source of antivenin for the species of snakes that are of concern in that locale, often the antivenin may be inaccessible. The use of a class of compounds called anticholinesterases can be lifesaving when dealing with neurotoxic envenomations if no antivenin is available. For physician use only, a suggested protocol is the administration of 0.6 mg of atropine IV (0.05 mg/kg for children) to control intestinal cramping, followed by 10 mg of Tensilon (0.25 mg/kg for children). If there is improvement, further control of symptoms can be obtained by titration of a dose of neostigmine, 0.025 mg/kg/hour by IV injection or continuous infusion. These medications are not included in the recommended Rx Injectable Kit.

SPIDER BITES

Generally, spiders will make a solitary bite, not several. If you wake with multiple bites, you have probably collided with some other arthropod. While only some spiders are considered poisonous, all spiders have venom that can cause local tissue inflammation and even slight necrosis or destruction. Most spiders are unable to bite well enough to inject the venom.

Black Widow Spider

The black widow (*Latrodectus mactans*) is usually glossy black with a red hourglass mark on the abdomen. Sometimes the hourglass mark is merely a red dot, the two parts of the hourglass do not connect, or the coat is not shiny and it may contain white. The bite may only be a pinprick, but generally a dull cramping pain begins at the site within 15 minutes, which may spread gradually until it involves the entire body. The muscles may go into spasms and the abdomen becomes board-like. Extreme restlessness is typical. The pain can be excruciating. Nausea, vomiting, swelling of eyelids, weakness, anxiety (naturally), and pain on breathing may all develop. A healthy adult can usually survive, with the pain abating in several hours and the remaining symptoms disappearing in several days.

An ice cube on the bite, if available, may reduce local pain. A specific treatment for relieving muscle spasm is methocarbamol (Robaxin), 100 mg given as a bolus into an IV line at 1 ml/min. After the initial bolus, a constant infusion of 200 mg/hr IV, or 500 mg by mouth every 6 hours, can be used. This medication has not been included in the Ship's Medicine Chest, but adequate pain relief can be given by using medications from the Non-Rx Oral Medication Kit, or Norco-10/325.

Similar spiders are found throughout the world. The South African knoppie, the New Zealand katipo, and the Australian red black spider bites have the same symptoms and can all be treated as described earlier. A specific antivenin is available in those countries.

Brown Recluse Spider

A brown coat with a black violin marking on the cephalothorax, or top part, identifies the brown recluse spider (*Loxosceles reclusa*). The initial bite is mild and may be overlooked at the time. In an hour or two, a slight redness may appear; by several hours, a small bleb appears at the bite site. Sometimes the wound appears as a bull's eye with several rings of red and blanched circles around the bite. The bleb ruptures, forming a crust, which then sloughs off; a large necrotic ulcer forms, gradually enlarging. Over the first 36 hours, vomiting, fever, skin rash, and joint pain may develop, and hemolysis of the blood may be massive.

Apply ice to the wound as soon as possible. Dapsone, 100 mg twice daily (a medication used in the treatment of leprosy), has been used, but its effectiveness is unlikely. Dapsone, once thought to be effective during the early stages of treatment to decrease the severity of the inflammation, is not included as a routine component of the Rx Medical Kit. Prophylactic use of antibiotics does no good. Avoid the application of heat to this wound, even though it is inflamed and necrotic.

Give ibuprofen, 200 mg, 4 tablets every 6 hours, to help with pain and to reduce inflammation. From the Rx Oral/Topical Kit, give Decadron, 4 mg every 6 hours. It is doubtful that steroid therapy is of benefit after 24 hours. Apply triple antibiotic ointment from the Topical Bandaging Kit and cover with gel dressing.

TICKS

More vector-borne diseases are transmitted in the United States by ticks than by any other agent (see table 19.1 on page 222). Ticks must have blood meals to survive their various transformations. It is during these meals that disease can be transmitted to humans and other animals.

Two families of ticks can transmit disease to humans: the Ixodidae, or hard ticks, and the Argasidae, or soft ticks. The lifecycle of the hard tick takes two years to complete: from the egg to the six-legged larva or seed tick, the eight-legged immature nymph, and finally the eight-legged mature adult. They must remain attached for hours to days while obtaining their blood meal. Disease will not be transferred if the tick can be removed before 24 hours. The soft ticks can live many years without food. They have several nymphal stages and may take multiple blood meals. They usually stay attached less than 30 minutes. Of the soft ticks, only the genus *Ornithodoros* transmit disease in the United States, namely relapsing fever. The 24-hour rule does not apply in this case.

Prevention of attachment is the best defense against tick-borne disease. DEET insect repellents are very effective against ticks. Permethrin 0.5% spray-treated clothing kills ticks upon contact, and remains active on clothing for 2 weeks. Then it's probably about time to wash those camping clothes anyway and respray them. The combination of permethrin on clothing and DEET on skin is 100% effective against tick attachment.

OK, so you didn't follow my advice and you find a tick attached. How do you remove it? A tried-and-true method is to grasp the skin around the insertion of the tick with a pair of fine-point tweezers and pull straight outward, removing the tick and a chunk of skin. For some reason this doesn't hurt. A recent study has shown the effectiveness of three products on the market in the United States, sold under the brand names of the Original Ticked Off, the Pro-Tick Remedy, and the tick plier, which is also sold under the name Tick Nipper. Hot wires, matches, glue, fingernail polish, Vaseline—none of them work. Burning the tick might cause it to vomit germs right into the victim, yet it will not let go. Be careful not to grasp the tick body—crushing it might also cause germs to be injected into the victim.

CATERPILLAR REACTIONS
The puss caterpillar (*Megalopyge opercularis*) of the southern United States and the gypsy moth caterpillar (*Lymantria dispar*) of the Northeast have bristles that cause an almost immediate skin rash and welt formation. Treatment includes patting the victim with a piece of adhesive tape to remove the bristles. Further treatment is discussed on pages 158–159 (Skin Rash).

MILLIPEDE REACTIONS
Millipedes do not bite, but contact can cause skin irritation. Cold packs can reduce discomfort. Wash thoroughly and treat as indicated on pages 158–159.

CENTIPEDE BITES
Some larger centipedes can inflict a painful bite that causes local swelling and a painful red lesion. Treatment with a cold pack is usually sufficient. Some bites are severe and regional lymph node enlargement may occur, which will be a swelling of the nodes generally at the joints along the blood flow pattern toward the heart from the bite site. Swelling at the bite location may persist for weeks. Adequate treatment consists of pain medication. Infiltration of the area with lidocaine 1% from the Rx Injectable Kit provides instant relief and is justified in severe cases.

MOSQUITOES
You have arrived at that secluded harbor on the perfect tropical island. Enjoying a solid-ground campout on shore, you begin to notice the mosquitoes. What are your options, other than heading back out to sea?

Mosquitos "see" by three different mechanisms: chemical sensors, visual spectrum, and infrared sensors. Countering these we can use three protective strategies to prevent their bites: behavioral, barrier, and chemical.

Behavior techniques are the least known, yet are very important. You produce a carbon dioxide plume that travels up to 150 feet (48 m) depending upon the wind speed. If you can camp where the wind blows your plume into a lake as opposed to the forest, you will decrease mosquito bites. Once they pick up your plume, they will then in turn use visual spectrum to locate brightly color flower mimics. Avoid Hawaiian shirts when camping! Wear white or light colors. The green of a Scout uniform is ok. Wear long sleeve shirts, long pants and socks—all treated with permethrin. Once closer to you, they activate their chemical sensors to detect the byproduct of your oil gland secretions being degraded by common skin bacteria. The highest bacteria content on your skin is located in your armpits and on your feet. Keeping clean decreases this smell and decreases bites significantly. When very near to you they turn on their infrared sensor and home in on the juiciest place to successfully chomp and get that delicious human blood meal. Sounds like a scary campfire story, but it is true. You are surrounded by tiny insect vampires that want to turn you into—if not the living dead—real dead people with some of these diseases. It has been estimated that simply using the above techniques can decrease mosquito bites by 85%.

And third, we come to what most people regard as their primary means of suppressing insect bites: chemical. Treating your clothing before a trip with 0.5% permethrin, a chrysanthemum derivative, is 100% effective to prevent tick bites. A tick crawls around on you before attaching. Treating clothing, including socks and underwear solves tick disease problems. A single clothing treatment lasts for 6 weeks. Mosquitos require additional skin protection for bite prevention. Generally, this can be achieved with 20% picaridin or DEET in concentrations of 30%, repeated as required. Lemon eucalyptus in 30% concentrations works almost as well. Other herbals, wrist bands, and electronic devices, do not match the effectiveness of those products.

The best mosquito repellent invented to date has been DEET (*n,n* diethyl-m-toluamide). This product has undergone a revolution since it was developed in 1946, ranging from the earliest preparations of 12% strength to numerous products marketing 100% DEET concentration. Between 10% and 15% of DEET applied to the skin surface is excreted in the user's urine. This fact, coupled with a few reports of convulsions in children using DEET, generally when also simultaneously sunburned, indicates we should probably minimize the total amount placed on the skin.

I never use 100% DEET except to soak either my head netting or a "bug jacket." Bug jackets are a very loose weave of cotton fabric that soaks up DEET. The loose weave allows air circulation, which is a real lifesaver during hot, mosquito-laden summer days. Buy one with a hood. Avoid buying the tight "no-see-um proof" mosquito suits, as you can sweat to death in them. Even during monstrous mosquito moments, it is possible to be relatively comfortable in a treated bug jacket. The hood can be pulled over your head when you are eating, and your cup or bowl brought very near your face so that you can gulp down food that is relatively free of mired insects (except for those that fall into the pot during the cooking process). Treat the bug jacket by pouring 100% DEET into a ziplock plastic bag and soaking the jacket overnight. Rather than wearing tight-weave net pants, I find it best to treat my trousers with permethrin, as indicated earlier, and my ankles or exposed legs with the DEET.

Picaridin in 20% strength provides relatively good black fly and mosquito protection for up to 8 hours.

Adequate mosquito netting for the head and for the tent or cot while sleeping is essential. Spraying netting and clothing with 0.5% permethrin increases the effectiveness of the netting and decreases bug bites enormously. Permethrin is an insecticide, not a repellent. It kills mosquitoes, ticks, black flies, and the like, and does not simply chase them away. It will not work if applied to the skin, as an enzyme in the skin destroys it. Not only is there no absorption through the skin, it is safe to use on both natural and synthetic fibers.

Vitamin B1 (thiamine) is not an effective preventative oral agent. Electronic sound devices to repel these critters have never dented mosquito buzzing or biting enthusiasm in the far north in my experience.

A considerable number of bites, or sensitivity to bites, may require an antihistamine, such as diphenhydramine, 25 mg capsules every 6 hours, from the Non-Rx Oral Medication Kit. Triple antibiotic ointment with pramoxine applied every 6 hours can provide local itch relief, but that is only due to the pramoxine component. Triple antibiotic ointment by itself is of no value. From the Rx Oral/Topical Kit, use Topicort 0.25% ointment twice daily, or Lanacane® cream.

BLACK FLIES

DEET compounds will work on black flies, but the concentration must be 30% or greater, and even the pure formula will work only a short time. It is best to use a specific black fly repellent.

For years, Skin So Soft, a bath oil marketed by your local Avon representative, has been mentioned as a black fly repellent. It does work, but only poorly and requires frequent applications, approximately every 15 minutes.

Netting and heavy clothes that can be sealed at the cuffs may be required. All black fly species like to land and crawl, worming their way under and through protective clothing and netting. Spray clothing and netting with 0.5% permethrin as mentioned in the section on mosquitoes.

Black fly bites can result in nasty sores that are usually self-limited, although at times slow healing. If infection is obvious, treat as indicated in the section on skin infection on page 157. Treat symptoms as indicated under Mosquitoes above.

NO-SEE-UMS AND BITING GNATS

These two examples of insect life are the scourge of the North Country, or any country in which they may be found. Many local people refer to any small black fly as a "no-see-um," but the true bug by that name is indeed very hard to see. They usually come out on a hot, sticky night. The attack is sudden and feels like fire over your entire exposed body surface area. Under the careful examination of a flashlight, you will notice an incredibly small gnat struggling with its head down, merrily chomping away. Make that bug portion of the previous sentence plural, please. You may need to resort to a strong DEET product of 35% or greater. Immersion in cold water will help relieve symptoms temporarily. One remedy for the sting, which I understand works quite well but have never had along to try, is an application of Absorbine Jr.!

Gnats, on the other hand, are small black flies whose bite is seldom felt. But these gentle biters leave behind red, pimple-like lesions to remind you of their visit. A rash of these pimples around the neck and ankles attests to their ability to sneak through protective clothing. Treat bites as described under Mosquitoes above. Without a head net or treated hooded bug jacket, hordes of gnats can suffocate you. Treat clothing with permethrin and a bug jacket with 100% DEET, as described in the section about mosquitoes.

SCORPION STINGS

Most North American scorpion stings are relatively harmless. Stings usually cause only localized pain and slight swelling. The wound may feel numb. Diphenhydramine, 25 mg 4 times daily, and Percogesic, 2 tablets every 4 hours, may be all that is required for treatment. A cold pack will help relieve local pain.

The potentially lethal *Centruroides sculpturatus* is the exception to this rule. This yellow-colored scorpion lives in Mexico, New Mexico, Arizona, and on the California side of the Colorado River. The sting causes immediate, severe pain with swelling and subsequent numbness. The neurotoxin injected with this bite may cause respiratory failure. Respiratory assistance may be required (see page 19). Tapping the wound lightly with your finger will cause the patient to withdraw due to severe pain. This is an unusual reaction and does not occur with most insect stings. A specific antivenin is available in Mexico and is also produced by the Poisonous Animals Research Laboratory at Arizona State University for local use.

In addition to the antivenin, atropine may be needed to reduce muscle cramping, blurred vision, hypertension, respiratory difficulty, and excessive salivation. Methocarbamol may be given, as described in the section on black widow spider bites (pages 210–211). Neither of these medications is included in the Prescription Kit. Narcotics such as Demerol and morphine can increase the toxicity and should be avoided. Percogesic from the Non-Rx Oral Medical Kit may be safely given.

ANTS/FIRE ANTS

While many ants alert you to their presence with a burning bite, fire ants can produce an intensely painful bite that pales the bite of any other ant—and many other bugs—to insignificance. While holding on tightly with a biting pincer and pivoting around, the fire ant stings repeatedly in as many places as the stinger can reach, causing a cluster of small, painful blisters to appear. These can take 8 to 10 days to heal. Treatment is with cold packs and pain medication. Large local reactions may require use of an antihistamine such as diphenhydramine, 25 mg, 2 capsules every 6 hours, or even Decadron, 4 mg twice daily. Local application of Spenco 2nd Skin can provide some relief. Treat with pain medication as required.

The greatest danger is to the hypersensitive individual who may go into anaphylactic shock (see pages 203–205).

AQUATIC STINGS, CUTS, AND RASH

Sea Urchin
Punctures from sea urchin spines cause severe pain and burning. Besides trauma from the sharp spines, some species inject venom. The wound can appear red and swollen, or even blue to black from harmless dye that may be contained in the spines. Generalized symptoms are rare but may include weakness, numbness, muscle cramps, nausea, and occasionally shortness of breath.

The spines should be removed thoroughly, a very tedious process. Very thin spines may be absorbed by the body without harm, but some may form reactive tissue around them (granulomas) several months later. Spines may migrate into joints and cause pain and inhibit movement, or lodge against a nerve and cause extreme pain. The discoloration of the dye causes no problems but may be mistaken for a thin spine. Relief may be obtained by soaking in hot water (110°F to 113°F or 43°C to 45°C) for 20 to 30 minutes. Vinegar or acetic acid soaks several times a day may help dissolve spines that are not found. Evacuation and treatment by a physician is also advisable if possible.

JELLYFISH
An extensive number of species of jellyfish in the world pose varying degrees of danger to people. Jellyfish tentacles in contact with human skin can cause mild pricking to burning, shooting, terrible pain. The worst danger is shock and drowning.

Pouring vinegar on the wound (4 to 6% acetic acid) inhibits the venom from being fired into the skin. Alcohol (or ideally formalin) poured over the wound may also prevent the nematocysts from firing more poison. Avoid the use of hot water in treating this injury, as water of any temperature activates the nematocysts. Try to remove the tentacles with gloved hands.

Powder the area with a dry powder such as flour or baking powder. Gently scrape off the mess with a knife, clamshell, or other sharp instrument, but avoid cutting the nematocysts with a sharp blade. Apply hydrocortisone 1% cream 4 times daily from the Topical Bandaging Kit, or Topicort 0.25% ointment twice daily from the Rx Oral/Topical Kit for inflammation. Severe stings can be treated with pressure/immobilization. Provide rescue breathing as required.

CORAL STINGS

These injuries are treated as indicated under Jellyfish.

Coral and Barnacle Cuts

Clean the wound thoroughly. Trivial wounds can later flare into real disasters that may go on for years. Scour thoroughly with a coarse cloth or soft brush and surgical scrub or soapy water. Then apply hydrogen peroxide to help bubble out fine particles and bacteria. Apply triple antibiotic ointment from the Topical Bandaging Kit. Manage this wound as discussed in the section on laceration care, page 124 (the Bleeding Wound). If an infection ensues, treat as indicated on pages 157–158 (Cellulitis).

Stingray

The damage is done by the stingray's barbed tail, which lacerates the skin, embedding pieces of tail material and venom into the wound. The wound bleeds heavily; pain increases over 90 minutes and takes 6 to 48 hours to abate.

Immediately rinse the wound with seawater and remove any particles of the tail sheath that are visible, as these particles continue to release venom. Hot water is the treatment of choice, applied as soon as possible and as hot as the patient can stand it (110°F to 113°F or 43°C or 45°C). The heat will destroy the toxin rapidly and remove the pain that the patient is experiencing. After hot water has been applied and all tail particles removed, the wound may be closed with taping techniques (see page 135). Elevation of the wound is important. If particularly dirty, leave the wound open and continue to use intermittent hot soaks as described on page 157.

Questionably dirty wounds should be treated with Levaquin, 750 mg daily, or doxycycline, 100 mg twice daily, from the Rx Oral/Topical Medication Kit. As these are nasty, painful wounds, treat for shock from the onset.

Catfish

Apply hot water as indicated under Stingray. The wound, caused by a puncture from one of its whiskers protruding from near its mouth, must be properly cleaned and irrigated using surgical scrub, if available, or soap. Place the patient on oral antibiotics for several days to decrease the chance of wound infection, which is common with this injury. Treat an infected wound as described on page 157.

Scorpion Fish

Scorpion fish spines have poisonous venom located in their fins, which usually cause wounds when unwary individuals step on them or otherwise accidentally contact them with their hands. Use the same treatment as under Stingray.

Sponge Rash

Sponges handled directly from the ocean can cause an allergic reaction that appears immediately. Fine spicules may also break off in the outer layer of skin, causing inflammation. It will be difficult to tell whether your victim is suffering from the allergic reaction or the spicules, or both. Soak the affected skin by applying vinegar to a cloth and covering for 15 minutes. Dry the skin and pat with the adhesive side of tape to remove sponge spicules. Again, soak in vinegar for 5 minutes. An application of rubbing alcohol for 1 minute has been suggested. Then apply hydrocortisone 1% cream 4 times a day from the Topical Bandaging Kit, or Topicort 0.25% ointment twice daily from the Rx Oral/Topical Medication Kit for several days, until the inflammation subsides.

CHAPTER 19

INFECTIOUS DISEASE

DIAGNOSIS OF INFECTIOUS DISEASES

There are three things that will prevent success in treating an infection. One is not having the correct diagnosis, so the proper antibiotic or other management is not used. The second is having a correct diagnosis but not having an available medication. The third, the infection becomes overwhelming regardless due to many factors.

Sir William Osler, one of the greatest teachers of medicine, gave a lecture at the Harvard Medical School is which he stated that of the three basic principles of medicine, the most important was diagnosis. After the lecture he was asked, "What are the other two principles?" he answered, "The second is diagnosis, and the third is diagnosis."

Diagnosis of an illness can sometimes be done by noting the time of onset of symptoms when the exposure to the new germs occurred. This is most feasible when you first come into contact with a foreign shore and an illness suddenly appears within your group. Otherwise, after being in an area for more than several months, or when dealing with indigenous people in that area, you are going to rely on knowing what diseases are the most prevalent and evaluate symptoms to work out a probability of what you are treating.

Table 19.1 Onset of Infectious Disease from Time of Exposure

Incubation time less than 2 weeks:

		Usual Incubation Period	Range of Time
1.	Chikungunya	2–4 days	1–14 days
2.	Dengue	4–8 days	3–14 days
3.	Encephalitis	3–14 days	1–20 days
4.	Enteric (typhoid) fever	7–18 days	3–60 days
5.	Acute HIV	10–28 days	10 days—6 weeks
6.	Influenza	1–3 days	1–5 days
7.	Legionellosis	5–6 days	2–10 days
8.	Leptospirosis	7–10 days	2–26 days
9.	Malaria, *P. falciparum*	6–30 days	within 6 months
10.	Malaria, *P. vivax*	8–30 days	within 12 months
11.	Spotted fever rickettsiosis	3 days -2 weeks	within 3 weeks
12.	Zika	3–14 days	14 days

Incubation time 14 days to 6 weeks

13.	Note several above		
14.	Amebic liver abscess	weeks to months	
15.	Hepatitis A	28–30 days	15–50 days
16.	Hepatitis E	26–42 days	2–9 weeks
17.	Schistosomiasis	4–8 weeks	

Incubation time greater than 6 weeks

18.	Note several above		
19.	Hepatitis B	90 days	60–120 days
20.	Leishmaniasis (visceral)	2–10 months	10 days to years
21.	Tuberculosis (TB)	Primary, weeks	Latent, years

So, What Is the Approach to Infectious Disease?

Identify the potential geographical risk of the diseases, where are they lurking? Let us look at the vector that spreads the disease; how do we block it from attacking us? If someone gets ill; how do we identify the most likely cause and what is the best treatment available to us? THAT is what this chapter is about. You can see why it is important in your planning, particularly if you are heading to sea, to study this chapter even before you sail.

Table 19.2 Herd Immunity

	TRANSMISSION	HERD IMMUNITY REQUIRED (%)
Measles	Airborne	92–95
Pertussis (whooping cough)	Airborne droplet	92–94
Diphtheria	Saliva	83–86
Rubella	Airborne droplet	83–86
Smallpox	Airborne droplet	80–86
Polio	Fecal–oral route	80–86
Mumps	Airborne droplet	75–86
SARS	Airborne droplet	50–80
Ebola	Bodily fluids direct contact	33–60
Influenza	Airborne droplet	33–44%
SARS-CoV-2 (COVID-19)	Airborne droplet	? probably 90%

The following tables summarize diseases found in North America and high-risk illnesses encountered in world travel. Table 19.3 on page 224 summarizes the disease of North American and Table 19.4 on page 225 the diseases of the world, areas where you find yourself when leaving your normal harbor. The individual sections of this chapter discuss these diseases in greater detail, including treatments when using the items suggested for the ship's medicine chest. Management of issues such as pain, fever, vector control, water purification, and other preventative measures are covered elsewhere in this book and must be considered important to preventing and managing these diseases.

The roles of having a crew immunized against infectious diseases cannot be overemphasized. Loss of adequate immunization of childhood diseases, resulting in decreased immunization rates have resulted in loss of herd immunity in some communities. If the percentage of a group losses it "herd immunity" above a certain percentage, a single case can spread like wildfire through the entire group, even infecting those who have some immunity due to the overwhelming number of germs that a massive flare in the infection causes. Depending upon how virulent the germ is, how easily it spreads, various levels of immunity must be present to prevent this "wild-fire" spread.

Table 19.3 Significant Diseases of North America

ILLNESS	MODE	PAGE NUMBER
Anaplasmosis tick		226
Babesiosis	tick	226
Blastomycosis	soil	226–228
Coccidioidomycosis	soil	228
Colorado Tick Fever	tick	228–229
Coronavirus		229–230
Echinococcus	water	230–231
Ehrlichiosis	tick	231–232
Encephalitis	mosquito	232
Giardiasis	water	232–233
Hantavirus	rodents/soil	233
Hepatitis A,E	water, food	233–234 & 235
Hepatitis B, C, D, G	blood, sex	234, 235, 236
Lyme Disease	tick	236, 237, 238
Leptospirosis		236
Measles (RubeolA)		239–240
Mumps		240–241
Meningococcal Meningitis	people	240
Plague	rodents/fleas, people	241
Rabies	mammals	241–242
Relapsing Fever	tick	242–243
Rocky Mountain Spotted Fever	tick	243–244
Rubella (German Measles 3 day measles)		244
STARI tick		245
Tetanus	soil	246
Tick Paralysis	tick	246–247
Trichinosis	food	247
Tuberculosis	people	249
Tularemia	tick, fly	250
Typhus, endemic	fleas	251
West Nile Virus	mosquito	252

This is not an all-inclusive list. Also, many of these diseases have worldwide distribution.

Table 19.4 Significant Diseases of the World

ILLNESS	MODE	PAGE NUMBER
Cholera	water	227–228
Chikungunya Fever	mosquito	227
Dengue	mosquito	230
Malaria	mosquito	238
Schistosomiasis	snail/water	244–245
Tapeworms	food/water	245–246
Trypanosomiasis, African	fly	247–248
Trypanosomiasis, American	+	248
Typhoid Fever	water/food	250–251
Typhus, Epidemic	lice	251–252
YellowFever	mosquito	252–253
Zika	mosquito	253

+*See text for vector description.*

It is interesting that some of the most dangerous diseases have a relatively low herd immunity required for the group protection from disease acceleration. Ebola has a high case-fatality rate of 60% to 90% in the case of the Zaire strain and 40% to 60% in the Sudan variety. But for potential number of deaths on the planet, it is hard to beat the danger of influenza. An aggressive strain of influenza could reach a mortality rate of 2.5%, but as the disease spreads easily among non-immune persons, where virtually everyone catches it (unlike Ebola, which no one should catch when implementing simple body fluid precautions), the death toll can be astounding. And we have now witnessed the destruction that a novel, or unfamiliar strain of a virus, such as SARS-CoV-2 can do to the world.

Sometimes herd immunity does not protect you from a disease such as tetanus as you catch this from spores when they enter your body via the skin from the environment and not from another person.

Prevention is simple, basic, and critical. It consists of proper hygiene (washing hands), water sourcing, food preparation and storage, insect protection, and immunizations. Beyond the commonly recommended infant, childhood, and adult immunizations, the sailor should consider typhoid, as it commonly explodes during natural disasters.

Anaplasmosis

Caused by the bacterium *Anaplasma phagocytophilum*, previously known as human granulocytic ehrlichiosis, this has more recently been renamed human granulocytic anaplasmosis. It is transmitted primarily from the black-legged tick (*Ixodes scapularis*) and the western black-legged tick (*Ixodes pacificus*). Symptoms of fever, headache, chills, and muscle aches occur within 1 to 2 weeks of a tick bite. Lab tests can eventually confirm the diagnosis, but symptoms are similar to the other tick-borne diseases. The first-line treatment for adults and children of all ages is doxycycline.

Babesiosis

First discovered in Yugoslavia in 1957, and discovered in the United States in 1968, this malaria-like illness is caused by a protozoan parasite that invades red blood cells. Two species have been identified, *Babesia microti*, causing disease in the northeastern United States, and *B. equi*, causing disease in California. An unidentified species caused this disease in a patient in Washington State. Of the approximately 2,000 cases reported in the United States, 95% were reported by Connecticut, Massachusetts, Minnesota, New Jersey, New York, Rhode Island, and Wisconsin. Tick-borne transmission of Babesia parasites is well established in these states.

Symptoms gradually begin 1 week after a tick bite with fatigue and loss of appetite, giving way in several days to fever, drenching sweats, muscle ache, and headache. The illness ranges from mild to severe, with death occurring in about 10% of patients. Treatment is available with oral quinine plus clindamycin (not included in the recommended medical kit). Protection from tick bites is best accomplished by treating clothing with permethrin (see page 212).

Blastomycosis

This infectious disease is caused by a fungus, *Blastomyces dermatitidis*. Outbreaks usually cluster, with multiple members of a party becoming ill. It is found in the Mississippi River Valley and the southeastern United States. It is also found in various parts of Africa. Wisconsin may have the highest incidence of blastomycosis of any state, with yearly rates ranging from 10 to 40 cases per 100,000 persons in some northern counties. In the United States, it has been associated with beaver lodges and digging in contaminated soil. It can also result from dog bites.

Onset of illness is slowly progressive, usually starting with a cough and developing into pneumonia with fevers, shortness of breath, chest pain, and drenching sweats. The symptoms generally present 3 weeks to 3 months after breathing in the fungal spores.

Infected blood carries the fungus to the skin and other tissues. Skin lesions enlarge with a collapsed center, purplish-red border, and frequent ulcerations.

Treatment is with specific antifungal medications.

Chikungunya Fever

This viral infection is spread by the Aedes mosquito (see Mosquitos, pages 213–216). Not related to dengue fever, it is very similar clinically, with particularly miserable, virtually crippling joint aches, particularly of the ankles, wrists, and hands. Since it mimics dengue and Zika virus, it is best to avoid treating with nonsteroidal anti-inflammatory medications such as ibuprofen or aspirin, as there can be bleeding complications with these diseases. Use Tylenol or Ultram for pain management. The painful effects of this disease can last for months.

Cholera

This intestinal infection, caused by the bacterium *Vibrio cholerae*, produces profuse, cramping diarrhea. Death can come from dehydration; indeed, the death toll can reach the tens of thousands during an epidemic. Ingestion of water contaminated with the bacterium spreads the disease. Humans are the only documented hosts for this disease. A cholera vaccine is available in the United States and many countries.

The most important treatment is to use oral rehydration as indicated on page 113. Antibiotics can reduce the shedding of cholera in the stool and can reduce diarrhea volume and duration by 50%, but these are not required for treatment, only adequate rehydration is necessary. A single dose of doxycycline, 3 100 mg tablets, from the Rx Oral/Topical Medication Kit is adequate to treat shedding.

Coccidioidomycosis

Also called San Joaquin fever or valley fever, coccidioidomycosis is a fungal infection caused by *Coccidioides immitis*. Found in the San Joaquin Valley of California and throughout the southwestern United States, this disease is caught by inhaling the fungal spore in dust.

Symptoms can be delayed in travelers until after leaving the endemic area. The primary symptoms are those of an upper respiratory infection, bronchitis, or pneumonia. Incubation time varies and a progressive form may occur weeks, months, or years after the original infection in people with decreased immunity (AIDS patients, people on steroids, or those receiving chemotherapy).

Treatment is not required for those with upper respiratory infection symptoms. The diagnosis should be made with special blood tests to avoid missing other treatable pneumonia. Progressive disease must be treated with IV antifungal medications.

Colorado Tick Fever

A viral disease spread by ixodid (hard-shelled) ticks, this disease is 20 times more common than Rocky Mountain spotted fever in Colorado. It is also found in the other states of the western Rocky Mountains and in provinces of western Canada. It is most frequent in April and May at low altitudes, and in June through July at high altitudes. Onset is abrupt, with chills, fever of 100.4°F to 104°F (38 to 40°C), muscle ache, headache, eye pain, and eye sensitivity to light (photophobia). The patient feels weak and nauseated, but vomiting is unusual. During the first 2 days, up to 12% of the victims develop a rash. In half the cases, the fever disappears after 2 to 3 days and the patient feels well for 2 days. Then a second bout of illness starts, lasting intensely for 2 to 4 days. This second phase subsides, with the patient feeling weak for 1 to 2 additional weeks.

This disease requires no treatment other than bed rest, fluids to prevent dehydration, and medications to treat fever and aches.

However, as the same ticks can also spread potentially dangerous Rocky Mountain spotted fever, treatment with doxycycline (100 mg twice daily), as described in that section, should be started immediately, and this therapy continued for 14 days. Do not wait for the characteristic rash of Rocky Mountain spotted fever or the fever pattern of Colorado tick fever to develop, or for a firm diagnosis of either to be established by a physician.

Coronavirus

There are many coronavirus infections found in animals and humans, most causing common cold problems. Several have leaped from animal hosts to humans and have caused great concern. Recently COVID-19 and in the past several years MERS and SARS. SARS, severe acute respiratory syndrome, was eliminated after initially spreading from Mainland China into Hong Kong, Toronto, and elsewhere. MERS is still a danger in the Arabian Peninsula. The causative virus of COVID-19 (SARS-CoV-2) became the world threat it did due to the long incubation period during which people had no symptoms yet were contagious. The incubation period is 14 days. The most contagious risk is 4 days prior to symptom onset until probably 10 days after the fever has resolved. With a large population naïve to the illness—that is to say, no herd immunity—such a disease would naturally spread like wildfire until a vaccine is widely available and enough survivors of the illness develop immunity. The immunity from this illness may last 2 years, more or less. The greatest danger to the sailing vessel in the immediate future could be the demand for quarantine or refusal to allow disembarkation in various ports.

For members of the crew who become ill with possible COVID-19, most will do perfectly well after a brief period of illness and require only rest and treatment with acetaminophen or other fever treatment. Those developing respiratory distress will benefit from oxygen therapy or lacking that as much fresh, moving air as possible. This illness will not develop in a crew member after 14 days of incubation, but could start very soon after embarkation as they were already presymptomatic with the disease. On a small boat, it will probably be impossible to prevent spreading but will not prove a significant illness to most, but to those it does affect strongly, it can indeed be lethal—generally the most at risk being those over the age of 70.

Dengue

Dengue—also called "break bone fever" or "dandy fever"—is a viral infection caused by a virus (Group B arbovirus or flavivirus) and is spread by bites from the *Aedes aegypti* mosquito. Dengue is endemic throughout the tropics and subtropics and can be expected to work its way into the southern United States due to the spread of the mosquito vector.

After an incubation period of 3 to 15 (usually 5 to 8) days, there is a sudden onset of fever (104°F or 40°C), chills, headache, low back ache, pain behind the eyes with movement of the eyes, and extreme aching in the legs and joints. The eyes are red and a transient flushing or pale pink rash occurs, mostly on the face. There is a relatively slow pulse rate for the temperature (see page 10). The fever lasts 48 to 96 hours, followed by 24 hours of no fever and a sense of well-being. A second rapid temperature increase occurs, but generally not as high as the first. A bright rash spreads from the arms/legs to the trunk, but generally not the face. Palms and soles may be bright red and swollen. There is a severe headache and other body aches as well. The fever, rash, and headache constitute the "dengue triad." The illness lasts for weeks, but mortality is nil. Treatment is rest and the use of pain and fever medication.

A condition called dengue hemorrhagic fever shock syndrome *is* lethal, and usually occurs in patients younger than 10, generally infants under 1 year of age. Dengue may be confused with Colorado tick fever, typhus, yellow fever, or other hemorrhagic fevers such as the Ebola virus or Rift Valley fever in Africa. This is a reaction to having had a dengue infection in the past and developing a partial immunity. A second infection of the disease (there are 4 serotypes that are closely related) can result in an autoimmune reaction that attacks the kidneys and causing other evidence of bleeding.

Echinococcus

Also called hydatid disease, the echinococcus infection is caused by the larval stage of a tapeworm found in dogs (with sheep as an intermediate host) or in wolves in wilderness areas (with moose as the intermediate host). This disease is worldwide, but most commonly a problem in Europe, Russia, Japan, Alaska, Canada, and the continental United States, particularly Isle Royale in Lake Superior. When ingested by sheep, moose, or humans, the eggs form embryos that pass through the intestinal circulation into the liver, and sometimes beyond into the lungs, brain, kidneys, and other tissue. There a fluid-filled cyst forms, which contains scolices, brood capsules, and second-generation (daughter) cysts containing infectious scolices. The hydatid cysts maintain their presence, sometimes bursting and spreading in a malignant fashion, causing destruction of liver, lung, and other critical tissues. After remaining without symptoms for decades, abdominal pain, jaundice, or chest pain and coughing may commence.

If the intermediate host is eaten by a carnivore (dog, wolf, or man), the infectious scolices are released into the GI tract, where they develop into adult worms and the lifecycle continues.

Most hydatid disease is from the tapeworm *Echinococcus granulosis*, but a rapidly progressive form develops when infection is caused by the *Echinococcus multilocularis* tapeworm. This tapeworm is carried primarily by foxes and domestic dogs and cats. Numerous small cysts form that multiply rapidly. The result is often fatal. There is no adequate medical treatment; attempts at surgical removal of multiple cysts are the only reliable hope for cure.

Ehrlichiosis

Since its discovery in 1987, the incidence of ehrlichiosis has increased to approximately 1,000 cases per year. The time of greatest risk is May through July. This is a rickettsial infection caused by *Ehrlichia chaffeensis* and is spread by several species of ticks.

The incubation time ranges from 1 to 21 days (mean 7 days). It presents with high fever and headache, with other common symptoms being tiredness, nausea, vomiting, muscle ache, and loss of appetite. About 20% of victims develop a rash, but this rash is seldom on the feet or hands. This disease can range from mild, flu-like symptoms to its extreme, which can be fatal.

The drug of choice is doxycycline, 100 mg twice daily for at least 3 days, beyond fever detection and until evidence of clinical improvement, typically 5 to 7 days total duration.

Encephalitis

Encephalitis from Group A arbovirus (western equine encephalitis, eastern equine encephalitis, Venezuelan equine encephalitis) in the United States and Canada and from Group B arbovirus (St. Louis encephalitis) in the United States can be prevented by liberal use of repellent and covering exposed areas with netting or clothing to prevent bites from infected mosquitoes. Symptoms of these illnesses include high fever (104°F or 40°C) and generally headache, stiff neck, and vomiting and, at times, diarrhea. These cases can be fatal and require evacuation to medical help.

Cool the patient with external means (cool water, fanning), and the use of aspirin or Mobigesic. The disease occurs in epidemics; be very careful with mosquito exposure when the disease becomes prevalent.

Giardiasis

Intestinal infection by *Giardia lamblia*, a single-cell parasite that causes giardiasis or beaver fever, is becoming a significant problem in wilderness travel in the United States and is a very common cause of traveler's diarrhea worldwide. The stools of infected individuals contain the infective cyst form of the parasite. These cysts can live in water for longer than 3 months. Other mammalian vectors, such as the beaver, are responsible for much of the wilderness spread of this disease. In many underdeveloped countries, the major spread is from untreated human waste found in the rivers and emptying into the sea.

In the active disease, the trophozoite form attaches itself to the small bowel by means of a central sucker. Multiplication is by binary fission or division. Approximately 2 weeks after ingestion of the cysts, there is either a gradual or abrupt onset of persistent watery diarrhea, which usually resolves in 1 to 2 weeks, but may persist less severely for several months. Abdominal pain, bloating, nausea, and weight loss from malabsorption may occur. Giardiasis is often without symptoms at all and a chronic carrier state exists. In the United States, about 4% of stools submitted for parasitology examination contain *G. lamblia* cysts.

Diagnosis is by finding cysts in stools, or trophozoites from gastric suction, or the "string test" from the duodenum. This latter test is performed by having the patient swallow a string, allowing the far end to pass into the first part of the bowel, or duodenum. When the string is pulled out, a microscopic examination may demonstrate the presence of trophozoites. In active disease, the cysts are routinely secreted, but in the chronic carrier state repeated stool examinations (at least 3) are required to provide a 95% accuracy of test results. Treatment is with one of several drugs available in the United States, the most commonly used being Flagyl (metronidazol), 250 mg 3 times daily for 5 days. A better drug is tinidazole, 2 g taken as a single dose. Prevention is by proper filtration of water, adequate chemical treatment, or heating water to 150°F (66°C). See page 113, for a full discussion of water treatment.

Hantavirus

Hantavirus was the cause of death among members of the Navaho Indian Nation in New Mexico in 1993. The virus has been identified in serum samples from 690 people in 12 states, with the greatest concentration in the western United States. It is caught by inhaling dust contaminated with feces from an infected deer mouse (*Peromyscus maniculatus*).

The onset of illness is a period of fever, muscle ache, and cough, followed by an abrupt onset of acute respiratory distress. The mortality rate has been 60%! There is no specific treatment available. Avoiding breathing dust that may contain the contaminated mouse feces is the preventative measure. When cleaning out cabins, use a wet mop and avoid sweeping dry debris.

Hepatitis A

A viral infection of the liver, hepatitis A (infectious hepatitis) has worldwide distribution. It is transmitted by ingestion of infected feces, in water supplies contaminated by human sewage, in food handled by persons with poor hygiene, or in contaminated food such as raw shell-fish grown in impure water. Contaminated milk, and even infusion of infected blood products (see hepatitis B), can spread this disease.

The period from the time of exposure to the appearance of symptoms takes 15 to 50 days. The disease can range from minor flu-like symptoms to fatal liver disease. Most cases resolve favorably within 6 to 12 weeks. Symptoms start abruptly with fever, lethargy, and nausea. Occasionally a rash develops. A characteristic loss of taste for cigarettes is frequent. In 3 to 10 days, the urine turns dark, followed by jaundice, with yellowing of the whites of the eyes and the skin. The stool may turn light-colored. There is frequently itching and joint pain. The jaundice peaks within 1 to 2 weeks and fades during the 2- to 4-week recovery phase. The hepatitis A patient stops shedding virus in the stool prior to the jaundice developing and is therefore not contagious by the time the diagnosis is normally made. Personal hygiene helps prevent spreading, but isolation of the patient is not strictly required.

In most cases, no specific treatment is required. After a few days to 2 weeks, appetite generally returns and bed confinement is no longer required, even though jaundice remains. The best guideline is the disappearance of the lethargy and feeling of illness that appeared in the first stages of the disease. Restrictions of diet have no value, but a low-fat diet is generally more palatable.

If profound prostration occurs, the trip should be terminated for the patient and he should be placed under medical care. If possible, unimmunized contacts should be immediately given the hepatitis A shot but the only practical solution is to immunize everyone against hepatitis A prior to leaving on a voyage.

Hepatitis B
Another viral infection of the liver, hepatitis B (serum hepatitis) is also worldwide in distribution. Transmission is primarily through infusion of infected blood products, sexual contact, use of contaminated needles or syringes, or even sharing contaminated razor blades. Dental procedures, acupuncture, and ear piercing and tattooing with contaminated equipment will also spread this disease.

Incubation period from time of exposure to the development of symptoms is longer than with hepatitis A, namely 30 to 180 days. The symptoms are similar, but the onset is less abrupt, and the incidence of fever is lower. There is a greater chance of developing chronic hepatitis (5% to 10% of cases). Mortality is higher, especially in elderly patients, where it ranges from 10% to 15%.

Immunization is available and is very effective.

Hepatitis C

A form of hepatitis, with similar manifestations to hepatitis B, has been designated as hepatitis C (formerly "non-A, non-B" since blood tests for evidence of exposure to those virus particles was not previously found). The transmission is probably the same as for hepatitis B. Incubation period is from less than 2 weeks to more than 25 weeks, with an average of 7 weeks for the development of clinical disease. Immunization is available. Specific treatment is available for this disease.

Hepatitis D

Hepatitis D, or the "delta agent," can only infect a person who has hepatitis B. The presence of this mutated RNA particle causes the infection to be more fulminant. It spreads only by contaminated needle use. No specific treatment exists. Prevention of hepatitis A with immunization is recommended.

Hepatitis E

An epidemic form of hepatitis (i.e., not A or C) has been termed hepatitis E. Spread by ingestion of contaminated food or water, the incubation period from time of contact ranges from 2 to 9 weeks, with a mean of 45 days. The disease mimics hepatitis A. The fatality rate in pregnant women is highest, about 20%. Outbreaks have been confirmed throughout developing areas of the old world. There is no immunization or specific treatment available.

Hepatitis G

A new virus has been identified as the hepatitis G virus. A member of the family Flaviviridae, it can be spread by blood and sexual contact, just as with hepatitis B. There is no immunization or specific treatment available.

Leptospirosis

This disease is caused by a spirochete, genus *Leptospira* (a similar organism causes syphilis and Lyme disease). Like those diseases, this organism can attack virtually any organ system, yet 90% of those infected have no symptoms. The organism can live in damp soil, vegetation, and mud, but dies almost instantly upon drying. It spreads into the environment due to contaminated urine from ill animals. This germ is located all over the world, including the northern United States. Cuts and abrasions on the skin increase the risk of illness, while wearing protective footwear or clothing decreases it.

The incubation period is 7 days, with a range of 2 to 29 days. Initially it can present with high fever, headache, chills, muscle aches, red eyes, abdominal pain, diarrhea, rash, and jaundice. It may occur in two phases. Recurrent fevers of up to 102°F (38.9°C) are noted. After the first phase, the patient may recover, then relapse in 6 to 12 days later with similar symptoms. About 200 cases are identified in the United States (50% in Hawaii), but this is considered the most widely spread disease from an animal in the world. About 1% to 5% of cases are fatal. The most serious form is called Wiel's disease, which includes jaundice and severe lung, kidney, and bleeding disorders. It is treated with doxycycline, 100 mg twice daily for 2 weeks, but recent studies are unclear if antibiotics help. However, I subscribe to the old adage: You should not die in the tropics unless you die on doxycycline.

Lyme Disease

Lyme disease is caused by a spirochete, *Borrelia burgdorferi*. The disease lives in various mammals but is transmitted to humans by the bite of several species of ticks. The disease is most common in the Northeast, extending through Connecticut and Massachusetts down to Maryland, in Wisconsin and Minnesota, throughout the states of California and Oregon, and in various South Atlantic and southcentral states, with cases reported from 43 of the lower 48 states. A map showing the reported incidence of Lyme disease per county by state within the United States is located at www.cdc.gov. It has been found in other countries as well, in the former Soviet Union, China, Australia, and Japan as well as several European countries.

The disease goes through several phases. In stage one, after an incubation of 3 days to a month, probably 95% of victims develop a circular lesion in the area of the bite. It has a clear to pink center, raised border, is painless, and ranges from 1 to 23 inches in diameter. There are usually several such patches. The patient feels lethargic, has headache, has muscle and joint pain, and has enlarged lymph nodes. In stage two, 10% to 15% of patients can develop a meningitis, and less than 10% develop heart problems. Symptoms may last for months but are generally self-limited. Approximately 60% enter stage three, the development of actual arthritis. Frequently a knee is involved. The swelling can be impressive. Stage three can start abruptly several weeks to 2 years after the onset of the initial rash.

Treatment of stage one Lyme disease is tetracycline, such as doxycycline, 100 mg taken twice daily for 21 days. Alternate drugs are penicillin and erythromycin. Treatment of choice for stages two and three Lyme disease consists of Rocephin, 2 g given IV daily for 14 to 21 days.

For prevention of Lyme disease after a recognized tick bite, routine use of antimicrobial prophylaxis or serologic testing is not recommended. A single dose of doxycycline may be offered to adult patients (200 mg) if (1) the attached tick can be reliably identified as an adult or nymphal *I. scapularis* tick that is estimated to have been attached for more than 36 hours on the basis of the degree of engorgement of the tick with blood or of certainty about the time of exposure to the tick; (2) prophylaxis can be started within 72 hours of the time that the tick was removed; (3) ecological information indicates that the local rate of infection of these ticks with *B. burgdorferi* is more than 20%; and (4) doxycycline treatment is not contraindicated.

One manifestation of Lyme disease is the development of a facial paralysis on one side, called Bell's palsy. The involved side is expressionless since the patient is unable to move the muscles of the forehead, around the eye, and so on. While there are other causes of Bell's palsy, in North America this problem must be considered as Lyme disease until ruled out by a physician. Treatment of Bell's palsy caused by Lyme disease is with oral antibiotic for 21 days.

Malaria

Human malaria is caused by five species of a protozoan: *Plasmodium falciparum*, *P. vivax*, *P. ovale*, and *P. malariae*, and, rarely, by *P. knowlesi* in Southeast Asia. The infection is acquired from the bite of an infected female Anopheles mosquito. It may also be spread by blood transfusion. Falciparum malaria is the most serious. While all forms of this disease make people ill and may be lethal, *P. falciparum* is the one that kills.

Regions of the world where malaria may be acquired are sub-Saharan Africa, parts of Mexico and Central America, Haiti, parts of South America, the Middle East, the Indian subcontinent, and Southeast Asia. Resistance to chloroquine by the deadly *P. falciparum* has become widespread. For travelers in resistant areas, there are several prophylactic medications that are currently used: Malarone®, Lariam, and doxycycline. To use Lariam (mefloquine), 250 mg, take 1 tablet weekly, starting 1 week prior to departure and continuing for 4 weeks after return. An alternate drug regimen, especially necessary when *P. falciparum* has become resistant to mefloquine, is the use of doxycycline, 100 mg to be taken once daily for prevention. This must be started the day before exposure, continued daily and for 4 weeks after exposure.

In areas with relapsing malaria (*P. vivax* and *P. ovale*), primaquine should be taken 1 tablet daily during the last 2 weeks of chloroquine therapy. This is usually appropriate for anyone faced with long exposure in areas with a high concentration of these strains of malaria. IAMAT (www.iamat.org) provides the percentage of *P. falciparum* versus *P. vivax* and *P. ovale*, as well as current information on resistance to chloroquine for each country.

If you are traveling into an area with malaria, taking a very long term (multiple years) of an antimalarial drug, while safe, may be impractical. Your best approach is strict mosquito protection with permethrin treatment of clothing, bed netting, residual spraying of building interiors, and skin protection—and the use of a treatment

Table 19.5 Pediatric Treatment Dose of Malarone for Malaria—Given for 3 Days

WEIGHT	TABLETS
5 to 8 kg (11 to 18 pounds)	2 pediatric tabs once daily
9 to 10 kg (19 to 23 pounds)	3 pediatric tabs once daily
11 to 20 kg (24 to 44 pounds)	1 adult tab once daily
21 to 30 kg (45 to 66 pounds)	2 adult tabs once daily
31 to 40 kg (67 to 88 pounds)	3 adult tabs once daily
Over 41 kg (over 89 pounds)	4 adult tabs once daily

dose of medication if someone comes down with possible malaria. In children malaria frequently presents with diarrhea and abdominal pain, but in all expect severe fever with profuse sweating, headache, nausea, and vomiting. This can lead to convulsions and death. A good treatment is to use Malarone (250 mg atovaquone + 100 mg proguanil), 4 tablets once daily (take with food or milk and the same time each day—repeat the dose if patient vomits within 1 hour of taking the dose). A pediatric treatment dose is also devised based upon weight. The pediatric tablet of Malarone is 62.5 mg atovaquone + 25 mg proguanil.

Measles (Rubeola)

A viral disease that spreads easily by inhalation and is one of the most contagious viral diseases with 90% of unimmunized persons who are exposed catching it. Onset is usually 1 to 3 weeks after exposure, usually 2 weeks. Onset is with a high fever 105°F (40.6°C), and usually conjunctivitis, runny nose, and cough. Three to seven days after, the fever a rash appears on the face, then covers the entire body, lasting for 4 to 7 days. It is contagious 4 days before until 4 days after the rash breaks.

One per 1,000 cases can develop deadly brain infections. It can cause diarrhea, middle ear infections, and pneumonia, which can also become fatal. Persons with ear infections and pneumonia may have a secondary bacterial infection as well due to their weakened condition and these can be treated with antibiotics, but an antibiotic will not help if the cause is just from the measles. There is no specific treatment. Only use acetaminophen (Tylenol) and not aspirin or non-steroidal anti-inflammatory medications (NSAIDs) like ibuprofen when treating the fever. You can treat cough and runny nose symptoms. Children who contract this disease should receive 200,000 units of vitamin A (50, units and under 6 months; 100,000 units 6 to 11 months), with a repeat dose in 2 to 4 weeks. If this breaks out in a group, any nonimmunized persons will catch it.

Immunization is protective and is provided by the MMR vaccine.

Meningococcal Meningitis

This acute bacterial infection caused by *Neisseria meningitidis* results in inflammation of the brain and central nervous system. Many cases are without symptoms or consist of a mild upper respiratory illness. Severe cases begin with sudden fever, sore throat, chills, headache, stiff neck, nausea, and vomiting. Within 24 to 48 hours, the victim becomes drowsy and mentally confused, followed by convulsions, coma, and death. Immediate and appropriately large doses of the proper antibiotic are critical to save the patient's life (the medical kit only has Rocephin, which must be given in large amounts: 1 g IM twice daily). The disease is spread by contact with the nasal secretions of infected persons (sneezing and coughing).

While the disease is found worldwide, large epidemics are more common in tropical countries, especially sub-Saharan Africa in the dry season, New Delhi (India), and Nepal.

In 80% of healthy young adults, bacterial meningitis is caused by the meningococci bacteria discussed in this section or by a pneumococci bacterium. Vaccines are available against both organisms.

Mumps

This virus infection spreads by respiratory droplets either by inhalation or touching them on surfaces. The incubation period is 16–18 days (range: 12–25). The disease starts with fever, headache, loss of appetite, and muscle ache. The hallmark of the disease is swelling of one or both parotid (salivary) glands. People are the most contagious from a few days before illness until 5 days after the onset of parotid gland swelling. The complications can be infections of the testicle, hearing loss, meningitis, encephalitis, and pancreatitis. Treat the fever with acetaminophen (Tylenol) and avoid aspirin.

Immunization is protective and is provided by the MMR vaccine. Unfortunately, the mumps component of this shot is the least effective and provides only about 88%. This protection may gradually decline and in case of outbreaks, the MMR should be boosted.

Plague

Plague is caused by a bacterium (*Yersinia pestis*) that infects wild rodents in many parts of the world, including the western United States and parts of South America, Africa, and Asia. Epidemics occur when domestic rats become infected and spread the disease to humans. Bubonic plague is transmitted by infected fleas, while pneumonic plague is spread directly to other people by coughing. Plague is accompanied by fever, enlarged lymph nodes (bubonic plague) and, less commonly, pneumonia (pneumonic plague).

Treatment is with doxycycline, 100 mg twice daily. Treat fever as necessary. Isolate the patient, particularly if coughing. Drainage of abscesses (buboes) may be necessary (see page 153). Exposed persons should be watched for 10 days, but incubation is usually 2 to 6 days.

Rabies

Rabies can be transmitted on the North American continent by several species of mammals, namely skunk, bat, fox, coyote, raccoon, bobcat, and wolf. Obviously, if removing an animal from a trap, jogging past an animal, separating mother from child, or taking food from a critter causes an attack, the most likely cause is not rabies. An attack by a wounded animal is cause for concern, as the animal may be wounded due to loss of coordination from rabies. Any unprovoked attack by one of these mammals should be considered an attack by a rabid animal. Dogs and cats in the United States have a low incidence of rabies. Information from local departments of health will indicate if rabies is currently of concern in your area.

Animals whose bites have never caused rabies in humans in the United States are livestock (cattle, sheep, horse), rabbits, gerbils, chipmunks, squirrels, rats, and mice. A significant epidemic of raccoon rabies has now extended from Florida to Connecticut, with isolated reports from New Hampshire and Ohio showing an expansion of this epidemic north and west. Hawaii is the only rabies-free state. Canada's rabies occurs mostly in foxes and skunks in the province of Ontario.

The rabies vaccine available in the United States is very effective, with low side effects. It is expensive, but much less expensive than having to acquire postexposure rabies immune globulin in addition to the complete series of shots.

The incubation can be brief or take months. It is caused when the virus is able to reach a peripheral nerve synapse—it then penetrates it and moves toward the brain at the rate of 4 inches (10 cm) per day! Once the virus is in the nerve, the patient is doomed. Rabies is a vicious, virtually 100% fatal disease once it develops clinically. It is called "hydrophobia" because the person appears to be afraid of water. They will be very thirsty but will choke when trying to swallow. Spasms, high fever, terrible headache, rapidly progress to death. Because of this, there is generous use of rabies vaccine and immune globulin. Approximately 16,000 to 39,000 people are vaccinated in the United States yearly to prevent this disease. Persons having to work with potentially rabid animal populations can be immunized with the vaccine and given yearly booster shots. It is possible to obtain the disease by merely being contaminated with the saliva or blood of an infected animal if it encounters a break in the skin or mucous membranes, and possibly even by breathing in dust infected with the virus. The first aid treatment will always be to irrigate the wound area, especially with a viricidal material, such as a saturated iodine water solution used for water purification (page 114), soap and water, or the other methods indicated for wound cleansing (page 131).

Relapsing Fever

This bacterial infection is caused by several species of Borrelia spirochete and is spread by body lice in Asia, Africa, and Europe, or by soft-bodied ticks in the Americas (including the western United States), Asia, Africa, and Europe. Symptoms occur 3 to 11 days from contact with the tick or louse vector, and start with an abrupt onset of chills, headache, muscular pains, and sometimes vomiting. A rash may appear and small hemorrhages present under the skin surface. The fever remains high from 3 to 5 days, and then clears suddenly. After 1 to 2 weeks, a somewhat milder relapse begins. Jaundice is more common during relapse. The illness again clears, but 2 to 10 similar episodes reoccur at intervals of 1 to 2 weeks until immunity fully develops.

Antibiotics are available for effective treatment. Mortality is low, less than 5% in healthy adults. Treatment is with doxycycline, 100 mg twice daily for 5 to 10 days. Personal hygiene is effective in preventing louse-borne disease, while control of ticks with insect repellent and frequent body checks and tick removal minimize the chance of tick-borne disease. Unlike many tick-borne diseases that will not spread to humans unless the tick has been attached for longer than 2 days, relapsing fever can be caught soon after attachment.

Rocky Mountain Spotted Fever

This is an acute and serious infection caused by a microorganism called *Rickettsia rickettsii* and transmitted by ixodid (hard-shelled) ticks. It is most common in North Carolina, Virginia, Maryland, the Rocky Mountain states, and the state of Washington. The peak incidence of cases is from May to September. Onset of infection is abrupt, after a 3- to 12-day incubation period (average 7 days from the tick bite). Fever reaches 103°F to 104°F (40°C) within 2 days. There is considerable headache, chills, and muscle pain at the onset. In 4 days, a rash appears on the wrists, ankles, soles, and palms, and then spreads to the trunk. Initially pink, this rash turns to dark blotches and even ulcers in severe cases.

Any suspected case of Rocky Mountain spotted fever should be considered a medical emergency. Do not wait for the rash to develop; rather, start the patient on antibiotics from the Rx kit. Give doxycycline, 100 mg, 1 tablet every 12 hours, and keep on this dosage schedule for 14 days. This is a drug of choice and its early use can cut the death rate from 20% to nearly zero. Prevention is by the careful removal of ticks and the use of insect repellent and protective clothing. Obviously, anyone suspected of having this disease needs to be seen immediately by a physician.

Rubella (German Measles, 3-day Measles)

A viral disease (unrelated to measles) that is highly contagious and is spread by person 7 days before and for 5 to 7 days after the onset of the characteristic rash that starts on the face and spreads to the body. Frequently there are aching joints, especially in young women. Incubation from exposure averages 14 days (range 12 to 23 days). The illness may start with a low-grade fever and lymph node enlargement. Some people will not have symptoms, but they will also be contagious. It is extremely dangerous to a pregnant woman's baby, even more so than Zika virus.

There is no treatment. Avoid aspirin for fever and use acetaminophen (Tylenol). It is prevented with immunization using the MMR vaccine.

Schistosomiasis

Blood trematodes or flukes are responsible for schistosomiasis (bilharziasis, safari fever). The eggs are deposited in freshwater and hatch into motile miracidia, which infect snails. After developing in the snails, active cercariae emerge, which can penetrate exposed human skin. Swimming, wading, or drinking freshwater must be avoided in infected areas.

Schistosoma mansoni is found in tropical Africa, part of Venezuela, several Caribbean islands, the Guianas, Brazil, and the Middle East. *S. japonicum* is encountered in China, Japan, the Philippines, and Southeast Asia. *S. haematobium* is in Africa, the Middle East, and small portions of India and islands in the Indian Ocean. The former two species are excreted in the stools and the latter in urine. Shedding may occur for years. No isolation is required of patients. Specific treatments for the various species are available. Initial penetration of the skin causes an itchy rash. After entry, the organism enters the bloodstream, migrates through the lungs, and eventually lodges in the blood vessels draining either the gut or the bladder, depending upon the species. While the worms are maturing, the victim will have fever, lethargy, cough, rash, abdominal pain, and often nausea. In acute infections caused by *S. mansoni* and *S. japonicum*, victims develop a mucoid, bloody diarrhea, and tender liver enlargement. Chronic infection leads to fibrosis of the liver with distension of the abdomen. In *S. haematobium* infections, the bladder becomes inflamed and eventually fibrotic. Symptoms include painful urination, urgency, blood in urine, and pelvic pain.

STARI

Southern tick-associated rash illness (STARI) develops around the site of a lone star tick bite and develops within 7 days of the bite. It can expand to a diameter of 8 cm (3 inches). Patients possibly experience fatigue, headache, fever, and muscle pains. Lone star tick bites almost always cause a local small inflamed area, and that by itself is not an indication that patient has STARI. Lone star ticks do not carry Lyme disease. While the CDC does not recommend, at the time of this writing, the use of antibiotics in treating STARI, since the causative organism is not known, studies have shown that taking an antibiotic such as doxycycline clears the symptoms quicker.

Tapeworms

Three species of tapeworm infect humans: *Taenia saginata* larvae found in beef; *Taenia solium* in pork; and *Diphyllobothrium latum* in fish. In all three, the human ingests undercooked flesh of the host animal, acquiring the infective cysts.

The beef tapeworm can be huge, forming lengths of 10 to 30 feet (3 to 10 m) inside the human host. It is common in Mexico, South America, Eastern Europe, the Middle East, and Africa. Symptoms can include stomach pain, weight loss, and diarrhea, but frequently the human host has no clue of the infestation.

The pork tapeworm infects victims in South America, Eastern Europe, Russia, and Asia. Generally, it is without symptoms; at times vague abdominal complaints are noted. A complication of this disease is cysticercosis: the tapeworm larvae penetrate the human intestinal

246 DOCTOR ON BOARD

wall—after the human drinks infected water—and invade body tissues, frequently skeletal muscle and the brain. There they mature into cystic masses. After several years, the cysts degenerate and produce local inflammatory reactions that can then cause convulsions, visual problems, or mental disturbances. In this case the human replaces the pig in the maturation cycle of the tapeworm, and it is the human flesh that is contaminated by the tapeworm cyst. This is an unlucky break for the involved human and any cannibals he might meet. Any water filtration or purification system can prevent cysticercosis.

The fish tapeworm occurs worldwide but is particularly a hazard in Scandinavia and the Far East. A single tapeworm, usually without symptoms, develops. The worm's absorption of vitamin B12 may cause pernicious anemia in the host.

Tetanus

Caused by a bacterium, *Clostridium tetani*, that is located worldwide, most cases of tetanus occur from very minor wounds such as a paper cut, rather than from rusty barbed wire, as so many people think. In fact, a hiker on the Appalachian Trail got tetanus from a blister on his heel and inadequate immunization. Onset is gradual, with an incubation period of 2 to 50 (usually 5 to 10) days. The earliest symptom is stiffness of the jaw, then sore throat, stiff muscles, headache, low-grade fever, and muscle spasm. As the disease progresses, the patients are unable to open their jaw and the facial muscles may be fixed in a smile with elevated eyebrows. Painful generalized spasms of muscles occur with minor disturbances such as drafts, noise, or someone jarring the patient's bed. Death from loss of respiratory muscle function, or even unknown causes, may ensue. The disease is frequently fatal. Prevention is obtained by adequate immunization.

Tick Paralysis

Five species of ticks in North America produce a neurotoxin in their saliva that can paralyze their victims. Most cases are found in the Pacific Northwest, Rocky Mountain States, and 7 southern states, as well as Australia. Spring and summer are the times of highest risk. The toxin is usually carried by an engorged, pregnant tick. Symptoms begin 2 to 7 days after the tick begins feeding. Throughout the ordeal, the patient's mental function is usually spared. Symptoms start as weakness in the legs, which progressively ascends until the entire body is paralyzed over several hours to days. At times the condition presents as ataxia (loss of coordination) without muscle weakness.

The diagnosis is made by finding an embedded tick. After removing the tick, symptoms resolve in hours to days, rarely longer. Untreated tick paralysis can be fatal, with mortality rates of 10% to 12%.

Trichinosis

Trichinosis is caused by eating improperly cooked meat infected with the cysts of this parasite, the roundworm *Trichinella spiralis*. It is most common in pigs, bears (particularly polar bears), and some marine mammals. Nausea and diarrhea or intestinal cramping may appear within 1 to 2 days, but it generally takes 7 days after digestion. Swelling of the eyelids is very characteristic on the 11th day. After that, muscle soreness, fever, pain in the eyes, and subconjunctival hemorrhage (see page 57) develop. If enough contaminated food is ingested, this can be a fatal disease. Most symptoms disappear in 3 months.

Treatment is with pain medication (Percogesic from the Non-Rx Oral Medication Kit, or Norco-10/325 from the Rx Oral Medication Kit). The use of steroids such as Decadron (20 mg/day for 3 or 4 days, followed by reduced dosage over the next 10 days) is indicated in severe cases. Specific drugs are available for treatment of this disease (albendazole and, when available, mebendazole). The best prevention is cooking suspected meat at 150°F (66°C) for 30 minutes for each pound (0.5 kg) of meat.

Trypanosomiasis, African (African Sleeping Sickness)

If you are heading to Africa, the African variety of trypanosomiasis is interesting as it is so different from the American variety, which you may encounter if you are heading to Central America or South America. Two species of trypanosomes cause African sleeping sickness (African trypanosomiasis), which is transmitted by the bite of the tsetse fly. The severity of the disease depends upon the species encountered. The infection is confined to the area of Africa between 15 degrees north and 20 degrees south of the equator—the exact distribution of the tsetse fly. Humans are the only reservoir of *Trypanosoma gambiense* found in West and Central Africa, while wild game is the principal reservoir of the *T. rhodesiense* of East Africa.

T. gambiense infection starts with a nodule or a chancre that appears briefly at the site of a tsetse fly bite. Generalized illness appears months to years later and is characterized by lymph node enlargement at the back of the neck and intermittent fever. Months to years after this development, invasion of the central nervous system may occur, noted by behavioral changes, headache, loss of appetite, backache, hallucinations, delusions, and sleeping. In *T. rhodesiense* infection, the generalized illness begins 5 to 14 days after the nodule or chancre develops. It is much more intense than the Gambian variety and may include acute central nervous system and cardiac symptoms, fever, and rapid weight loss. It has a high rate of mortality. If untreated, death usually occurs within 1 year. Specific, but frequently toxic, therapy is available.

Trypanosomiasis, American (Chagas Disease)

Chagas disease (American trypanosomiasis), caused by *Trypanosoma cruzi*, a protozoan hemoflagellate, is transmitted through the feces of a brown insect called the "kissing bug," or the "assassin bug" in North America. This bug is a member of the family Reduviidae. A name popular in South America is vinchuca, derived from a word which means "one who lets himself fall down." These bugs live in palm trees or the thatching in native huts and like to drop onto their sleeping victim's face or exposed arms. When biting victims, the bug defecates. The itch of the wound causes bitten patients to scratch the wound, rubbing the feces into the bite site, thus causing the inoculation of the infectious agent. This disease is located in parts of South and Central America, but the vector for the disease (the kissing bug) is located in the Southwestern United States. At first this disease may have no symptoms. A chagoma, or red nodule, develops at the site of the original infection. This area may then lose its pigmentation. After

1 to 2 weeks, a firm swelling of one eyelid occurs, known as Romana's sign. The swelling becomes purplish in color, and lymph node swelling in front of the ear on the same side may occur. In a few days a fever develops, with generalized lymph node swelling. Rapid heart rate, spleen and liver enlargement, swelling of the legs, and meningitis or encephalitis may occur. Serious conditions also can include acute heart failure. In most cases, however, the illness subsides in about 3 months and the patient appears to live a normal life. The disease continues, however, slowly destroying the heart, until 10 to 20 years later chronic congestive heart failure becomes apparent. The underlying cause may never be known, especially in a traveler who has left the endemic area. In some areas of Brazil, the disease attacks the colon, causing flaccid enlargement with profound constipation.

This disease is a leading cause of death in South America, generally due to heart failure. As many as 15 million people in South America may be infected.

Tuberculosis

TB is caused by one of two bacteria, *Mycobacterium tuberculosis* or *M. bovis*. The infection results in a very chronic illness that can reactivate many years after it has been apparently killed. In the United States, there are 20,000 new cases, with 1,800 deaths, yearly. Worldwide there are 8 to 10 million new cases, with 2 to 3 million deaths yearly. This disease is spread primarily by inhalation of infected droplets. The disease also spreads by drinking infected milk or eating infected dairy products such as butter. If milk cannot be pasteurized, the animals form which it is sourced (cows, goats, etc.), should be tuberculin-free. In my practice, I once treated an elderly lady from southern Indiana who had widespread TB which she had caught from drinking goat's milk.

Active pulmonary disease usually develops within a year of contact. The early symptoms of fever, night sweats, lethargy, and weight loss can be so gradual that they are initially ignored. TB usually infects the lungs, but it can spread throughout the body, causing neurological damage, bone infections, and overwhelming infection. Diagnosis is usually made with a chest X-ray.

Tularemia

Tularemia (rabbit fever, deerfly fever) can be contracted through exposure to ticks, deerflies, or mosquitoes. Cuts can be infected when working with rabbit pelts. Eating improperly cooked infected rabbits can result in onset. Similarly, muskrats, foxes, squirrels, mice, and rats can spread the disease via direct contact with their carcasses. Stream water may become contaminated by these animals.

An ulcer appears when a wound is involved, and lymph nodes become enlarged, first in nearby areas and then throughout the body. Pneumonia normally develops. The disease lasts 4 weeks in untreated cases. Mortality in treated cases is almost zero, while in untreated cases it ranges from 6% to 30%.

Treatment of choice is streptomycin, but the doxycycline suggested for the Rx Oral/Topical Medication Kit works extremely well. The average adult would require an initial dose of 2 tablets, followed by 1 tablet every 12 hours. Continue therapy for 5 to 7 days after the fever has been broken.

Typhoid Fever

Caused by the bacterium *Salmonella typhi*, typhoid fever is spread by contaminated food and dairy products. Prevention is proper food storage, the thorough cooking of food, and avoidance of unrefrigerated dairy products.

The disease is characterized by headache, chills, loss of appetite, backache, constipation, nosebleed, and tenderness of the abdomen to palpation. The temperature rises daily for 7 to 10 days. The fever is maintained at a high level for 7 to 19 more days, then drops over the next 10 days. With typhoid fever, a pulse rate of only 84 may occur with a temperature of 104°F (40°C), when one might otherwise expect a pulse rate of over 120. Between the 7th and 10th days of the illness, rose-colored splotches, which blanch when pressure is applied, appear in 10% of patients.

The drug of choice for treating this illness is Rocephin, given 30 mg/kg of body weight/day IM in 2 divided doses per day for 2 weeks. An oral drug that can be used is Levaquin, 750 mg given once daily. Diarrhea may be severe in the latter stages of this illness. Replacement of fluids is especially important during the phases of high fever or diarrhea (see pages 90–93). Patients with relapses should be given another 5-day course of the antibiotic. Immunization prior to departure to endemic areas is useful in preventing or curtailing the severity of this infection and should be taken by anyone traveling to an endemic area. This disease is very common after mass disaster situations and, while immunization is not usually indicated for living in the United States, it is a disease to be prepared for during international travel.

Endemic Typhus, Flea-Borne

This disease is also known as murine typhus, rat-flea typhus, New World typhus, Malaya typhus, and urban typhus. It is one of the several diseases caused by rickettsia, which resemble both viral and bacterial infections. Other diseases caused by this order are Rocky Mountain spotted fever, Q-fever, trench fever, and the various typhus diseases. Endemic typhus is due to *Rickettsia typhi*. It is located worldwide, including the southern Atlantic and Gulf Coast states of the United States. It is spread to humans through infected rat flea feces.

After an incubation period of 6 to 18 days (mean 10), shaking chills, fever, and headache develop. A rash forms, primarily on the trunk, but fades fairly rapidly. The fever lasts about 12 days. This is a mild disease and fatalities are rare. Antibiotic treatment with doxycycline, 100 mg given twice daily, is very effective. Prevention is directed toward vector (rat and flea) control.

Epidemic Typhus, Louse-Borne

This malady is also called classic typhus, European typhus, and jail fever. It killed 3 million people during World War II. On the positive side, no American traveler has contracted this disease since 1950. It is most likely to be encountered in mountainous regions of Mexico, Central and South America, the Balkans, Eastern Europe, Africa, and many countries of Asia. The causative agent is *Rickettsia prowazekii*, which is transmitted by infected lice.

Following a 7- to 14-day incubation period, there is a sudden onset of high fever (104°F or 40°C), which remains at a high level, with a usual morning decrease, for about 2 weeks. There is an intense headache. A light pink rash appears on the 4th to 6th day, soon becoming dark red. There is low BP, pneumonia, mental confusion, and bruising in severe cases. Mortality is rare in children less than 10 years of age but may reach greater than 60% in those over 50. Antibiotics, such as doxycycline, 100 mg twice daily, are very effective if given early in the disease. Prevention is proper hygiene and delousing when needed. A vaccine was formerly made in the United States but is no longer available and is not needed due to the low incidence observed.

West Nile Virus

This is an arbovirus that primarily infects birds, especially crows, ravens, and robins. Mosquitoes then spread this virus to all mammals, which unfortunately includes humans. A sign of local West Nile virus activity can be dead birds, especially crows, ravens, and robins. In North America, the mosquito vector is the culex, which is unfortunate as these mosquitoes do not usually announce their presence by buzzing in your ears or leaving welts when they bite. They are silent, stealth biters. If you are being buzzed and welt up, you don't have to worry about it being from a culex mosquito.

West Nile virus was first identified in the United States in 1999 and has presented in all states and in all provinces of Canada (with rare exceptions). The disease is usually without symptoms, but when more severe it results in fever, headache, stiff neck, nausea or vomiting, muscle ache and weakness, even coma and death. It does not spread from person to person, except via blood transfusion. Support is accomplished with adequate pain medication, evacuation if possible, and generally helping with normal body functions.

Yellow Fever

An arbovirus, yellow fever is found in tropical areas of South and Central America and Africa. This viral disease is contracted by the bite of the *Aedes aegypti* mosquito (and other species). Onset, about 2 weeks after the bite, is sudden, with a fever of 102°F to 104°F (40°C). The pulse is usually rapid the first day, but becomes slow by the second day. In mild cases, the fever falls suddenly 2 to 5 days after onset.

This remission lasts for hours to several days. Next the fever returns, but the pulse remains slow. Jaundice, vomiting of black blood, and severe loss of protein in the urine (causing it to become foamy) occurs during this stage. Hemorrhages may be noted in the mouth and skin (petechiae). The patient is confused, and the senses are dulled. Delirium, convulsions, and coma occur before death in approximately 10% of cases. If the patient is to survive, this last febrile episode lasts from 3 to 9 days. With remission, the patient is well, with no aftereffects from the disease.

Immunization is available and required or recommended for travel to many countries. It was once a common disease in the United States and we have the mosquito here that can spread it again.

Zika Virus

This is a viral disease spread by a daytime-biting mosquito that frequently lives in human habitats, the *Aedes alopictus*. As the range of this beast is well into the northern areas of the United States, and it can also carry dengue, chikungunya, and West Nile virus, febrile illness associated with muscle and joint pain, and at times rash and/ or eye irritation, could be any one of these diseases. Avoid the use of aspirin or meloxicam but treat instead with Tylenol or Ultram. Due to possible birth defects from this disease, pregnant women will need to have a careful specialist follow-up. Prevention is the use of mosquito protection as indicated on pages 213–216 and since this disease can be spread sexually, use condoms for at least 6 months after exposure or illness. Persons traveling into a Zika-infested area should continue to wear mosquito repellant at least 2 weeks after they leave to prevent a mosquito in a disease-free area from biting and spreading this illness into the community. Frequently the ache and other symptoms of Zika are very mild, and a person can contract it without even knowing they have had it or are carrying it and are possibly contagious.

CHAPTER 20

ENVIRONMENTAL INJURIES

No matter where you go sailing, while ankle sprains, bumped heads, blisters, and diarrhea are the most common problems that will probably bother you, environmental conditions pose the most likely threat to life. Foremost among these dangers is hypothermia. Death from heat exposure is still the second leading cause of death among high school athletes (discounting the highway). Unless you live right on the Pacific Coast, lightning can do more than scare you—it can destroy the integrity of your boat and disrupt navigation and communications.

Table 20.1 Environmental Injuries

ENVIRONMENTAL INJURIES ()

Hypothermia	256
Chronic Hypothermia	256–258
Acute Hypothermia	258–259
Cold water submersion	260
Cold stress injuries	260
Frostnip	260–261
Frostbite	261–262
Cold-induced bronchospasm	262–263
Immersion foot, Trench Foot, Cockpit Foot	263–264
Chilblains	264
Heat stress injuries	264
Heat cramps	268

Dilutional Hyponatremia	267
Heat exhaustion	268
Heat stroke	269
Prickly heat	270
Lightning	270

HYPOTHERMIA

The term "hypothermia" refers to the lowering of the body's core temperature to 95°F (35°C); profound hypothermia is a core temperature lower than 90°F (32°C). Hypothermia onset applies to two distinctly different onsets of pathology. Chronic hypothermia is the slow onset of hypothermia in the sailor exposed to conditions too cold to be protected by his equipment. Acute hypothermia, or immersion hypothermia, is the rapid onset of hypothermia of a person immersed in cold water.

In acute hypothermia—when the onset of cold core temperature takes less than 2 hours—the body cannot produce the complex physiological responses that it is capable of when it has more time. In chronic hypothermia—when body temperature takes 6 hours or longer to arrive at the cold core—the responses are quite dramatic and include profound dehydration, exhaustion, and complex chemical changes in the blood. The ideal treatment is quite different in the hospital setting; in the field, our treatment options are reduced to basic techniques of preventing further heat loss and some passive reheating maneuvers.

Chronic Hypothermia

You do not have to be in a bitterly cold setting to die of hypothermia. In fact, most chronic hypothermia deaths occur in the 30°F (0°C) to 50°F (10°C) range. This temperature range places almost all open water sailing in a high-risk status all year long. To survive hypothermia, be prepared to prevent it, recognize it if it occurs, and know how to treat it. Dampness and wind are the most devastating factors to be considered: Dampness can reduce the insulation of clothing and cause evaporative heat loss, and the increased convection heat loss caused by wind can readily strip away body energy—the so-called wind chill effect. Currently, many television weather forecasters discuss a "feels-like temperature" to indicate either a coolness noticeable at cold temperatures by wind or a warmness felt at hot temperatures with associated humidity. But wind chill is an incredibly important concept in understanding the importance that even a slight breeze has with regard to stripping body heat away from you and knowing to immediately consider whatever shelter you can find to minimize this loss if clothing is inadequate.

Factors important in preventing hypothermia are a high level of physical conditioning, adequate nutritional and hydration status, avoiding exhaustion, and availability of adequate insulation. There is an increased risk of "trauma hypothermia" in the case of injury, especially shock. Even in mild temperature conditions, a person in shock can become hypothermic. It is very important to insulate persons who are injured from the environment, particularly by providing surface insulation.

An initial response to cold is vasoconstriction, or the clamping down of surface blood vessels. This prevents heat from being conducted to the surface by the blood, and effectively increases the thickness of the mantle, or outer layer depth, for increased insulation. Those who become profoundly hypothermic, with a core temperature below 90°F, have concentrated their blood volume into a smaller inner core. The amount of dehydration in these persons can be profound, approaching 5 to 6 quarts (5.5 liters) in someone below 90°F, equivalent to the entire circulatory volume. This fluid loss comes not only from the vascular space but also from fluid between the cells and within the cells as the body slowly adjusts to the continuing heat loss by shrinking blood circulation into the core and increasing the thickness of the mantle layer. Cold diuresis, an increased urination, is part of this response. At this point rapid, sudden rewarming can lead to rewarming shock. Hospital methods of rewarming must be coupled with tight metabolic control by adjusting blood factors such as clotting, electrolytes, blood sugar levels, and the like.

In chronic hypothermia, rewarming shock and loss of metabolic control are the causes of death, not the so-called afterdrop phenomenon. Afterdrop, or the further lowering of core temperature after rewarming has started, is due to the combination of conduction equilibration of heat and a circulation component. By far the most important aspect is conduction equilibration. This physical property of conduction results in an equilibration of thermal mass as the higher warmth of the core leaches into the colder mantle layer. The amount of afterdrop that occurs is primarily dependent upon the rate of cooling prior to the rewarming process, not the method of rewarming!

The treatment of the chronic hypothermic victim is to prevent further loss of heat; this generally means providing shelter and/or more adequate clothing. Persons who are cold may well become hypothermic and, if they are not exhausted, the best method of warming would be to continue exercise. If the victim is exhausted, she will require rest and food. She is dehydrated and requires fluids. If she can stand, a roaring fire can provide adequate, controlled heat. Since chronic hypothermia victims are usually exhausted, they will then not be able to exercise themselves to warmth. Exercise is a method of generating heat, as is shivering, but when energy stores are consumed, exhaustion commences, and significant hypothermia will begin unless further heat loss is stopped.

Deepening hypothermia will lead to a semicomatose state and worse. This victim needs to be evacuated and hospitalized. Obviously, the real salvation of this situation is a warm shelter, but if you are stuck in the elements, wrap to prevent further heat loss and transport to warmth as soon as possible. Chemical heat packs, and the like, can be added to the wrap to help offset further heat loss, but this will not add much heat to rewarm the patient and having these items on your boat is practically worthless. When heating bottles of water to provide external heat, care must be taken not to burn the victim. If evacuation is not feasible, add heat slowly to avoid rewarming shock. A warm cabin is ideal. Huddling the victim between two rescuers in an adequate sleeping bag or blankets may be the only alternative.

Acute Hypothermia

Afterdrop is, however, a real problem for the acute or immersion hypothermic who has had a significant exposure to cold water. As a rule of thumb, a person who has been in water of 50°F (10°C) or less for a period of 20 minutes or longer is suffering from a severe amount of heat loss. That individual's thermal mass has been so reduced that he is in potentially serious condition. He should not be allowed to move around, as this will increase the blood flow to his very cold skin and facilitate a profound circulatory-induced afterdrop—one so great as to be potentially lethal. If this same person is simply wrapped in a litter and not provided with outside heat, there is a real danger his core temperature will cool down to a lethal level because of this profound amount of heat loss.

The ideal treatment is rapid rewarming of the acute hypothermic by placing him in hot water (110°F or 43°C) to allow rapid replacement of heat. The acute hypothermic may have an almost normal core temperature initially, but it is destined to drop dramatically as his body equilibrates his heat store from his core to his very cold mantle. A heated cabin can be a lifesaver. If not available, huddling two rescuers with the victim in a large sleeping bag may be the only answer—the same therapy that might have to be employed in the field treatment of chronic hypothermia under some conditions.

The person who has been immersed for less than 20 minutes in cold water can do anything he wants to rewarm. He can run around like crazy, sit in a warm cabin, or just wrap up in warm, dry insulation. The total body thermal mass is still high enough that the temperature equilibration by both the conductive and circulatory components will not reduce the core temperature to a dangerous level.

To review, the person who has been in cold water longer than 20 minutes has experienced such a profound heat loss that allowing him to run around or even wrapping him without additional significant heat will cause a tremendous drop in his core temperature—into a lethal range. The person who is fished out of cold water after 2 hours or longer must be considered as approaching chronic hypothermia. He has survived long enough that his physiological protective mechanisms have resulted in dehydration and other changes that are so complex that rapid rewarming can result in shock and death unless he is carefully monitored in a hospital setting.

Cold Water Submersion

Cold water submersion is always associated with asphyxiation and simultaneous hypothermia. Note that there is a distinct difference between immersion and submersion: submersion indicates that the victim is entirely underwater; immersion means that the head is above water.

Asphyxiation results in brain death, so prompt rescue and immediate implementation of CPR play an important role in the survival of the victim. Total submersion in cold water causes a rapid core cooling, which results in a lower oxygen demand by the brain and other body tissues and increases the chance of survival over that of a victim of warm water submersion. Full recovery after 10 to 40 minutes of submersion can occur. CPR must be continued until the body has been warmed to at least 86°F (30°C). If still unresponsive at that temperature, the victim may be considered dead. It may take several hours of CPR while the patient is being properly rewarmed to make this determination.

The rewarming process for immersion victims should not be attempted in the field. Hospital management of victims of cold-water submersion is very complex. They are best transferred to centers experienced with this problem, but they will never have a chance if rescuers do not implement CPR immediately. In remote location, the safest approach is rewarming any hypothermia victim is to place him or her in a warm room, be patient, hydrate if and when he or she becomes conscious, and know that there are stories of dead, hypothermic people, waking up when left for dead in a warm room.

COLD-STRESS INJURIES

Frostnip

Frostnip, or very light frostbite, can be readily treated in the field, if recognized early enough. This term is usually reserved for a form of superficial frostbite, but I am convinced there really is a separate entity that should be considered frostnip: the skin turns pure white in a small patch, generally the tip of the nose or ear edges. When detected, cup your hands and blow on the affected parts to effect total rewarming.

Under identical exposure conditions, some people are more prone to this than others. On one of my trips into subarctic Canada, a companion almost constantly frostnipped his nose at rather mild temperatures (20°F or 7°C). We frequently had to warn him, as he seemed oblivious to the fact that the tip of his nose would repeatedly frost.

Frostbite

Frostbite is the freezing of skin tissue. The temperature of the skin must be 24°F (4°C) before it will freeze. Risk of frostbite increases if the victim is hypothermic, dehydrated, injured, wearing tight-fitting clothing or boots or is not removing boots and changing socks or checking his feet at least nightly.

Traditionally, several degrees of frostbite are recognized, but the treatment for all is the same. The actual degree of severity will not be known until after the patient has been treated. In the field, most cases of frostbite are not identified until the area has already thawed and the blue, discolored skin is found when finally changing socks or actually looking at the area in question.

When superficial frostbite is suspected, thaw immediately so that it does not become a more serious, deep frostbite. Warm hands by withdrawing them into the parka through the sleeves—avoid opening the front of the parka to minimize heat loss. Feet should be thawed against a companion or cupped in your hands in a roomy sleeping bag or other insulated environment.

The specific therapy for a deeply frozen extremity is rapid thawing in warm water (approximately 110°F or 43°C). This thawing may take 20 to 30 minutes, but it should be continued until all paleness of the tops of the fingers or toes has turned to pink or burgundy red, but no longer. This will be very painful and will require pain medication (Rx: Norco-10/325, 1 tablet; nasal Stadol; or injectable Nubain will probably be required).

Avoid opening the blisters that form. Do not cut skin away but allow the digits to autoamputate over the next 3 months. Blisters will usually last 2 to 3 weeks and must be treated with care to prevent infections (best done in a hospital with gloved attendants, lacking that handled quite well using clean dressings to soak up the fluids).

A black carapace will form in severe frostbite. This is a form of dry gangrene. The carapace will gradually fall off with amazingly good healing beneath. Efforts to hasten the carapace removal generally results in infection, delay in healing, and increased tissue loss. Leave these blackened areas alone. The black carapace separation can take over 6 months, but it is worth the wait. Without surgical interference, most frostbite wounds heal in 6 months to a year. All persons heading to sea should have their tetanus booster prior to departure (within the previous 10 years is ideal—but see the discussion under immunizations). Treat for shock, with elevation of the feet and lowering of the head, as shock will frequently occur when these people enter a warm environment.

Once the victim has been thawed, very careful management of the thawed part is required. Refreezing will result in substantial tissue loss, and this must be avoided. The patient sometimes becomes a stretcher case if the foot is involved, but not always. For that reason, it may be necessary to leave the foot or leg(s) frozen and allow the victim to walk back to the evacuation point or the facility where the thawing will take place, realizing that the amount of damage is increasing the longer the area remains frozen. Early rapid thawing is essential to minimize tissue loss. Do not allow the extremity to remain frozen unless it is essential to preserve life. Peter Freuchen, the great Greenland explorer, once walked days and miles keeping one leg frozen, knowing that when the leg thawed, he would be helpless. He lost his leg but saved his life. And that's what will also happen to you. If you leave it frozen, you will lose the frozen part.

If a frozen foot has thawed and the patient must be transported, use cotton between toes (or fluff sterile gauze from the emergency kit and place between toes), and cover other areas with a loose bandage to protect the skin during sleeping bag stretcher evacuation. The use of Spenco 2nd Skin for blister care would be ideal (see page 139).

Cold-Induced Bronchospasm

Cold-induced bronchospasm, a form of asthma sometimes called "frozen lung" or pulmonary chilling, occurs when breathing rapidly at very low temperatures, generally below 20°F (29°C). There is burning pain, sometimes coughing of blood, frequently asthmatic wheezing, and, with irritation of the diaphragm, pain in the shoulder(s) and upper stomach that may last for 1 to 2 weeks. The treatment is bed rest, steam inhalations, drinking extra water, humidification of the living area, and no smoking. Avoid this condition by using parka hoods, face masks, or breathing through mufflers, which result in rebreathing warm, humidified, expired air. The differential diagnosis must include the possibility of pneumonia. Pneumonia patients will also have high fevers (see pages 81–82 for treatment).

Immersion Foot (Trench Foot, Cockpit Foot)

Immersion foot results from wet, cool conditions with temperature exposures from 68°F (20°C) down to freezing. This is an extremely serious injury that can be worse than frostbite. There are two stages to this problem. In the first stage, the foot is cold, swollen, waxy, and mottled with dark burgundy to blue splotches. This foot is resilient to palpation, whereas the frozen foot is very hard. The skin is sodden and friable. Loss of feeling makes walking difficult. The second stage lasts from days to weeks. The feet are swollen, red, and hot; blisters form; infection and gangrene are common.

To prevent this problem, avoid nonbreathing (rubber) footwear when possible, dry the feet and change wool socks when they get wet or sweaty (certainly every night), and periodically elevate, air, dry, and massage the feet to promote circulation. Avoid tight, constricting clothing. At a minimum, remove boots and socks nightly, drying the feet and warming them before sleeping.

Treatment differs from frostbite and hypothermia in the following ways: (1) give the patient 10 grains (650 mg) of aspirin every 6 hours to help decrease platelet adhesion and the clotting ability of the blood; (2) give additional Norco-10/325 every 4 hours for pain, but discontinue as soon as possible; (3) provide 1 ounce of hard liquor (30 ml) every hour while awake and 2 ounces (60 ml) every 2 hours during sleeping hours to vasodilate or increase the flow of blood to the feet. There are no data concerning the value of using Plavix as an antiplatelet agent in treating immersion foot but, if you have it in your cardiac kit, use it. If you are unsure whether you are dealing with immersion foot or frostbite, or if the victim may have suffered both, treat for frostbite.

Chilblains

Chilblains result from the exposure of dry skin to temperatures from 60°F (16°C) to freezing. The skin is red, swollen, frequently tender, and itching. This is the mildest form of cold injury and no tissue loss results. Treatment is the prevention of further exposure with protective clothing over bare skin and the use of ointments if available, such as A+D Ointment or Vaseline (white petrolatum). The hydrocortisone 1% cream from the Topical Bandaging Kit will help when applied 4 times daily.

HEAT STRESS INJURIES

High environmental temperatures are frequently aggravated by strenuous work; humidity; reflection of heat from rock, sand, or other structures (even snow!); and the lack of air movement. It takes a human approximately 10 days to become heat acclimated. Once heat stress adaptation takes place, there will be a decrease in the loss of salt in the sweat produced to conserve electrolytes. Another major change is the rapid production of sweat and the formation of larger quantities of sweat. Thus, the body is able to start its efficient cooling mechanism—sweating—more fully and with less electrolyte disturbance to the body.

Table 20.2 Risk Factors for Heat Stress Injuries

1. High humidity
2. Overweight
3. Very young or very old
4. Unaccustomed to heat
5. Illness with fever or taking drugs such as antihistamines
6. Clothing or equipment that interferes with heat loss (certain helmets, too much or restrictive clothing)
7. Dehydration (drinking to prevent thirst will keep dehydration above 2%)

Salt lost in sweat during work can normally be replaced at meal-time. An unacclimated man working an 8-hour shift would sweat 4 to 6 liters. The salt content is high, 3 to 5 g/liter of sweat. With acclimatization, salt concentration drops (1 to 2 g/liter). An acclimatized man might lose 6 to 16 g of salt during an 8-hour shift in 6 to 8 liters of sweat. The unacclimated man could lose 18 to 30 g of salt in 4 to 6 liters of sweat. The average American diet contains 10 to 15 g/day of salt. This means that an unacclimated worker could be suffering from a 3 to 20 g of salt deficit per day. In the 10 days that it would take his body to become conditioned to heat stress, the total salt deficit could become substantial.

A concern in heat illness prevention is that a heat-stressed individual must obtain adequate fluid replacement. If we focus on salt replacement, to the exclusion of adequate water intake, the individual may become salt loaded and accelerate his dehydration. Generally, an excess of salt or water over actual needs is readily controlled by kidney excretion.

Depletion of body salt can lead to progressive dehydration because the body will attempt to maintain a balance between electrolyte concentrations in tissue fluids with that in the cells. Deficient salt intake, with continued intake of water, tends to dilute tissue fluid. This suppresses the antidiuretic hormone (ADH; vasopressin) of the pituitary gland, preventing the kidney from reabsorbing water. The kidney will then excrete a large volume of very dilute urine. The salt concentration of body fluids will be maintained, but at the cost of increasing the depletion of body water, with a rapid onset of dehydration. Under heat stress, this can result in symptoms of heat exhaustion similar to those resulting from water restriction, but with more severe signs of circulatory insufficiency and notably little thirst. Absence of chloride in the urine (less than 3 g/liter) is diagnostic of salt deficiency, a test not performable in the field.

An opposite defect in the regulation of ADH can lead to severe loss of sodium by the body, resulting in hyponatremia. A deficiency of ADH causes water retention by the kidney and hyponatremia with rather low amounts of water ingestion. Another cause of hyponatremia would be overhydrating, basically causing water intoxication. The discovery of hyponatremia as a reason for the collapse of hikers in the Grand Canyon has been blamed on overhydration. But it is hard to imagine carrying that much water. Their condition may have resulted from ADH deficiency. Military personnel during training have also suffered from hyponatremia collapse, but in the case of an individual being allowed multiple breaks for water whenever he felt like it (unrestricted access to limitless water), overhydration as the cause for hyponatremia makes sense.

The ideal replacement fluid for the unacclimated worker in heat would be lightly salted water (0.1% or 1 teaspoon/gallon; 1 g/liter) to prevent water or salt depletion. He needs 13 to 20 ounces (400 to 600 ml) of water before activity, and 3 to 6 ounces (90 to 180 ml) of water every 10 to 15 minutes during an active period. Do not go longer than 30 minutes between drinks of water. Replacement fluids should not contain sugar concentrations greater than 6 g per 100 ml, as higher concentrations slow gastric emptying. Acclimatized subjects need only water as a replacement fluid, but need 32 ounces (1 liter) per hour in activity during hot weather. Thirst develops when a person is about 2% dehydrated, so "drinking to thirst"—that is, drinking to satisfy thirst—is a safe way to prevent dehydration and avoid overhydration.

With no water available, how long could a person expect to survive? The answer is generally dependent upon the temperature and the amount of activity. At a temperature of 120°F (49°C) with no water available, the victim would expect to survive about 2 days (regardless of activity). This temperature is so high that survival would not be increased beyond 2 days by even 4 quarts (3.7 liters) of water. Ten quarts (9.5 liters) might provide an extra day. At 90°F (32°C) with no water, the person could survive about 5 days if she walked during the day, 7 days if travel was only at night or if no travel was undertaken at all. With 4 quarts (3.7 liters) of water, survival would extend to 6.5 days with day travel and to 10 days with only night travel. With 10 quarts, days of survival would increase to 8 and 15, respectively. If the highest temperature was 60°F (15.5°C) with no water, the active person could expect to survive 8 days, the inactive person 10 days.

Can a person survive by consuming urine if there is not water available? The short answer is yes, for an amazing period of time. While seawater (water at about 0.9% salinity) will cause dehydration, the lower solute content of urine does not, even when it has a very high specific gravity from being concentrated. For a practical proof of this, refer to the excellent book *Skeletons on the Zahara* for the account of the crew of the American brig *Commerce* led by Captain James Riley during a survival epic after being shipwrecked in 1815. The physiology is solid, but the concept is repulsive.

PREVENTING HEAT ILLNESS

- Drink to prevent thirst.
- Avoid alcohol.
- Wear baggy clothing that promotes evaporation of sweat.
- Cover the head and shade the face.
- Keep physically fit and allow time for heat acclimatization.
- Avoid exercising during hottest time of day.

Dilutional Hyponatremia

This is a condition in which the blood sodium level falls too low to maintain normal body function and is typically caused by drinking too much water and not consuming adequate salt-containing food. Drinking only to treat thirst can prevent overhydration.

Symptoms include headache, weakness, fatigue, lightheadedness, muscle cramps, nausea with or without vomiting, sweaty skin, normal core temperature, normal or slightly elevated pulse and respirations, and a rising level of anxiety. These patients appear to have heat exhaustion or heat stroke since the signs and symptoms overlap. Treating it like heat exhaustion by just adding water will harm the hyponatremia patient, making it worse. Increased severity of hyponatremia includes disorientation, irritability, and combativeness, which gives the problem a more common name: water intoxication. Untreated, the ultimate result will be seizures, coma, and death.

Note that heat-exhausted patients have a typically low output of yellowish to brown urine (urinating every 6 to 8 hours) combined with thirst. Hyponatremia patients urinate a clear stream frequently. Hyponatremia patients deny thirst and will admit to have been drinking lots of water.

Patients with mild-to-moderate symptoms and a normal mental status may be treated in the field: the treatment for this condition is rest in shade with no fluid intake (even sports electrolyte drinks) and a gradual intake of salty foods while the kidneys reestablish a sodium balance. The ideal treatment fluid would be an approximately 9% salt solution, which would be the equivalent of 3 to 4 bouillon cubes in 1/2 cup of water. Once a patient develops hunger and thirst combined with normal urine output, the problem is solved. Restriction of fluids for someone who is well hydrated, fortunately, is harmless. Patients with an altered mental status require rapid evacuation to a medical facility.

Heat Cramps

Salt depletion can result in nausea, twitching of muscle groups, and at times severe cramping of abdominal muscles, legs, or elsewhere. Treatment of heat cramps consists of stretching the muscles involved (avoid aggressive massage), resting in a cool environment, and replacing salt losses. Generally, 10 to 15 g of salt (a pinch per quart—liter) and drinking to satisfy thirst should be adequate treatment.

Heat Exhaustion

Heat exhaustion is a classic example of compensatory shock (see page 15), and is encountered while working in a hot environment. The body has dilated the blood vessels in the skin to divert heat from the core to the surface for cooling. However, this dilation is so pronounced, coupled with profuse sweating and loss of fluid (also a part of the cooling process) that the BP to the entire system falls too low to adequately supply the brain and the visceral organs. The patient will have a rapid heart rate and other findings associated with the compensatory stage of shock: pale color, nausea, dizziness, headache, and a lightheaded feeling. Generally, the patient sweats profusely, but this may not always be the case. The temperature may be elevated, but often not at all.

Treat as for shock. Have the patient lie down immediately, elevate the feet to increase the blood supply to the head, and remove from direct sunlight and the hot environment. Provide copious amounts of water, a minimum of 1 to 2 quarts (1 to 2 liters). Lightly salted water would be best. Obviously, fluids can be administered only if the patient is conscious. If unconscious, elevate the feet above head level and protect from aspiration of vomit. Give water when the patient awakens.

Heat Stroke

Heat stroke (sun stroke) represents the complete breakdown of the heat control process (thermal regulation) in the human body. With the loss of the ability to sweat, core temperatures rise over 105°F (40°C) rapidly and soon exceed 107.6°F (42°C), resulting in death if not treated aggressively. This is a true emergency. It is a progressive stage of shock. The patient will be confused, very belligerent, and uncooperative, and will rapidly become unconscious. Immediately move into shade or erect a hasty barrier for shade. Spray with water or other suitable fluid and fan vigorously to lower the core temperature through evaporative cooling. Lacking other available fluid, this is the one time in medicine when it may be justifiable to urinate on your patient. Massage the limbs to allow the cooler blood of the extremities to return to core circulation more readily, and fan to increase evaporative heat loss. Carefully monitor the core temperature and cease cooling when it lowers to 102°F (39°C). The temperature may continue to fall or suddenly rise again.

The most significant finding in heat stroke is the altered mental status of the victim. While heat exhaustion victims can be confused, this should resolve rapidly when they are in the shock treatment position (head down, feet up). The confusion and very often belligerent behavior of heat stroke victims make them very hard to handle. While their skin is normally dry and hot, this is not always the case. Suspect heat stroke in anyone who becomes confused and erratic in behavior, or unconscious, during exercise in a hot environment.

This person should be evacuated as soon as possible, since his thermal regulation mechanism is quite unstable and will remain so for an undeterminable length of time. He should be placed under a physician's care as soon as possible. Return to the shore if possible. Otherwise, treat as above.

Prickly Heat

Prickly heat is a heat rash caused by the entrapment of sweat in glands in the skin. This can result in skin irritation and frequently severe itching. Treatment includes cooling and drying the involved area and avoiding conditions that may induce sweating for a while. Providing several hours in a cool, dry environment daily is the only reliable treatment for prickly heat, but you may treat for itch as indicated on pages 35–36.

LIGHTNING

For a sailor, lightning has significant risks, one of personal danger and the other potential significance for the ship ranging from structural to electronic component damage. Lightning is much more common over land, as the earth soaks up more heat rapidly and usually reflects less of it than water. This allows warm air masses to rise, meeting cooler air masses, stimulating thunderstorms.

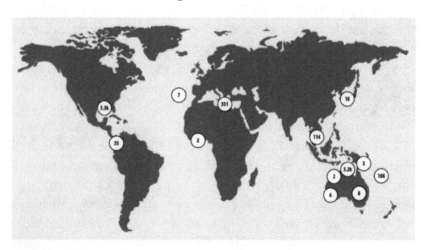

Figure 20.1
Maps indicating greatest lightning risk can be found real-time as indicated in the text

To observe real-time lightning strikes go to www.lightningmaps. org/?lang=eng.

Ships frequently get struck by lightning, especially in the high-intensity coastal areas.

Boats place you at a peculiar disadvantage when it comes to lightning. You can run, but you can't hide, unless it is along a shoreline that has much higher structures than your ship placing you into a cone of protection (see below). We all know that this is not always practical or safe.

When looking at the world lightning frequency strike map below, it can be easily seen that there are considerably more strike over and near land masses. This map is a composite of strikes between 1995 and 2002.

To observe real-time lightning strike on a worldwide data base, go to www.lightningmaps.org

Data taken from ship insurance claims provide the information shown in tables 20.3 and 20.4 below.

Table 20.3 The Probability of a Lightning Strike by Type of Boat, 2003–2013

TYPE OF BOAT	CHANCES PER 1,000
Multihull sailboat	6.9
Monohull sailboat	3.8
Trawler/motor yacht	1.5
All—overall average	0.9
Bass boat, runabout, pontoon boat	0.1

Table 20.4 The Probability of a Lightning Strike by Size of Boat, 2003–2013

TYPE OF BOAT	CHANCES PER 1,000
0–15 feet (up to 4.5 m)	0
16–25 feet (up 7.5 m)	0.2
26–39 feet (up to 12 m)	2.1
40–64 feet (up to 20 m)	6

Ship Damage

Lightning can blow a hole right through the hull of a boat, but more commonly its passage through metal fitting damages the surrounding fiberglass. This can be severe enough that the boat sinks. Extreme damage from lightning is the exception, not the rule.

According to the Boat US Marine Insurance files, over the past decade, more than 75% of lightning claims in were for less than 30% of the insured value of the boat consisting primarily of damaged electronics. The integration of electronics into navigation and communications to propulsion and maneuvering makes these systems vulnerable to damage.

The "fuzzy" lightning dissipation terminals and the early streamer emission terminals are not evidence-based equipment. A well-designed lightning protection system provides an appropriate discharge path out of the boat having a lightning rod wired properly to a submerged metal plate (grounding terminal) via special wires (down conductors) installed specifically for that purpose. Prevention of secondary flashes from any large metal structures would require side flash conductors. A brief, technical description of this technology is available at www.boatus.com/seaworthy/magazine/2016/january/lightning-protection.asp and in the same magazine at www.boatus.com/magazine/2017/april/lightning-strikes.asp.

Besides checking the electronics used in navigation and operation of the ship, certainly check communications devices for damage. Communications are an integral part of the medical treatment protocol for ship operation due to the potential need for medivac, telemedical advice, or other assistance and instructions on returning to a port. Electronic instruments should be turned off before an impending storm, if possible, even stored in a metal box or microwave oven to act as a Faraday box to prevent damage.

Hull damage may not be readily apparent. The damage to the boat is determined by how the strike exits. A ship struck by lightning needs its hull checked and needs to be at least short-hauled to a port facility to accomplish this if possible.

Crew Injury

Other than being totally toasted, cardiopulmonary arrest is the most significant lightning injury to humans. People who can scream from fright or pain after an electrical bolt has struck are already out of immediate danger. Their wounds may be dressed later. Those who appear dead must have immediate attention, as they may be saved. Normally, when dealing with mass casualties, the wounded are cared for preferentially while the dead are left alone. Not in this instance! The victim is highly unlikely to die unless cardiopulmonary arrest occurs. If cardiopulmonary arrest does happen, 75% will die unless CPR is performed. As the heart tends to restart itself due to its inherent ability (automaticity), the heartbeat may return spontaneously in a short time. However, the respiratory system may be shut down for 5 to 6 hours before being able to resume its normal rhythm. Lack of oxygen will cause a person whose heart has restarted spontaneously to die.

When administrating CPR, take precautions with the cervical spine, as the explosion may have caused fractures of the neck or other portions of the body. While CPR is being performed, check for the pulse periodically. When the heart restarts, maintain ventilations for the patient until respirations also resume. Attempt to continue this as long as possible; a victim may be revived even after many hours with no neurological defects—but only if CPR or respiration ventilation has been properly performed. Remember, after a lightning strike, the victim's eyes may be fixed and dilated, respirations ceased, heart stopped, BP 0/0—all signs of clinical death. Pay no attention to these findings and administer CPR as long as physically possible.

Lightning frequently causes vascular spasms in its victim. This can result in faint, or even nonpalpable, pulses. When the vasospasm clears, which it generally does within a few hours, the pulses return.

Neurological defects are the second major consequence of lightning hits. Approximately 72% of victims suffer loss of consciousness, and three-quarters of these people will have a cardiopulmonary arrest. Direct damage to the brain can result, but frequently the neurological defects, including seizure activity and abnormal brainwave studies, eventually revert to normal. Two-thirds of victims will have neurological defects of the lower half of their bodies; one-third will suffer from paralysis of the upper half. Amnesia and confusion of events after the accident are common, but usually transient.

Most will have amnesia, confusion, and short-term memory loss that may last 2 to 5 days. These effects are similar to those experienced by electroconvulsive shock therapy patients. The person may be able to talk intelligently, but shortly thereafter not remember the conversation had taken place.

Burns from lightning itself are generally not severe. Very high voltage is carried over the surface of conductors. The high voltage of lightning is similarly carried over the surface of the body with minimal internal burn damage, the so-called flashover effect.

Direct electrical burn damage can occur, however, and when it does it usually consists of one of several types. Linear burns start at the head, progress down the chest, and split to continue down both legs. These burns are usually 1/2 to 1 1/2 inches in width and are first and second degrees. They follow areas of heavy sweat concentration. Punctate burns look like a buckshot wound. These are full thickness, third-degree burns that are discrete, round wounds, measuring from a few millimeters to a centimeter in width. These seldom require grafting as the area is so small. Feathering or ferning burns are diagnostic of lightning injury. They fade within a few hours to days and require no treatment. This phenomenon is not a true burn, but the effect of electron showers on the skin. They have a characteristic reddish fern appearance that covers the skin surface—especially the trunk. Thermal burns also result from vaporization of surface moisture, combustion of clothing, heated metal buckles, and the like. Thermal burns are the most common type of lightning-associated burn, and they can be first, second, or third degree.

The flashover effect saves most victims from burn trauma. However, as noted, burns do occur. Persons with head burns are two and a half times more likely to die than those without. Possibly more surprising, persons with leg burns are five times more likely to die than those who do not have them. This is probably related to a ground or step current phenomenon.

The four mechanisms of direct lightning injury are (1) direct strike, (2) splash, (3) step current, (4) blunt trauma. To minimize the chance of lightning injury, the following should be noted about these mechanisms:

1. Direct strikes are most likely to take place in the open, especially if carrying metal or objects above shoulder level. Shelter should be taken within the cone of safety, described as a 45-degree angle down from a tall object, such as a tree or cliff face. But that cone of safety isn't quite true. Being too close to the mast can result in increased exposure to splash current or ground current; too near the outer edge, and the zone of safety simply fails and you have increased exposure to direct strike. The strike can easily jump 30 feet (10 m) to strike the mast lower than its actual top (the so-called air terminal). And one must consider the area adjacent to the object being struck as dangerous because of splash injuries and step current.

2. Splash injuries are perhaps the most common mechanism of lightning hit—the current strikes an object and jumps to a person whose body has less resistance than the object the lightning initially struck. Splash injuries may occur from person to person, when several people are standing close together. It has jumped from wires after having struck the fence some distance away. It has splashed to people from plumbing fixtures inside houses that were struck. Avoid close proximity to walls, fences, plumbing, or other items that could be struck. Inside a ship, this risk is minimized by proper ship grounding.

3. Step current is also called stride voltage and ground current. The lightning current spreads out in a wave along the ground from the struck object, with the current strength decreasing as the radius from the strike increases. If the victim's feet are at different distances from the point of the strike, and the resistance in the ground is greater than through his body, he will complete a circuit. Large groups

of people can be injured simultaneously in this manner. Keeping feet and legs together, while squatting down, minimizes the chances of step voltage injury.

4. Blunt trauma, or the sledgehammer effect, results from the force of the lightning strike, or the explosive shock wave that it produces. The victim may be forcibly knocked to the ground. Over 50% of victims will have their eardrums ruptured in one or both ears. This may result from direct thermal damage, the thunder shock wave, or even skull fractures from the blunt trauma. Barotrauma to the ears may be reduced by keeping the mouth open during times of great danger.

Naturally, the injuries that result (ear pain, burns, blunt trauma, cardiac or pulmonary arrest) are all managed as indicated elsewhere in this book.

CHAPTER 21
THE SHIP'S MEDICINE CHEST

Many maritime regulations, including the country of your ship's registry and the ports at which you call, can influence the content and your management of the ship's medicine chest. U. S. federal legislation had been enacted in 1790, which required every American flag vessel over 150 tons with a crew of 10 or more to carry a medicine chest. In many jurisdictions, there are exclusions for private boats not accepting paying passengers or crew members in certain categories regarding the design and contents of the ship's medicine chest. If you are visiting foreign ports of call, you must be cognizant of these regulations.

In this section we will be looking at the most practical development of a compact medical chest to serve the purposes of both offshore and extend cruises in a private ship, generally with a crew ranging from 3 to 25. Medical care and medicine chest recommendations for commercial ships are subject to specific requirements of the country of their registry. This book would provide a valuable guide as far as diagnosis and provide treatment plans that would be of value to commercial concerns as the official publications developed for the merchant marine are not symptom-based. There are expanded discussions of this topic available at www.doctor-on-board.com.

The most appropriate ship's medicine chest would be compact, containing both multifunctional and cross-functional components. This requires the minimal number of medications but provides in-depth coverage when a medication is consumed.

Taking the above into account, study the potential first aid material requirements, anticipate the most likely serious events that could conceivably occur, but also tailor the kit to the medical skill level of the participants. Additional factors to consider are the weight, cost, bulk, and availability of components. Take into consideration the number in the party, length of survival situation, degree of risk anticipated, and whether or not there is a potential that other people beyond those of the immediate shipboard party will be treated.

When companies design commercial kits, two additional factors must also be considered. One is what real estate agents call "curb appeal." It must look impressive at first glance. The other is to plan for various price points to target different markets. These constraints give commercial kits a disadvantage over the kit you put together yourself. They always contain a shallow amount of multiple line items to look impressive.

While commercial kits are usually an anathema to practical use, they can prove to be a necessity to the commercial ship master due to convenience of acquisition and to match complex requirements of some maritime laws.

The ship's medicine chest includes state-of-the-art items that will provide ideal treatment. As this book has been written for those who may be isolated without ready access to professional medical care, the treatments discussed go beyond normal first aid. The kits described in this chapter go beyond what would be considered a "first aid" kit, but many components are easily usable under first aid conditions. The ship's medicine chest consists of 7 units: Topical Bandaging Kit, Non-Rx Oral Medication Kit, Rx Oral/Topical Medication Kit, the Rx Injectable Medication Kit, the Rx Cardiac Medication Kit, the Dental Kit, and the Lifeboat Survival Kit.

As a minimum, the Topical Bandaging Kit and Non-Rx Oral Medication Kit will generally fulfill the vast majority of emergency treatment requirements. The prescription kits are designed for long-term and more advanced patient care. All items listed in the kits can be obtained without a prescription, except in the kits clearly marked "Rx."

All nonprescription medications have packaging that describes the official dosages and appropriate warnings or precautions concerning their use. Prescription medications usually have elaborate package inserts with this same information. When obtaining a prescription drug for your medical kit, request this insert from your physician or copy the information from the Physicians' Desk Reference or from the Tarascon Pharmacopoeia©, available at libraries and even as smartphone apps.

The quantities of all items can be split into minimal amounts that would be included in a special kit, which you would want to repack for your lifeboat, to last 2 to 3 weeks. Due to the suggested list having items with multifunctional capability (the item can be used for more than one purpose) and items with cross-functional uses (one condition can be treated by several of the items), the quantities of items in the kit can be reduced. Cost is also a factor in recommending products. When significant treatments are required, such as implementing the use of antibiotics, the patient should be evacuated if possible. A patient with any injury, symptom, or infection that does not improve within 48 hours should be evacuated to definitive medical care. For those of you preparing for a situation where evacuation is unlikely or impossible, evaluate the stock requirements and plan accordingly.

Most medications will have an expiration date of 1 to 5 years from the date of purchase. The expiration dates have been calculated to guarantee the product will not have degraded more than 3% of the active ingredient. A study has reported that an evaluation of 8 products stored in their original containers for 28–40 years past their expiration date retained greater than 90% of their potency. Storage affects shelf life—generally heat and sunlight degrade products, but a study release in 2019 in the *Journal of Wilderness and Environmental Medicine* evaluated a wide range of items that were stored in very unfavorable conditions over a year beyond expiration date and were found to have lost none of their potency. Commercial ships must pay stick attention to medication expiration dates by law. Many countries you may enter will require that all medications brought into their jurisdictions have at least a 6-month period until expiration.

All items should be obtained in stock bottles, which usually come in 90 or 100 count. In stock bottles, the items listed should last at least 5 to 10 years beyond their expiration date. Some medications listed are too expensive for a stock bottle or need to be ordered individually, such as the injection medications. Obtain what you can—having more than you require could prove useful during a voyage as these items will be invaluable and might be useful in barter circumstances (which is frankly illegal in most jurisdictions but sometimes necessary in isolated circumstances).

Aspirin does degrade rather fast and will soon smell like vinegar, indicating it is losing potency. Epinephrine solution turns brown as it degrades into norepinephrine, which fortunately is an active metabolite but works to a lesser degree in treating anaphylaxis. Avoid capsules and choose tablets, since the former are very sensitive to heat and dampness. Liquids usually degrade faster than solids.

There can be variations in generic names among American, Canadian, and British sources. Professional vendors for stocking the ship's store are listed as ship's chandlery in yellow pages listings. And always give the Internet search engines and major online supply sources a look.

ALTERNATIVE IMPROVISATION

Alternatives to the use of the medications listed below are outlined in the treatment discussions for various problems throughout the book. Alternatives to medical supplies are also discussed below and are indicated by a check mark. Granted, resources at sea will be limited on your ship, but many galley items and other assorted materials can substitute for standard medical supplies in a pinch.

LIFEBOAT KIT VERSUS SHIP'S MEDICINE CHEST

The ship's medicine chest should have routine inventories made and rotation of medications to prevent expirations being exceeded. The Lifeboat kit should be sealed, located, and attached within the lifeboat and not disturbed. The outside should be marked with an expiration date of the shortest dated medication inside. Figuring that the ambient temperatures the kit will be exposed to will be severe at times, this kit should be repackaged and updated yearly. Beside the medications suggested below, the lifeboat will obviously require signal equipment, water, food, environmental protective and other survival gear. This book concentrates on the medical/surgical supplies only. Familiarize yourself with discussions on hydration, environmental injuries such as heat and cold, and eye and skin protection and have necessary gear and supplies for protection prepacked in the lifeboat.

Regarding both the lifeboat and the ship supplies, the medical items have been divided into subgroups, primarily responding to their being prescription or not, but also oral, topical, or injectable.

While it is not feasible to think you will need an automatic external defibrillator (AED)prepacked aboard a lifeboat. A portable AED should be on every boat and readily available to transfer to the lifeboat if appropriate and possible during evacuation.

TOPICAL MEDICATION AND BANDAGING KIT

ITEM	LIFEBOAT KIT	SHIP'S MEDICINE CHEST
Coverlet® bandage strips	6 strip	100 strips
Spenco 2nd Skin	1 package	10 packages
Hemostatic dressings	2 packages	5 packages
Nu-Gauze pads	4 sterile	100 sterile packages
Silverlon bandages	1 pack	10 packs
Waterproof tape 1	1 roll	10 rolls
SAM Splint	1 each	3 reach
Elastic stretch roll bandages	1 3" roll	6 of each 2", 3", 6" roll
Maximum strength triple antibiotic ointment with pramoxine, 1 oz tube	1 tube	12 tubes
Lanacane Cream™ 1 ounce (30 g) tube	1 tube	6 tubes
OpCon-A ophthalmic drops 5 ml	1 bottle	4 bottles
Hydrocortisone cream 1%, 1 oz (30 gram) tube	1 tube	24 tubes
Clotrimazole Cream 2%, ½ oz (15 gram) tube	0	12 tubes
Cavit dental filling paste	0	3 kits
Protective gloves	0	2 dozen
Irrigation syringe 30 ml capacity	0	1 each

Coverlet Bandage Strips

A Beiersdorf product, these common 1″ × 3″ bandage strips are the best made. They stick even when wet, will last through days of hard usage, stretch for compression on a wound, and conform for better application.

✓ Duct tape, climbing tape.

Spenco 2nd Skin

Truly a major advance in field medicine. This inert hydrogel consists of 96% water and 4% polyethylene oxide. It is used on wet, weeping wounds to absorb fluids and protect the injury. This is a perfect prevention or cure for friction blisters. It revolutionized the field treatment of first-, second-, and third-degree burns, as it can be applied to all three as a covering and for pain relief. This item should be in every medical kit. The ideal covering pad is the Spenco Adhesive Knit Bandage. If used in treating blisters, remove only the outer covering of cellophane from the 2nd Skin, cover with the Knit Bandage, and occasionally dampen with clean water to maintain the hydrogel's hydration. It will last a lot longer this way when in short supply. There are a variety of similar dressing sold in virtually all drugstores which are labeled as

✓ The cooling technique for burns (see page 148) and a piece of tape over hot spots (see page 147) can simulate the benefits of Spenco 2nd Skin. Cellophane, plastic food wrappers, or plastic sheeting of any kind makes an excellent wound covering. Secure with tape of any type. A cellophane dressing is nonadherent, seepage leaks from the unsealed edges, the wound can be observed, and the increased and appropriate moisture level of the dressing increases the rate of wound healing.

Hemostatic Dressings

There are now three hemostatic dressings approved by the military. Since the addition of Quick Clot Combat Gauze (Z-Medica Corporation, Wallingford, CT, USA; http://www.quickclot.com) in

April 2008 to the TCCC Guidelines, based on the recent battlefield success, Celox Gauze (Medtrade Products Ltd, Crewe, UK; www.celoxmedical.com) and ChitoGauze (HemCon Medical Technologies, Portland, OR, USA; www.tricolbiomedical.com) have been added. When used they must be placed into the wound on top of the bleeding vessel, and not on top of other bandage material. Direct pressure must be applied continuously for a minimum of 5 minutes or as per the manufacturer's recommendation. QC Combat Gauze has an "official" shelf life of 2 years.

✓ Gauze dampened with epinephrine or nasal decongestant can help decrease oozing blood.

Nu-Gauze Pads
Johnson & Johnson (J&J) Company has developed a gauze that is 2-ply yet absorbs nearly 50% more fluid than conventional 12-ply gauze pads. This may not seem important until a rapidly bleeding wound needs care. For years J&J has made a "Nu-Gauze" strip packing dressing; the Nu-Gauze Pads are a completely different material. They are a wonderful advance in gauze design.

✓ Cotton T-shirts or other clothing; bandannas.

Silverlon Bandage
This is a proprietary dressing that is over 99% silver-bonded to a flexible polymer backing that has extremely effective antiseptic properties. This dressing can remain in place for 5 days at a time. If it becomes saturated with pus or drainage, it can be removed, rinsed off, and reinserted. It is amazing but true—a bandage that can be used days at a time and then reused, and still be fully effective regarding its germicidal properties. From both a theoretical reason and my personal experience, on any long voyage I would make this my dressing of choice.

In case of puncture wounds or deep abscesses that must be opened (see page 153), this same product is available as a non-adhesive packing strip. For wounds requiring packing, this is the most modern go-to product to use, for the same reasons I mentioned earlier. Additionally, this material is now available as a face mask for Sars-Cov-2 protection. Refer to their website at www.silverlon.com.

Waterproof Tape

A tough tape that can be used for splinting or bandage application. There are no brand advantages that I can determine. A 1″ × 15′ roll on a metal spool is a usable size.

✓ Duct tape, climbing tape.

Sam Splint

A padded, malleable splint that provides enough comfort to be used as a neck collar. It is adequately rigid to splint any extremity and universal, so that only one of these needs to be carried for all splinting needs. This item replaces ladder splints, etc. It weighs less than 5 ounces.

✓ Malleable splints can frequently be made from stays found in internal backpack frames. Other stiff materials can be used, such as strips of Ensolite foam pads or inflatable pads, held in place with tape or torn cloth.

Elastic Bandages

Elastic bandage 2″

Elastic bandage 3″

Elastic bandage 6″

Obtain good-quality bandages that stretch without narrowing and that provide firm, consistent compression.

✓ Elastic bandages can be replaced with almost any cloth that is firmly wrapped in place. The most stretchy form of cloth usually available is a cotton T-shirt.

Maximum Strength Triple Antibiotic Ointment with Pramoxine, 1 oz Tube

Each gram of this ointment contains bacitracin, 500 units, neomycin sulfate, 3.5 mg, polymyxin B sulfate, 10,000 units, and an anesthetic pramoxine hydrochloride, 10 mg. For use as a topical antibiotic in the prevention and treatment of minor infections of abrasions and burns, this formulation also is an anesthetic that numbs the skin. A light coat should be applied twice daily. Neomycin can cause skin rash and itch in some people. If this develops, discontinue use and apply the hydrocortisone cream to counter this effect.

- ✓ Honey or granulated sugar placed on wounds is painless and kills germs by dehydrating them. A strong sugar solution draws the fluid from the bacteria, but human cells are able to actively avoid the dehydration process and are not injured with this technique.

Lanacane Cream 1 oz (30 g) Tube

This brand-name cream is used to treat burns, hemorrhoids, and reduce the itch of insect bites and stings. This product consists of benzocaine (20%) as an anesthetic and benzethonium chloride (0.2%) as an antiseptic.

Chlorhexidine Surgical Scrub

This Mölnlyce Health Care product, chlorhexidine gluconate 4% (Hibiclens), far surpasses hexachlorophene (pHisoHex®) or povidone-iodine scrub (Betadine) with regard to its antiseptic action. This item is now available as a generic. The onset and duration of its action is much more impressive than either of those two products.

- ✓ Many surgical scrubs are available without prescription and are ideal for use, but they can all be replaced with potable (drinkable) water irrigation. Remember, "the solution to pollution is dilution."

Opcon-A Eye Drops

This product is a combination of naphazoline (0.0267%) and pheniramine maleate (0.315%) made by Bausch and Lomb. These eye drops are used for allergy relief, to remove redness, and to alleviate discomfort from smoke, eye strain, and the like. They will not cure infection or disguise the existence of a foreign body. Place 1 drop in each eye every 6 hours.

✓ Rinse eyes with clean water. A wet, cold compress relieves eye itch and pain.

Hydrocortisone Cream 1%, 1 oz Tube

This non-Rx steroid cream treats allergic skin rashes, such as those from poison ivy. A cream is ideal for treating weeping lesions, as opposed to dry scaly ones but will work on either. For best results, cover with an occlusive dressing (plastic cover) overnight.

✓ Blistery rashes can be soothed, and the leaking fluid dried, by applying a cloth made wet with concentrated salt solution.

Clotrimazole Cream 2%, ½ oz Tube

This is one of the most effective antifungal preparations available for foot, groin, or other body fungal infections. Brand names are Lotrimin® and Mycelex® (vaginal cream). The vaginal cream in a 2-ounce tube is less expensive and works well on the skin surface as well as vaginally.

✓ Dry, itchy lesions of any type respond to a soothing coating of cooking oil.

Cavit Dental Filling Paste

For temporary filling of cavities and repair of broken bridgework. Without being able to drill out the underlying decay, the cavity will need to be seen as soon as possible by a dentist for proper care or an abscess may form.

✓ Use oil of cloves to line the cavity for pain relief. A mixture of zinc-oxide powder (not the ointment) and oil of cloves, made up as a thick paste, can also be used as a temporary filling.

Protective Gloves

Due to concerns with blood-borne pathogens (hepatitis B and C and AIDS), it is prudent to carry protective gloves for first aid use. These can be nonsterile (they are readily sterilized by boiling or treating with antiseptics). Vinyl gloves will last much longer in a kit than latex gloves, but the best are nitrile gloves.

✓ Use an empty food bag or waterproof stuff sack as a glove or wrap your hand in the most waterproof material available.

Irrigation Syringe

Required for forceful irrigation of wounds. The best would have a protective spray shield, such as the ZeroWet Supershield; otherwise, wear glasses to protect your eyes from splash contamination discussed in chapter 16.

✓ The solution to pollution is dilution. Forceful irrigation is the best method for cleaning a wound and diluting the germ count enough so that the body's immune system can kill the remaining germs. Without a syringe, augment the volume of water you are pouring on the wound with a brisk scrubbing action using a soft, clean cloth.

Surgical Kit

	LIFEBOAT KIT	SHIP'S MEDICINE CHEST
Quantity		
Needle holder	0	1
Adson w/teeth	0	1
Adson w/o teeth	0	1
3–0 Ethilon sutures	0	12
5–0 Ethilon sutures	0	12
3–0 gut sutures	0	6

This consists of 1 needle holder, 1 Adison forceps with teeth and 1 without teeth, 3–0 Ethilon sutures, 5–0 Ethilon sutures, and 3–0 gut sutures. The 3–0 and 5–0 sutures should have 3/8 circle, cutting needles. The gut sutures are best placed with a ½ circle for use potentially within the mouth.

- ✓ Many surgical kits are available from Amazon, including practice kits. Once in the field, butterfly bandages can be fashioned from tape as described on page 135. Lacking other means of fastening gaping wounds together, use the technique of open packing the wound with a wet-to-dry dressing described on page 141.

- ✓ Surgical kit consists of 1 needle holder, Adson tissue forceps (1 with teeth, one without). 3–0 Ethilon sutures, 5–0 Ethilon sutures, and 3–0 gut (dissolvable) sutures.

Foley Catheter Kit

	LIFEBOAT KIT	SHIP'S MEDICINE CHEST
Quantity		
Foley catheter insertion kit	0	2 kits

See chapter 11, for description of use of the Foley catheter.

Automatic External Defibrillator

	LIFEBOAT KIT	SHIP'S MEDICINE CHEST
Quantity		
Automatic external defibrillator	0	1

NON-RX ORAL MEDICATION KIT

- ✓ Alternatives to the use of these medications are discussed in the treatment options throughout the book. Each medication is multifunctional and also has cross-therapeutic versatility. This means that each item can be used for more than one problem, and problems have more than one drug that can be used as treatment. This allows a minimal number of medications to be carried, yet provides depth of coverage if one medication is in short supply.

ITEM	LIFEBOAT KIT	SHIP'S MEDICINE CHEST
Percogesic tablets	12 tablets	200 tablets
Ibuprofen 200 mg tablets	12 tablets	500 tablets
Diphenhydramine 25 mg tablets	0 (use Percogesic)	500 tablets
Bisacodyl 5 mg tablets	0	100 tablets
Loperamide 2 mg tablets	12 tablets	200 tablets
Famotidine 20 mg tablets	12 tablets	500 tablets

Percogesic Tablets (Pain, Fever, Muscle Spasm, Sleep Aid, Anxiety, Congestion, Cough, and Nausea)

Relieves pain, fever, and muscle spasm. Each tablet contains 325 mg of acetaminophen and 12.5 mg of citrate diphenhydramine. Ideal for injuries of joints and muscles, as well as aches from infections. Diphenhydramine is also a decongestant and cough suppressant. It also induces drowsiness and can be used as a sleeping aid or to calm a hysterical person. These indications are not included on the packaging information. Dosage is generally 2 tablets every 4 hours as needed. One of the most useful non-Rx drugs obtainable.

Ibuprofen Tablets (200 mg) (Pain, Fever, Bursitis, Tendonitis, Menstrual Cramps)

Brand names are Advil®, Nuprin®, Motrin®, and others. It relieves pain, fever, menstrual cramps, and inflammation. Overuse syndromes such as bursitis and tendonitis are common in nautical-related activities, and this is an ideal treatment. The non-Rx dosage is 2 tablets 4 times a day. It should be taken with food to prevent stomach irritation or heartburn. The Rx dosage is 4 tablets taken 4 times daily, a dose that may be necessary for severe inflammation.

Diphenhydramine Tablets (25 mg) (Antihistamine, Antianxiety, Cough, Muscle Cramps, Nausea, Motion Sickness Prevention)

The brand name is Benadryl; many variations are sold containing more ingredients than just the diphenhydramine. For antihistamine action, these capsules can be taken 1 or 2 every 6 hours. To use as a powerful cough suppresser, the dose is 1 tablet every 6 hours. For muscle spasm relief, take 1 or 2 tablets at bedtime alone, or in combination with 2 ibuprofen 200 mg tablets. For nausea or motion sickness, take 1 tablet every 6 hours as needed. For sleep induction, take 1 or 2 tablets after going to bed. The Percogesic included in this kit also contains diphenhydramine.

Bisacodyl Tablets (5 mg) (Constipation)

This laxative works on the large bowel to form a soft stool within 6 to 10 hours. Use 1 tablet as needed. It is very gentle, so do not expect rapid results. The brand-name product motto is: "Take one in the PM for a BM in the AM."

Loperamide Tablets (2 mg) (Diarrhea)

An anti-diarrheal with the brand name of Imodium®. Dosage for persons 12 or older is 2 tablets after the first loose bowel movement, followed by 1 tablet after each subsequent loose bowel movement, but no more than 4 tablets a day for no more than 2 days. The prescription use of this medication is usually 2 tablets immediately, and 2 with each loose stool up to a maximum of 8 per day. Follow the package instructions for children's dosages.

Famotidine (20 mg) (Heartburn, Certain Allergic Reactions)

Brand name is Pepcid. This medication suppresses acid formation. It may be used to treat certain allergic reactions. The non-Rx dosage is 1 tablet daily. Prescription use goes as high as 40 mg daily for acid suppression. Stronger formulations of medications are available to treat stomach heartburn and reflux symptoms, such as the proton pump inhibitor (PPI) class of compounds, including over-the-counter

(OTC) omeprazole (Prilosec) and lansoprazole (Prevacid) and esomeprazole (Nexium). If you have severe problems with these conditions, substitute them for Famotidine.

RX ORAL/TOPICAL MEDICATION KIT

The ship's medicine chest also includes prescription kits. Obtaining prescription items can properly be requested from your family physician or from a physician who understands your special needs as a sailor. There are alternative sourcing possibilities. Many items can be purchased via the Internet internationally. Some materials may be obtained from aquarium stores or agricultural outlets. As these sources may be "moving targets," the best advice is for you to check sailing blogs and websites for the latest sourcing suggestions.

ITEM	LIFEBOAT KIT	SHIP'S MEDICINE CHEST
Doxycycline 100 mg tablets	14	200
Zithromax 500 mg tablets	0	60
Levaquin 750 mg tablets	0	60
Diflucan 150 mg tablets	0	48
Norco-10/325 tablets	24	100
Atarax 25 mg tablets	24	100
Mobic® (meloxicam) 15 mg tablets	24	240
Topicort 0.25% ointment	0	12
Tobradex ophthalmic drops	0	6
Tetracaine ophthalmic solution 0.5%,	0	2
Denavir (penciclovir) cream 1%,	1	6
Stadol nasal spray	1	6
Decadron 4 mg tablets	6	100
Flagyl 250 mg	0	24
Famciclovir 500 mg	0	100
Malarone (proguanil/atrovaquone)	0	100–> need 1/person/day when in malaria area

Doxycycline Tablets (100 mg) (Antibiotic)

The generic name of an antibiotic that is useful in treating many travel-related diseases. The various sections of the text dealing with infections will indicate the proper dosage, normally 1 tablet twice daily. Not to be used in children 8 years or younger, or during pregnancy. May cause skin sensitivity on exposure to sunlight, thus causing an exaggerated sunburn. This does not usually happen, but be cautious during your first sun exposure when on this product. Many people traveling in the tropics have used this antibiotic safely. Very useful in malaria prevention at a dose of 1 tablet daily, but this must be continued for 4 weeks after leaving the contact area. Common brand names are Vibramycin®, Vibra-tabs®, Doryx®, Doxycin®, and Monodox®.

Azithromycin Tablets (500 mg) (Antibiotic)

Zithromax is the brand name of azithromycin, a broad-spectrum antibiotic used to treat certain types of pneumonia, infected throats, skin infections, and venereal diseases due to *Chlamydia trachomatis* or *Neisseria gonorrhoeae*, and genital ulcer disease in men due to *Haemophilus ducreyi* (chancroid). Dosage is 1 tablet daily for 3 days. These 3 tablets result in a therapeutic blood level for the next 7 days, thus providing a total of 10 days of coverage.

Levofloxacin Tablets (750 mg) (Antibiotic)

Levaquin is the brand name of a broad-spectrum antibiotic of a group known as fluoroquinolones. This medication is useful in treating diarrhea and organisms resistant to the above antibiotics. It is useful in treating sinus infections, bronchitis, pneumonia, skin infections and skin ulcers, and complicated urinary tract and kidney infections. Avoid excessive sun exposure while on this medication. Avoid in persons under the age of 18, and during nursing and pregnancy. Drink extra water when on this medication. Do not take with antacids, vitamins containing minerals, and ibuprofen; otherwise, it may be taken at mealtimes. Some people are made dizzy by this medication. There is a possibility that it might cause tendonitis and should be stopped if muscle pain or tendon inflammation occurs, as a tendon rupture may result. While used to treat diarrhea, it may cause diarrhea, and it may result in vaginal monilia infection.

Diflucan Tablets (150 mg) (Antifungal)
One tablet of this medication is taken to eliminate vaginal yeast (candidiasis) infection. These infections are at greater risk after taking broad-spectrum antibiotics, as they can suppress normal, healthy bacteria in the vagina. Tropical conditions are also a risk factor in developing this condition. While this medication often reacts with other medications, none are included in the ship's medicine chest recommended in this book and short-term use of 1 pill will normally not be significant regardless. The most common side effects are headache, nausea, and cramping (and these are rare).

Norco-10/325 Tablets (Pain, Cough)
The brand name of the combination of 325 mg of acetaminophen and 10 mg of hydrocodone, the principal use of the drug is in the relief of pain. Hydrocodone is a powerful cough suppressor, and is also useful in treating abdominal cramping and diarrhea. The dosage of 1 tablet every 6 hours will normally control a severe toothache. Maximum dosage is 6 tablets per day. It may be augmented with Atarax (see below). This product is now a Class II scheduled prescription, which makes obtaining it, controlling it, and transporting it much more problematic. This is a good compound and safe when used properly. Unfortunately, misuse has caused very restrictive legislation, both nationally and internationally. It would be very hard to obtain a large quantity of this medication, yet it has many uses as indicated and is safe when used properly. A potential replacement for your medical kit is Ultram® (tramadol) 50 mg, which can be taken every 6 hours for pain. You may also take meloxicam, 15 mg daily, or acetaminophen, 500 mg 4 times per day, simultaneously. Tramadol is a Class IV scheduled medication, which will still require a prescription.

Hydroxyzine Tablets (25 mg) (Nausea, Anxiety, Antihistamine, Pain Medication Augmentation)

Atarax is a brand name of hydroxyzine hydrochloride (also note the listing under Vistaril in the Rx Injectable Medication Kit); these tablets have multiple uses. This is an immensely powerful anti-nausea agent, muscle relaxant, antihistamine, antianxiety agent, and sleeping pill and will potentiate a pain medication (make it work better). For sleep, take 50 mg at bedtime; for nausea, 25 mg every 4 to 6 hours; to potentiate pain medication, take a 25 mg tablet with each dose of the pain medication. This medication treats rashes of all types and has a drying effect on congestion. The injectable version, Vistaril, has identical actions.

Meloxicam (Mobic) 15 mg Tablets (Pain Medication, Anti-Inflammatory, Fever)

This anti-inflammatory, analgesic tablet is unique in that it does not inhibit platelets from aggregating together and thus does not increase the same bleeding tendencies in wounds that occur with aspirin or ibuprofen. For this reason, it is included in the blast first-aid kits for combat troops in Afghanistan and formerly in Iraq. Dosage is 1 tablet per day taken with food. This is an ideal pain medication, will reduce fever, and helps in the treatment of overuse injuries such as tendonitis or in cases of acute trauma (sprains, strains, fractures, contusions, broken bones).

Desoximetasone (Topicort) Ointment (0.25%, 0.5 oz Tube) (Skin Allergy)

This Rx steroid ointment treats severe allergic skin rashes. Dosage is a thin coat twice daily. Occlusive dressings are not required when using this product. It should be used with caution over large body surface areas or on children. Use should be limited to 10 days or less, particularly in the latter cases.

Tobradex Ophthalmic Drops (2.5 ml) (Eye and Ear Antibiotic, Anti-Inflammatory)

This is a combination of a powerful antibiotic (tobramycin 0.3%) and a steroid (dexamethasone 0.1%). It can be used to treat infections or allergies in the eye (for which it was designed) or the ear. It can be instilled in either location 2 to 3 times daily. This medication can cause complications in case of viral infections of the eye (which are rare compared to bacterial infections and allergy conditions).

Tetracaine Ophthalmic Solution (Drops), 0.5%, 15 ml Bottle (Eye and Ear Anesthetic)

This is a sterile solution for use in the eye or ear to numb pain. Do not reapply to an eye if pain returns without examining for a foreign body very carefully. Try not to use repeatedly in the eye, as overuse delays healing. Continued pain may also mean you have missed a foreign body. Do not use in ears if considerable drainage is present; an eardrum may have ruptured and if this medication gets into the middle ear through a hole in the eardrum, it will cause profound vertigo (dizziness).

Penciclovir (Denavir) Cream, 1%, 5 gm Tube (Antiviral, Lip and Mouth Sores)

An antiviral treatment useful for cold sores on the face and on the lips. While not approved for use inside the mouth, this product actually works well there and is not harmful if swallowed. This may be used at high altitudes, in desserts or land or oceans with high reflective light, to prevent cold sores caused by intense UV light. Apply every 2 hours during waking hours for 4 days.

Butorphanol (Nubain) Nasal Spray (Severe Pain)

This is a powerful pain medication formulated to be absorbed by the lining of the nose. It is 10 times stronger than morphine on a milligram-to-milligram basis. Use only one spray up a nostril and wait 60 to 90 minutes before using a second spray in the other nostril. This process may be repeated in 3 to 4 hours. It should be working effectively within 20 minutes after the first spray. Overspraying or allowing the medication to drain down the throat will waste it since it is inactivated by gastric fluids.

Dexamethasone (Decadron) Tablets (4 mg) (Allergy, Specific Trauma Situations)

For allergy, give 1/2 tablet twice daily after meals for 5 days. This medication can also be used in serious head and spine injuries as indicated on pages 174–175.

Metronidazole (Flagyl) Capsules (250 mg) (Trichomonas Or Giardia Infection)

Metronidazole is an antibiotic that is useful in treating diarrhea caused by giardia (see page 192) at a dose of 250 mg 3 times daily. It is also used in treating infections by *Entamoeba histolytica* and *Trichomonas vaginalis* (both protozoal parasites) and certain other bacteria. It may cause numbness and nausea. It should not be taken by people with central nervous system diseases. Do not drink alcohol with this drug, as it causes flushing and vomiting.

Famciclovir Capsules (250 or 500 mg) (Cold Sores, Herpes Viral Infections)

This may be taken as a single, 1,500 mg dose as prophylaxis to prevent herpes simplex lip lesions, which are often activated by high altitude or reflective UV light exposure. This medication should be included in the kit if persons are known to have recurrent problems. An alternative is to use the Denavir cream.

Atovaquone and Proguanil (Malarone) (250 mg/100mg for Adult; 62.5 mg/25 mg Pediatric)

For malaria prevention or prophylaxis, the adult dose is 1 tablet daily 1 to 2 days before the exposure, daily while exposed, and for 7 days after exposure. Repeat dose if vomiting occurs within 1 hour after the dose. The children's dose is determined by weight. However, two other dosing regimens may be appropriate: one, a terminal dose for a short exposure trip or a treatment dose for presumptive management of illness.

PEDIATRIC TABLETS	PATIENT'S WEIGHT
1	22–44 pounds (10–20 kg)
2	45–66 pounds (21–30 kg)
3	67–88 pounds (31–40 kg)
1 Adult Tablet	Over 88 pounds (40 kg)
See text, page 239.	

RX INJECTABLE MEDICATION KIT

Items will require syringes and needle to inject. While no injectable medications are suggested for the lifeboat kit, it is appropriate to have a box of 100 sterile 3.5 ml syringes fitted with 25 gauge needles 5/8 inch length.

ITEM	LIFEBOAT KIT	SHIP'S MEDICINE CHEST
Nalbuphine 20 mg/ml	0	2 vials
Lidocaine 1%, 10 ml	0	2 vials
Dexamethasone 4 mg/ml 5 ml vials	0	6 vials
Ceftriaxone 500 mg vial	0	24 vials
Hydroxyzine 50mg/ml 30 ml vials	0	4

Nalbuphine (Nubain) (20 mg/ml, 10 ml Vial)

A strong, synthetic narcotic analgesic, this is available only by prescription but it is not a controlled narcotic. It is equal to morphine in strength. Normal adult dose is 10 mg (0.5 ml) given IM every 3 to 6 hours. The maximum dose is 20 mg (1 ml) every 3 hours. It can be mixed with 25 to 50 mg of Vistaril in the same syringe for increased analgesia in severe pain problems.

Lidocaine 1% (10 ml Vial)

Injection for numbing wounds. Maximum amount to be used in a wound in an adult should be 15 ml. This fluid is also used to mix Rocephin. See the package insert that comes with Rocephin.

Dexamethasone (Decadron) (4 mg/ml, 5 ml Vial)

For use in allergic reactions, give 4 mg daily for 5 days IM.

Ceftriaxone (Rocephin) (500 mg Vial)

A broad-spectrum antibiotic of the cephalosporin class, the inject-able medication has a wide range of bactericidal activities, including for pneumonia and bronchitis, skin infections, urinary tract and kid-ney infections, gonorrhea, pelvic infection, bone and joint infections, intra-abdominal infections, and some types of meningitis. Each vial will require 0.9 ml of lidocaine 1% to mix the contents. The reconsti-tuted medication is stable at room temperature for 3 days.

Hydroxyzine (Vistaril) (50mg/ml, 10 ml Vial)

A brand name of hydroxyzine hydrochloride, its uses and dosages are the same as indicated for Atarax in the Rx Oral/Topical Medication Kit. Obviously, in the treatment of profound vomiting, injections of medication will work better than oral administration. This solution can be mixed in the same syringe as the Nubain for administration as one injection.

Epinephrine Auto Inject Pens (Epipen, Epipen Jr. and Symjepi®)

The EpiPen and EpiPen Jr. are automatic injection syringes. Use only on one person. The EpiPen delivers 0.3 ml (0.3 mg) of 1:1,000 epi-nephrine; the EpiPen Jr. delivers 0.3 ml (0.15 mg) of 1:1,000 epineph-rine. The EpiPen devices automatically give the medication IM. Due to the high cost of auto-injection syringes, I suggest that your physician order several vials of epinephrine 1:10,000 solution for injection, and the appropriate syringes for administration (see page 205). The Symjepi is a manually injected prefilled syringe approved in 0.3- and 0.15-mg strengths, in 2019 by the FDA and available commercially in early 2020.

CARDIAC MEDICATION KIT

This kit contains both prescription and nonprescription items. See chapter 3 for additional discussion with regard to managing a heart attack (MI).

ITEM	LIFEBOAT KIT	SHIP'S MEDICINE CHEST
Aspirin 81 mg chewable tablets	30	500
Nitroglycerine 0.4 mg tablets	25	100
Clopidogrel 75 mg tablets	30	100
Atenolol 25 mg tablets	60	200
Aspirin 81 mg chewable tablets		
Nitroglycerin 0.4 mg tablets, sealed bottle of 25 or 100 tablets; or nitroglycerin spray, 60-spray canister		
Clopidogrel 75 mg tablets		
Atenolol 25 mg tablets (beta blocker)		

Aspirin (81 mg Chewable Tablets)

Do not use enteric-coated tablets, which are slower to work than chewable tablets. A larger number of aspirin can be carried to treat fever, inflammation, and pain. Not for use in children or during pregnancy. This medication is used to prevent platelet aggregation during a heart attack. Aspirin treatment reduced mortality by 23% in acute MI in a published trial called ISIS-2. Aspirin is a platelet cyclooxygenase inhibitor (see also clopidogrel below).

Nitroglycerin Sublingual Tablets (0.4 mg)

Once the seal on the bottle is open, the medication must be used within 6 months, regardless of its original expiration date. Brand name Nitrostat® is stable for 24 months after the bottle is opened, or until the expiration date on the bottle, whichever is earlier. Nitroglycerin is degraded more rapidly by heat and moisture. In tropical environments, it is better to carry nitroglycerin spray. This remains stable for 2 years, even with use. It needs to be primed with a spray before use. Meta-analysis of pre-thrombolytic-era nitrate trials found that nitroglycerin treatment resulted in a 35% reduction in mortality from acute MI (vasodilator).

Clopidogrel (Plavix) Tablets (75 mg)

This is another platelet inhibitor. This medication is very expensive, so stocking a kit with more than 10 becomes an economical challenge. The CURE trial showed that clopidogrel therapy resulted in an 18% reduction in MI, death, or stroke in patients with acute coronary syndrome and non-ST-elevated MI treated medically. This medication is a platelet ADP-receptor inhibitor, so it works differently than aspirin and the effects are additive when both are taken.

If someone has a history of phlebitis, pulmonary embolism, they should be on this medication routinely for 6 months from the episode. Persons with cardiac stents need to be on it for life.

Atenolol (Tenormin®) Tablets (25 mg)

Atenolol is a beta blocker. ISIS-I and MIAMI trials showed that beta blocker therapy resulted in a 13% reduction in mortality with either atenolol or metoprolol. Its use reduces heart rate, BP, and ischemia, raises ventricular fibrillation threshold, and reduces the likelihood of malignant ventricular arrhythmias and sudden death. Do not give if the person has a slow heart rate (below 60 beats per minute).

Clinical Reference Index

A

abdomen, examining, 13
abdominal pain, 85–89
abdominal thrust, 17–18
abortion, spontaneous, 102, 103
abrasions, 142–43
abscesses, 74, 156–57
acetaminophen (Tylenol), 32, 208, 227, 240, 241, 244, 253
ADH (antidiuretic hormone), 265–66
Admundsen, Roald, 121
adult one-rescuer CPR, 18–21
adult two-rescuer CPR, 21–22
AEDs (automatic external defibrillators), 22, 281, 288
African sleeping sickness, 247–48
African trypanosomiasis, 247–48
afterdrop, 258–59
airways, 6–7, 19–20, 22
allergic conjunctivitis, 54, 56
allergic dermatitis, 159–60
American trypanosomiasis, 248–49
amoxicillin/clavulanate (Augmentin), 74, 75, 77, 79
anaphylactic shock, 203–5
anaplasmosis, 226
animal bites and stings. *See* bites and stings
ankle injuries, 199
antacid therapy, 86

anterior shoulder dislocations, 182–83
antibiotic guidelines, 134–35
antibiotic ointment with pramoxine, maximum strength triple, 284–85
anticholinesterases, 210
antidiuretic hormone (ADH), 265–66
ants, 217–18
aphthous ulcers, 73
appendicitis, 88–89
aquatic stings, cuts, and rash, 218–20
arms: examining, 13; forearm fractures, 188–89; upper arm fractures, 184–86
arthritis, 167
Aspercreme, 167
aspirin, 280, 299
assessment: and care, 3, 4–5; focused, 8–9; initial, 6–8; medical history and physical examination, 12–13; vital signs, 9–11
Atarax (hydroxyzine), 294
atenolol (Tenormin), 300
athlete's foot, 159
atovaquone and proguanil (Malarone), 296–97
atropine, 210, 217

Augmentin (amoxicillin/
   clavulanate), 74, 75, 77, 79
automatic external defibrillators
   (AEDs), 22, 281, 288
azithromycin (Zithromax), 73

B
babesiosis, 226
back, examining, 13
bacterial skin rash, 160–61
bandages, 141–42, 282, 283–84
barnacle cuts, 219
Basic Illustrated Wilderness First Aid
   (Forgey), 126–27
beef tapeworms, 245
Bell's palsy, 237–38
Benadryl (diphenhydramine), 290
birth control pills, 101
bisacodyl, 290
bites and stings, 203–20; about,
   152–53; anaphylactic shock,
   203–5; ants/fire ants, 217–18;
   aquatic stings, cuts, and rash,
   218–20; black flies, 216; caterpillar
   reactions, 213; centipede bites,
   213; human bites, 152; millipede
   reactions, 213; no-see-ums and
   biting gnats, 216–17; and rabies,
   241–42; scorpion stings, 217;
   snake bites, 205–10; spider bites,
   210–11; ticks, 212
black flies, 216
black widow spiders *(Latrodectus
   mactans)*, 210–11
bladder infection, 95–96
blastomycosis, 226–27
bleach, chlorine, 115
bleeding: checking for severe, 7;
   stopping, 126–31; from suture or
   staple use, 139

blisters, 147–48
blood pressure, 11
blood sugar, 111
blood under nail, 155–56
body ringworm, 159
boils, 74, 156–57
bone function and disorders. *See*
   orthopedics
"boxer's fracture," 192
bradycardia, 27
break bone fever, 230
breastfeeding, 104
breathing: checking, 6–7; and CPR,
   21, 22; rapid, 22–23
broken bones. *See* fractures
bronchitis, 81–82
bronchospasm, cold-induced,
   262–63
brown recluse spiders *(Loxosceles
   reclusa)*, 211
bulb syringes, 132
burns, 148–52, 274
bursitis, 167
butorphanol (Nubain) nasal
   spray, 295
butorphanol tartrate (Stadol), 34

C
candida infection, 100–101
canker sores, 73
cardiac evaluation and care, 23–27
Cardiac Medication Kit, 299–300
cardiopulmonary arrest, 273
cardiopulmonary resuscitation. *See*
   CPR
caterpillar reactions, 213
catfish, 220
Cavit dental filling paste, 286
cavities, 66, 76, 77–78
ceftriaxone (Rocephin), 298

cellulitis, 157–58
Celox Gauze, 283
centipede bites, 213
Centruroides sculpturatus, 217
cerumen, 69
cervical collars, 176, 177
cervical spine, 7–8, 12
chagas disease, 248–49
chalazia, 56–57
chest, examining, 12
chest compressions, in CPR, 19, 22
chest injuries, 200–201
chest pain, 81–83
chikungunya fever, 227
chilblains, 264
childbirth, 104
chills, 31
ChitoGauze, 283
Chlorhexidine surgical scrub, 285
chlorine, 115, 117
choking, 17–18
cholera, 227–28
ciguatera poisoning, 108
circulation, checking, 7
clavicle injuries, 179–81
clindamycin, 226
clopidogrel (Plavix), 300
clotrimazole cream (Lotrimin, Mycelex), 286
coccicioidomycosis, 228
cockpit foot, 263–64
cold-induced bronchospasm, 262–63
cold-stress injuries, 260–64
cold water submersion, 260
colitis, 91
collarbone injuries, 179–81
Colorado tick fever, 228–29
Combat Action Tourniquet, 128
Commerce (ship), 120

Compazine (prochlorperazine), 43
conduction equilibration, 258
congestion, 61, 69–70
conjunctivitis, 54–55, 56
constipation, 93
contact lenses, 49–52
copperhead bites, 207
coral cuts, 219
coral snakes *(Micrurus fulvius),* 206, 209–10
coronavirus, 229–30
Coverlet bandage strips, 282
COVID-19, 229–30
CPR: adult one-rescuer, 18–21; adult two-rescuer, 21–22; for cold water submersion, 260; for heart attack, 26; for lightning injury, 273
crepitation, 201
Cryptosporidium, 115–16
cyanosis, 201
cystitis, 95–96

D

dandy fever, 230
dapsone, 211
debridement, 133
Decadron (dexamethasone), 296, 298
deerfly fever, 250
DEET insect repellents, 160, 212, 214–15, 216, 217
defibrillators, 22, 281, 288
delivery (childbirth), 104
Denavir cream (penciclovir), 295
dengue, 230
dental care, 74–80; cavity, 66, 76, 77–78; dental pain, 76–77; filling, lost, 77; gum pain or swelling, 74–75; loose or

dislodged tooth, 78–79; mouth lacerations, 75–76; pulling a tooth, 79–80
dermatitis, allergic, 159–60
desoximetasone (Topicort), 294
dexamethasone (Decadron), 296, 298
diabetes, 23, 103, 111–12
diarrhea, 88, 90–93, 113–14
dibucaine, 34
Dickson, Murray, 78
diclofenac, 168
Diflucan, 293
dilutional hyponatremia, 265–66, 267–68
dinoflagellates, 108, 109
diphenhydramine (Benadryl), 290
dislocations: ankle, 199; elbow, 187–88; hip, 194–96; knee, 198–99; kneecap (patella), 197–98; shoulder, 181–83; wrist, 189–91
diuretics, 175
diverticulitis, 90–91
double vision, 58
doxycycline, 292
dressings, 127–31, 141–42, 282–83

E
ear problems, 65–70; earache, 66, 72; foreign bodies, 69; infections, 66–68; ruptured eardrum, 68, 69–70; TMJ syndrome, 70
Ebola, 225
echinococcus, 230–31
eclampsia, 103–4
ectopic pregnancy, 102–3
ehrlichiosis, 231–32
elastic bandages, 284
elbow trauma, 186–88

encephalitis, 232
endemic typhus, 251–52
Ensolite foam, 176, 179, 199, 284
environmental injuries, 255–76; about, 255–56; cold-stress injuries, 260–64; heat stress injuries, 264–70; hypothermia, 256–60; lightning, 270–76
epididymitis, 104–5
epinephrine (EpiPen, EpiPen Jr. and Symjepi), 205, 280, 298
epistaxis, 62–63
erupting wisdom tooth, 74–75
erythromycin, 237
eugenol (oil of cloves), 73, 76, 77, 79, 286
eyebrow wound closure, 140
eye pain and irritation, 45–59; abrasions, 52–53; blunt trauma, 57–58; conjunctivitis, 54–55, 56; contact lenses, 49–52; foreign body injury, 47–49; glaucoma, 58–59; iritis, 50, 55–56; patch and bandaging, 46, 54, 58; sties and chalazia, 56–57; subconjunctival hemorrhage, 57; ultraviolet eye injury, 53–54

F
falciparum malaria, 238
famciclovir (Famvir), 296
famotidine (Pepcid), 290–91
felon, 154–55
femur fractures, 196–97
fever: about, 30–32; relapsing, 242–43
fever blisters, 73
filling, lost, 77
finger and toe problems: blood under nail, 155–56; felon,

154–55; finger fractures and sprains, 192–93; ingrown nails, 153–54; paronychia, 154
fire ants, 217–18
fishhook removal, 144–47
fish tapeworms, 246
Flagyl (metronidazole), 296
flea-borne endemic typhus, 251
Flector, 168
flies, black, 216
fluid replacement, 113–14, 150–51
focused assessment, 8–9
Foley catheters, 96–97, 288
food poisoning, 107
foot injuries, 200
foreign bodies: and airway obstruction, 17–18; in ear, 69; in eye, 47–49; and mouth lacerations, 76; nasal, 61–62
Forgey, William, 126–27, 160
fractures: about, 170–72; ankle, 199; diagnosis and care protocols, 173–74; elbow, 186–87; finger, 192–93; forearm, 188–89; hand, 192–93; hip, 194–95; knee, 198–99; nose, 63; open, 172–73; ribs, 200–201; shoulder blade (scapula), 183–84; thigh (femur), 196–97; thumb, 192; tooth, 79; upper arm, 184–86; wrist, 189–90, 191
friction blisters, 147–48
frostbite, 261–62
frostnip, 260–61
"frozen lung," 262–63
fungal infections, 100–101, 159, 226–27, 228
furosemide (Lasix), 175
furuncles, 74, 156–57

G
gall bladder problems, 86–87
gardiasis, 232–33
gastritis, 85
gastroenteritis, 90
Gatorade, 89, 114, 151
German measles, 244
gestational diabetes, 103
Giardia lamblia, 115, 116
"GI jungle juice," 160
glass inomer, 78
glaucoma, 58–59
gloves, protective, 287
glucometers, 112
glycerin, sublingual, 24
gnats, 216–17
gonorrhea, 99
Grey Owl, 52–53
gum pain or swelling, 74–75
gypsy moth caterpillar *(Lymantria dispar)*, 213

H
halazone, 115
hand injuries, 192–93
hantavirus, 233
hard ticks (Ixodidae), 212
head, examining, 12
headache, 37
head injuries, 174–75
head velocity signal, 41
heart, 23–27, 273
heart attack, 23–26
heat stress injuries, 264–70; about, 264–67; dilutional hyponatremia, 265–66, 267–68; heat cramps, 268; heat exhaustion, 268–69; heat stroke, 269–70; prickly heat, 270
Heimlich maneuver, 17–18

help, requesting, 1–2
hemorrhoids, 93–94
hemostatic dressings, 127–31, 282–83
hepatitis, 72, 233–36
herd immunity, 223–25
hernia, 94–95
herpes, 100
herpes simplex, 73
hiccups, 37
hip, examining, 13
hip injuries, 194–96
hives, 36
Hubble, Frank, 8
human bites, 152. *See also* bites and stings
hydatid disease, 230–31
hydrocortisone cream, 286
hydrodynamics, law of, 196–97
hydroxyzine (Atarax, Vistaril), 294, 298
hyperglycemia, 111
hyperosmolar diuretics, 175
hyperventilation syndrome, 22–23
hyphema, 58
hypoglycemia, 111
hyponatremia, 265–66, 267–68
hypothermia, 256–60; acute, 256, 258–59; chronic, 256–58; cold water submersion, 260

I
ibuprofen, 289
Icy Hot, 167
immersion foot, 263–64
immunization, 223
Imodium (loperamide), 290
impetigo, 160–61
Infalyte, 114

infections: bladder, 95–96; dental, 75; ear problems, 66–68; fungal, 100–101, 159, 226–27, 228; intestinal, 227–28; monilia (candida), 100–101; nail base, 154; trichomonas, 101; urinary tract, 103; Vincent's, 73; wound, 156; *see also* infectious diseases
infectious diseases, 221–53; diagnosis of, 221; and herd immunity, 223–25; onset of, 222; prevention of, 225–26; *see also specific diseases*
influenza, 225
ingrown nails, 153–54
inguinal hernia, 94
initial assessment, 6–8
inline traction, 170–71, 176
insects in ear, 69
insulin storage, 111. *See also* diabetes
International Health Regulations, 2
intestinal infections, 227–28
iodine, 115–16, 117
iritis, 50, 55–56
irrigation of wounds, 133–34
irrigation syringes, 132, 287
itch, 35–36, 157–59

J
"jammed" fingers, 193
jellyfish, 218–19
"jock itch," 159
joint pain, 167–69. *See also* orthopedics
junctional tourniquets, 127

K
Katadyn Pocket Filter, 117
King, Dean, 120, 267

kneecap (patella) dislocation, 197–98
knee injuries, 198–99

L
labial frenum, laceration of, 75
Lanacane cream, 285
lansoprazole (Prevacid), 291
Lasix (furosemide), 175
legs, examining, 13. *See also* orthopedics
leptospirosis, 236
lethargy, 32–33
Levaquin (levofloxacin), 292–93
lidocaine, 297
lifeboat kit, 280–81. *See also* medicine chest
lightning, 270–76
lip wound closure, 140
loop diuretics, 175
loperamide (Imodium), 290
Lotrimin (clotrimazole cream), 286
louse-borne endemic typhus, 251–52
lunate dislocation, 190
Lyme disease, 236–38
lymph nodes, infected, 66

M
malaria, 238–39
Malarone (atovaquone and proguanil), 296–97
mal de mer, 39–43
mallet finger deformity, 193
mannitol, 175
Marcolongo, Lorenzo, 119
maximum strength triple antibiotic ointment with pramoxine, 284–85
"Mayday" assistance, 1–2

measles, 239–40
medical history, taking, 12
medicine chest, 277–300; about, 277–80; alternative improvisation, 280; automatic external defibrillator, 281, 288; Cardiac Medication Kit, 299–300; Foley Catheter Kit, 288; *vs.* lifeboat kit, 280–81; Non-Rx Oral Medication Kit, 288–91; Rx Injectable Medication Kit, 297–98; Rx Oral/Topical Medication Kit, 291–97; Surgical Kit, 287–88; Topical Medication and Bandaging Kit, 281–87
Medicine for the Backcountry (Tilton & Hubble), 8
meloxicam (Mobic), 294
meningococcal meningitis, 240
menorrhagia, 100–101
menstrual problems, 101–2
MERS, 229
methocarbamol (Robaxin), 211, 217
metoprolol, 25, 300
metronidazole (Flagyl), 296
millipede reactions, 213
miscarriage, 102, 103
Mobic (meloxicam), 294
Mobigesic, 232
Mobisyl, 167
moleskin, 148
monilia (candida) infection, 100–101
mononucleosis, infectious, 72
mosquitoes, 230, 238–39, 252, 253
motion sickness, 39–43
Motrix Wizard skin stapler, 136
mouth and throat problems, 71–80; dental care, 74–80; infectious mononucleosis, 72; mouth

lacerations, 75–76, 140; mouth sores, 72–73; sore throat, 71–72
multivitamins, 103, 151
mumps, 240–41
muscle function and disorders. *See* orthopedics
muscle pain, 164–66
muscle relaxants, 165
Mycelex (clotrimazole cream), 286
myocardial infarction, 23–26
Myoflex, 167

N
nail base infection, 154
nalbuphine (Nubain), 297
Nano Hybrid, 78
nasal congestion, 61
nasal foreign body, 61–62
Naturalyte, 114
nautical medicine, introduction to, 1–2
navicular fractures, 190, 191
neck, examining, 7–8, 12
neck injuries, 174, 176–77. *See also* spine injuries
Neosporin, 49, 55
neostigmine, 210
neurotoxic snakes, 206, 208–9
nitrofurantoin, 103
nitroglycerin spray, 24
nitroglycerin sublingual tablets, 299–300
Non-Rx Oral Medication Kit, 288–91
Norco-10/325 tablets, 293
no-see-ums, 216
nose problems, 61–63; congestion, 61; foreign bodies, 61–62; fracture, 63; nosebleed, 62–63
Nubain (nalbuphine), 297

Nubain (butorphanol) nasal spray, 295
Nu-Gauze pads, 283

O
oil of cloves (eugenol), 73, 76, 77, 79, 286
omeprazole (Prilosec), 86, 291
One-A-Day multiple vitamins, 151
Opcon-A eye drops, 285–86
open fractures, 172–73
oral fluid replacement, 113–14, 150–51
Oralyte, 114
orchitis, 104–5
organic phosphorus pesticides, 107–8
orthopedics, 163–201; about, 163–64; ankle, 199; chest, 200–201; collarbone, 179–81; elbow, 186–88; foot, 200; forearm, 188–89; fractures, 170–74; hand, 192–93; head, 174–75; hip, 194–96; joint pain, 167–69; knee, 198–99; kneecap (patella), 197–98; muscle pain, 164–66; neck, 174, 176–77; shoulder, 181–84; spine, 174, 177–79; thigh (femur), 196–97; thumb, 192; upper arm, 184–86; wrist, 189–91
Osler, William, 100, 221
otitis externa, 66–67
otitis media, 67–68
overuse syndromes, 165
oximeters, 11
oxygen saturation, 11

P
pain management, 33–35, 140–41
"Pan, Pan" assistance, 1–2

pancreatitis, 85–86
paracetamol. *See* acetaminophen (Tylenol)
paralytic shellfish poisoning, 109
paronychia, 154
paroxysmal atrial tachycardia (PAT), 26
Pascal's law of hydrodynamics, 196–97
patella dislocation, 197–98
Pedialyte, 114
pelvis, examining, 13
penciclovir (Denavir cream), 295
penicillin, 100, 237
Pennsaid, 168
Pepcid (famotidine), 290–91
Pepto-Bismol, 92
Percogesic, 289
pericoronitis, 74–75
perilunate dislocation, 190–99
periodontal abscess, 74
permethrin, 212, 214, 215, 216, 217, 226, 238
pesticides, organic phosphorus, 107–8
petroleum product poisoning, 107–8
pharyngitis, 71–72
Phenergan (promethazine), 43
physical exam, 8–9, 12–13
picaridin, 214, 215
piles, 93–94
pilocarpine, 59
pit vipers, 206, 207–8
placebo effect, 43
plague, 241
plant poisoning, 107
Plavix (clopidogrel), 300
pneumonia, 81–82
pneumothorax, 82, 201

poisoning, 107–9
Polar Pure, 116
Polysporin, 49, 55
pork tapeworms, 245–46
pre-eclampsia, 103–4
pregnancy, 102–4
pressure immobilization, 208–9
pressure packing, 131
Prevacid (lansoprazole), 291
Prevest DenPro Fusion Flo Dental-Cured Nano Hybrid, 78
prickly heat, 270
Prilosec (omeprazole), 86, 291
prochlorperazine (Compazine, Stemetil), 43
proguanil and atovaquone (Malarone), 296–97
promethazine (Phenergan), 43
proprioception, 41–42
pufferfish poisoning, 109
pulmonary chilling, 262–63
pulmonary embolus, 83
pulse, 10, 11, 15
puncture wounds, 143
puss caterpillar *(Megalopyge opercularis)*, 213

Q
Quick Clot Combat Gauze, 282–83
quinine, 226

R
rabbit fever, 250
rabies, 241–42. *See also* bites and stings
rash. *See* skin rash
rattlesnake bites, 207
refractometers, 119, 120
relapsing fever, 242–43

reproductive organs, 99–105; abortion, spontaneous, 102, 103; ectopic pregnancy, 102–3; menstrual problems, 101–2; pregnancy, 102–4; testicle, painful, 104–5; vaginal discharge and itching, 100–101; venereal diseases, 99–100
respirations, 10, 17–23, 81–83
responsiveness, level of, 10
rewarming shock, 257
ribs, fractured, 200–201
RICE technique (Rest, Ice, Compress, Elevate), 165–66, 169, 198, 200
rigors, 31
Riley, James, 120, 267
ringworm, body, 159
Robaxin (methocarbamol), 211, 217
Rocephin (ceftriaxone), 298
Rocky Mountain spotted fever, 243–44
rubella, 244
rubeola, 239–40
"Rule of Nines," 148, 149
ruptured eardrum, 68, 69–70
ruptured tendons, 193
Rx Injectable Medication Kit, 297–98
Rx Oral/Topical Medication Kit, 291–97

S
sailing injury statistics, 121–24
salt loss in sweat, 265
SAM splint, 284
San Joaquin fever, 228
SARS (severe acute respiratory syndrome), 229

SARS-CoV-2 (COVID-19), 229–30
Sawyer Products filters, 117–18
saxitoxin, 109
scalp wounds, 139–40
scapula fracture, 183–84
scene, surveying, 6
schistosomiasis, 244–45
scombroid poisoning, 108–9
scopolamine (Transderm Scop or Transderm-V), 42–43
scorpion fish, 220
scorpion stings, 217
sea anemone larvae, 161
seabather's eruption, 161–62
seasickness, 39–43
sea urchins, 218
seawater, drinking, 119–20
2nd Skin, 147–48, 151, 282
severe acute respiratory syndrome (SARS), 229
ship damage, from lightning, 272
shock: about, 15–17; anaphylactic, 203–5; rewarming, 257; treating for, 126, 150–51
shoulder injuries, 181–84
shoulders, examining, 13
Silverlon bandages, 141–42, 283–84
sinus congestion, 69–70
Skeletons on the Zahara (King), 120, 267
skin rash: about, 158–59; allergic dermatitis, 159–60; aquatic stings, cuts, and rash, 218–20; bacterial skin rash, 160–61; fungal infection, 159; seabather's eruption, 161–62; southern tick-associated rash illness (STARI), 245; sponge rash, 220
skin signs, 10

Skin So Soft, 216
sling and swathe, 179, 180, 181, 183, 184–85
snake bites, 205–10
snow blindness, 53–54
soft ticks (Argasidae), 212
soft tissue care and trauma management, 121–62; abrasions, 142–43; abscesses, 156–57; antibiotic guidelines, 134–35; bites, animal, 152–53; bites, human, 152; bleeding, 126–31, 139; cellulitis, 157–58; dressings, 141–42; eyebrow and lip closure, 140; finger and toe problems, 153–56; fishhook removal, 144–47; friction blisters, 147–48; mouth and tongue lacerations, 140; pain control, 140–41; puncture wounds, 143; sailing injury statistics, 121–24; scalp wounds, 139–40; skin rash, 158–62; splinter removal, 143–44; thermal burns, 148–52; types, 125–26; wound area, shaving, 139; wound cleaning, 131–34; wound closure techniques, 135–39; wound infection and inflammation, 156
Sopite syndrome, 39, 42
sore throat, 71–72
southern tick-associated rash illness (STARI), 245
Special Operations Forces Tactical Tourniquet Wide (SOFTT-W), 128–29
Spenco 2nd Skin, 147–48, 151, 282
spider bites, 210–11
spine injuries, 174, 177–79. *See also* neck injuries
splinter removal, 143–44

splints: for fractures, 170, 172, 176, 180, 181, 186–87, 188–89, 193; for neurotoxic snake bites, 209
sponge rash, 220
spontaneous subconjunctival hemorrhage, 57
sports creams, 167–68
sprains, 192, 193, 198, 199
square knots, 137, 138
stabilization of patient, 15–27; cardiac evaluation and care, 23–27; respirations, difficult, 17–23; shock, 15–17
Stadol (butorphanol tartrate), 34
stapling, 135–36, 139
STARI (southern tick-associated rash illness), 245
Stemetil (prochlorperazine), 43
SteriPEN, 118
Steri-strips, 135
sties, 56–57
Stimson maneuver, 183, 188
stinging nettle, 160
stingrays, 219–20
stings. *See* bites and stings
stitching, 136–39
stomach irritation, 85
strep throat, 71–72
streptomycin, 250
string test, 233
subconjunctival hemorrhage, 57
subungual hematoma, 155–56
sugar tong splints, 185, 186
sunglasses, 53
sun stroke, 269–70
Surgical Kit, 287–88
suturing, 136–39
Symjepi (epinephrine), 280, 298
symptom management, 29–37
syphilis, 99–100

T

tachycardia, 26
tachypnea, 22–23
Tactical Combat Casualty Care (TCCC), 1, 127, 129, 283
Tales of an Empty Cabin (Grey Owl), 52–53
tape, waterproof, 284
tape closure techniques, 135
tapeworms, 230–31, 245–46
TB (tuberculosis), 249
teeth. *See* dental care
temperature, 11, 30. *See also* chills; fever
temporomandibular joint syndrome (TMJ), 70
tendinitis, 167
tendons, ruptured, 193
Tenormin (atenolol), 300
Tensilon, 210
tension eye patch, 46
testicle, painful, 104–5
testicular torsion, 105
tetanus, 246
tetracaine ophthalmic solution, 295. *See also* eye pain and irritation
tetracycline, 237
thermal burns, 148–52
thermometers, 11
thigh (femur) fractures, 196–97
thimble jellyfish larvae, 161
3-day measles, 244
thumb injuries, 192
thumb spica wrap, 191, 192
tick paralysis, 246–47
ticks: about, 212; and infectious diseases, 226, 228–29, 236–38, 243–44, 245, 246–47
Tilton, Buck, 8, 104, 178
tinidazole, 233

TMJ (temporomandibular joint syndrome), 70
Tobradex ophthalmic drops, 294–95. *See also* eye pain and irritation
toe problems. *See* finger and toe problems
tongue, laceration of, 75–76
toothache, 76–77
Topical Medication and Bandaging Kit, 281–87
Topicort (desoximetasone), 294
torsion, testicular, 105
tourniquets, 127–30
traction splinting, 170–71, 176, 196–97
tramadol (Ultram), 227, 253, 293
Transderm Scop or Transderm-V (scopolamine), 42–43
traveler's diarrhea, 91–92
trench foot, 263–64
trench mouth, 73
trichinosis, 247
trichomonas infection, 101
triple antibiotic ointment with pramoxine, maximum strength, 284–85
trypanosomiasis, 247–49
tuberculosis (TB), 249
tularemia, 250
Tylenol (acetaminophen), 32, 208, 227, 240, 241, 244, 253
typhoid fever, 250–51
typhus, endemic, 251–52

U

ulcers, 85
Ultram (tramadol), 227, 253, 293
ultraviolet eye injury, 53–54
urinary retention, 96–98

urinary tract infection, 103
urine, drinking, 120, 267

V
vaginal discharge and itching,
   100–101
valley fever, 228
vasoconstriction, 257
vasopressin, 265–66
venereal diseases, 99–100
Vincent's infection, 73
visceral nerve signals, 41–42
Vistaril (hydroxyzine), 298
vital signs, 9–11
Voltaren, 168
vomiting, 90

W
water, need for, 266–67
water moccasin bites, 207
water purification, 114–19
wax plugs, 69
welts, 36
West Nile virus, 252

Where There Is No Dentist
   (Dickson), 78
Wiel's disease, 236
Wilderness First Responder (Tilton),
   104, 178
Wilderness Medicine (Forgey), 160
wisdom tooth, erupting, 74–75
wounds: bleeding from suture or
   staple use, 139; cleaning, 131–34;
   closure techniques, 135–39;
   infection and inflammation, 156;
   irrigation of, 133–34; shaving
   wound area, 139; *see also* soft tissue
   care and trauma management
wrist injuries, 189–91

X
X-Stat, 127

Z
Zerowet Supershield, 287
Zika virus, 253
zinc oxide, powdered, 77, 286
Zithromax (azithromycin), 73

About the Author

William W. Forgey, MD, is a fellow of the Academy of Wilderness Medicine and past president of the Wilderness Medical Society. He has been a fellow of the Explorers Club, New York City, since 1975. He was named as one of the 20 greatest American Explorers in 2004 by the Explorers Club and honored by having a subcamp named for him at the 2005 Boy Scouts of America National Jamboree. He holds a CTH® from the International Society of Travel Medicine. Dr. Forgey is a volunteer clinical professor of Family Medicine at the Indiana University School of Medicine and was awarded the AΩA Volunteer Faculty of the Year award in 2000. He is a Professeur Associé, Sciences de la santé, Universite d'etat d'Haïti, an overseas fellow of the Royal Society of Medicine (London), and a trustee and member of the Scientific Advisory Committee of the International Association for Medical Assistance to Travelers (Toronto), and advisor and founder of Health Corps Haiti—Medical Student Missions, Inc. He currently practices full-time as a family physician.

CPSIA information can be obtained
at www.ICGtesting.com
Printed in the USA
BVHW071222250421
605759BV00001B/1

9 781493 056637